Strategic Benchmarking
Reloaded with Six Sigma

Strategic Benchmarking Reloaded with Six Sigma

Improve Your Company's Performance
Using Global Best Practice

Gregory H. Watson

John Wiley & Sons, Inc.

Library of Congress Cataloging-in-Publication Data

Watson, Gregory H.
  Strategic benchmarking reloaded with six sigma : improve your company's performance using global best practice / Gregory H. Watson.
    p. cm.
  Includes bibliographical references and index.
  ISBN: 978-0-470-06908-0 (cloth)
  1. Benchmarking (Management) 2. Six sigma (Quality control standard) 3. Performance. I. Title.
  HD62.15.W38 2007
  658.4'013—dc22

                                                                      2006032784

Printed in the United States of America.

10 9 8 7 6 5 4 3 2 1

To the memory of my parents
Robert John Watson, Jr. (1916–1996)
Anne Faye Bellotte Watson (1919–1999)
in grateful appreciation for their lives
and the contribution that they made to mine.

Contents

CONTENTS

Preface

THE ORIGINS OF STRATEGIC BENCHMARKING

The idea of strategic benchmarking was developed while redesigning a business planning system for Xerox Corporation in the summer of 1992. At that time I was vice president for quality of the largest and most profitable business unit—Office Document Products—which contained the core Xerox copier business, and I had spent the first six months of this year in helping to establish the International Benchmarking Clearinghouse. Prior to this time, Xerox had not clearly separated the ideas of strategic and operational benchmarking, although it had done both types of studies. For example, in the seminal book on this subject by Robert C. Camp, there is no mention distinguishing in the scope of the study as strategic or operational, as he only focused on distinctions of the type of the study based on the characteristics of the benchmarking partner organization from which information was obtained.[1]

---

1. Robert C. Camp, *Benchmarking* (Milwaukee: ASQ Quality Press, 1989). Bob Camp described the early distinction that was made among the types of benchmarking studies that were defined as

This concept of linking strategic planning and benchmarking was further stimulated by my experience at Hewlett-Packard, where we introduced the Japanese planning system called *hoshin kanri* in the mid-1980s. It was this planning system that formed the basis of the new Xerox planning process, which they called *Managing for Results*.[2] Some 14 years ago, while on sick leave from this job as a vice president of quality at Xerox Corporation, I embarked on an intellectual journey to develop a book that John Wiley & Sons published—it was called *Strategic Benchmarking*. By most standards, this book was very successful: it was chosen as one of the 12 best business books of 1993 by *Library Journal, Fortune Magazine* selected it as an alternative book-of-the-month club offering, and *Executive Book Summaries* picked it as one of 30 books that they abridged for their synopsis of emerging executive thoughts. *Strategic Benchmarking* was also translated into nine languages and published worldwide. Subsequent to writing this book, I left Xerox to begin my own consulting company, and I became captured by some major projects that took most of my time and also introduced me to Six Sigma as a system of quality thinking. Out of this consulting experience grew a realization that significant improvements could be made to the method of strategic benchmarking if it were coupled with the statistical concepts that are included in Six Sigma.

Today, this new book expands upon the original subject by extending the concept of strategic benchmarking to *reload* it with the current wave

---

competitive, internal, industry, and generic—based primarily on the identity of the benchmarking partner.

2. I described the process for *hoshin kanri* in an introduction to a book edited by Dr. Yoji Akao, chair of the Policy Deployment Research Committee for the Union of Japanese Scientists and Engineers (JUSE), which was published in 1991 ("Understanding Hoshin Kanri," *Hoshin Kanri* (Portland, OR: Productivity Press, 1991). This book was a translation of the JUSE Research Committee's report, and Dr. Akao decided that he wanted an American experience with policy deployment to introduce the book. The introductory chapter that I contributed also described the combined experience of implementing this at Hewlett-Packard and Compaq as well as some early benchmarking results from sharing it with the Xerox Corporate Quality Office in 1990. The name of the Xerox process was borrowed from a book of the same title by Dr. Peter F. Drucker who was also very instrumental in creating this concept in Japan. The Xerox policy deployment system, which we developed, is documented in a speech that I gave at the American Society for Quality's Annual Congress ("Managing for Results," *Proceedings*, 48th Annual Quality Congress, 1994).

of Six Sigma thinking that has influenced so many American corporations. The idea to reload strategic benchmarking with Six Sigma leads to a natural question, What has changed or what circumstances are different at this time to warrant a new treatment of this subject? Allow me to summarize these changes as a preface to this book and also use this opportunity to introduce the organization of its contents.

BENCHMARKING AS A MANAGEMENT PRACTICE

This book approaches strategic benchmarking as a management practice. Why choose to write about this subject again? I decided to recreate a book on strategic benchmarking because in reflecting over the first 25 years of benchmarking practice, I saw that more companies have missed key opportunities by not applying the benchmarking methodology to assist in defining their strategic business issues. Some companies started out doing it right and dropped their focus as they became arrogant and self-confident in their ability to succeed, and they considered other organizations unworthy as examples of practices or behaviors that should be emulated. Indeed, in previous writings, I quoted a director of a major corporation, where he stated the reason why he didn't want his people to do benchmarking, "We don't want to taint our performance by learning how mediocre companies develop products."[3] But his comment totally misses the point of doing benchmarking. There are different lessons that must be learned at different levels of the organization, and organizations can learn from many different sources and then creatively adapt or imitate those lessons and practices that will advance their own performance. In doing benchmarking, it is an egregious error to copy and just do what others are doing—adopting their practices as best practice may lead to serious errors in execution! Also, if the same practices become widespread throughout an industry, then that industry can also stagnate and become noncompetitive due to lack of innovation. Of course, no serious manager would want his people to do this, but managers must

3. Gregory H. Watson, *Strategic Benchmarking* (New York: Wiley, 1993), 196.

recognize that such a simple approach isn't the most valuable way to conduct benchmarking.

As Peter F. Drucker pointed out so poignantly in his classic book on management, *The Effective Executive,* business leaders must lead their organizations in "doing the right things," and discovery of the right things is the objective of a blended application of strategic benchmarking and business planning while doing the right things right is the objective of operational benchmarking. Drucker commented, "To be effective is the job of the executive. To effect and to execute are, after all near synonyms. The executive is, first of all, expected to *get the right things done.* And this is simply that he is expected to be effective. For manual work, we need only efficiency; that is, the *ability to do things right* rather than the ability to get the right things done [italics added]."[4] How does strategic benchmarking work in a context of an organization's management process to help executives become more effective?

THE BUSINESS BENEFITS OF STRATEGIC BENCHMARKING

Strategic benchmarking is a key element in the transcendent system of core business planning processes that defines the strategic intent of an organization. It focuses on identifying those factors that must be changed for an organization to build the strength that assures its continuing success. What is it that stimulates change in an organization — is it change identified based upon Theory Opinion (Theory O) judgments, or is it based on a scientific, objective observation of the business environment as interpreted through the eyes of a seasoned judge of the business?[5] There is a big difference between a purely subjective approach to

4. Peter F. Drucker, *The Effective Executive* (New York: Harper, 1996), 1–12.

5. Gregory H. Watson, "Perspectives on Quality: Oh No! Theory O!" *Quality Progress* 22 no. 6 (2000): 16. This article introduced the concept of "Theory O" as a word play on Douglas McGregor's Theory X and Theory Y as management styles and the counter point of William Ouchi who introduced a midpoint with Theory Z. Theory O stands for Theory Opinion — a management decision that is driven purely by the subjective interpretation of an individual (usually the business leader or someone with positional authority) who wants to see things done their way — or take the highway if you don't agree! This style of decision making is prevalent in many businesses and is a problem be-

strategy development and one that is based on statistically sound observations, which are then subjected to a rigorous dialogue among the management team members, resulting in a collaborative perspective among the business leaders. This way of developing an understanding of the business environment develops organizational congruence through consensus on its direction and an aligned and integrated commitment of the organizations capabilities, competences, and resources to the change process in order to jointly obtain the desired state as they have agreed will most likely result in long-term success. By encouraging a broad involvement in the strategic benchmarking as a directed inquiry process, management not only develops consensus on the action to be taken but also engages the organization in the definition of the rationale for changes in the intent of its strategy direction that refines its business direction. Another benefit of broad participation in this process is that it enhances the level of flexibility of the team to adapt to unanticipated changes that crop up as they have fully analyzed the scenarios of the future and considered how contingent options could work out based on the moves of their competitors and introduction of newly emerging technologies.

Benchmarking applies objective measurement and the scientific method of analysis as the means to identify and discover ways that enhance the value of an organization's products, services, or processes. Benchmarking involves three major ingredients: First, it measures performance; second, it determines the causes for achieving that level of performance; and, finally, it extracts elements of that work practice that may be transferred to other organizations for the sake of improving their performance in the focus subject of the study. How does this recipe work?

- First, the linkage of benchmarking to strategic planning allows management to recognize what it must address as a change initiative. Once an improvement opportunity is identified, then the management team follows a basic tenant of total quality management:

---

cause it does not use the check and balance of management by fact to verify the opinion prior to the troops saluting and going off to accomplish the task.

The best way to improve performance results of a business outcome is to improve the process that produced it!

- The gap between the internal performance and the external best-practice performance identifies how much change must occur in the process to bring its performance to bring it up to a par level with the comparison group or to achieve leadership beyond this group.
- The fact that other organizations have achieved this degree of performance indicates that the improvement is possible and that the means they applied to achieve this level of performance provides an example of what can be done to make this improvement achievable and the results obtainable. Identifying a benchmark practice separates a best practice from a managerial hallucination, wish, hope, or dream—all of which are associated with a Theory O style of management.

The result of a benchmarking study should be the definition of a change management project to be implemented by a business process owner. It is through the execution of the change project that the benefits of the benchmarking study are realized, not just by doing the study! As Larry Bossidy, former CEO of AlliedSignal and Honeywell, said, "Many efforts at cultural change fail because they are not linked to improving business outcomes."[6] Excellence—being the best of the best—is achieved by execution!

THE CONTRIBUTION OF SIX SIGMA TO BENCHMARKING

How does inclusion of Six Sigma concepts and method enrich the process of strategic benchmarking? Six Sigma is an application of the scientific method, statistical analysis, lean thinking, process management, and systems engineering in a rigorous, integrated approach to problem solving and design of products, processes, and services. What is it specifically

6. Larry Bossidy and Ram Charan, *Execution: The Discipline of Getting Things Done* (New York: Crown Business, 2002), 85.

that Six Sigma contributes to strategic benchmarking that makes it such a worthwhile addition to justify reloading this methodology with it? There are a number of key contributions that Six Sigma makes to benchmarking that strengthen the ability of an organization to conduct these studies, draw valid conclusions from their analytical results, and make better informed choices about the direction it should pursue.

- Six Sigma provides an objective analysis standard by using a single measure to compare process performance for measures that have been operationally defined and specified in a way that assure consistency when contrast to cross-company performance for similar work or business processes. The use of sigma levels as a benchmark metric drives consistency in making judgments about the relative achieved performance level in observations and using both average and variation in performance indicates that a truly sustainable gain in the degree of performance has been achieved. Six Sigma can be used to implement statistical methods in benchmarking processes and to focus on using the management of variation as a way to make work more consistent and achieve higher performance in its outputs.
- Six Sigma delivers the scientific methods to a benchmarking study through the use of a disciplined analytical approach (called the *DMAIC process*)[7] that is overlaid on the Analyze step of the benchmarking process to tighten up the process of making effective comparative analyses.
- Six Sigma also assures traceability of the lessons learned from the measurement to the specific process-level activity through a thorough process mapping that breaks down the process into steps whose contribution to the overall performance is analyzed for quality, cost, and cycle time to enhance its effectiveness. In the language of Total Quality Management (TQM), this breakdown follows the SIPOC model where Customer expectations are designed into the

---

7. DMAIC is an acronym that stands for the first initial in each of the five steps of statistical problem solving process used during a Six Sigma project: Define, Measure, Analyze, Improve, and Control.

process in order for the outcomes to be consistently delivered in a way that meets them![8]

- Finally, Six Sigma conducts many small experiments to characterize and then optimize the performance of a business process and demonstrate the effectiveness of the proposed change in a way that builds confidence in its implementation.

The blending of these ingredients of Six Sigma into the strategic benchmarking process has resulted in a process that is different from both methodologies in their original states. Perhaps the greatest contribution of this book is in further defining the strategic process of "improvement opportunity discovery" that was called the *Recognize* step of Six Sigma by Dr. Mikel Harry.[9] This step precedes DMAIC and Design for Six Sigma and is used by management to develop a portfolio of change projects to which it will allocate its resources to manage change. It is in this prerequisite step of the Six Sigma methodology that strategic benchmarking plays such a vital role.

ORGANIZATION OF THIS BOOK

This book is organized into four parts, preceded by an introduction and followed by a set of appendixes that provide details that will help you in your implementation of the methods. The Introduction describes the history of benchmarking from its modern invention at Xerox in 1979 through its 25th anniversary in 2004. This chapter is supplemented by an appendix that identifies the 56 books that have been written about benchmarking during this period.

The first part of the book explains the business context of benchmarking, and it consists of two chapters that describe how strategic benchmarking and Six Sigma can be combined to stimulate business im-

---

8. SIPOC is an acronym that summarizes the typical flow of activity throughput as it moves from the Supplier as Input to the Process and then as Output to the Customer.

9. Dr. Mikel J. Harry, "Breakthrough Strategy Makes Factorial Dimensions of Quality Visible," *Quality Progress* April (2000).

provement. The second part defines a revised benchmarking process after integrating Six Sigma methods to enhance the way that a study is conducted. The third part presents case studies and is divided into three chapters. The first chapter reviews and updates the case studies from the original *Strategic Benchmarking* book and identifies lessons learned from hindsight into the practices of these management teams regarding how their use of benchmarking could have been improved. In the last two chapters are case studies for a strategic benchmarking study and an operational benchmarking study, in order to illustrate how these studies are performed in more detail. The fourth part of the book tells how to integrate or mainstream benchmarking and Six Sigma into strategic planning and uses these methods to improve performance as a routine aspect of the management process. This last part of the book is supplemented by appendixes that present templates that define the code of conduct for benchmarking, a standard operating procedure for conducting benchmarking studies, and an approach for using Internet resources to streamline the way research is conducted during benchmarking studies. Taken as a whole, this book describes a roadmap for integrating strategic benchmarking with Six Sigma in the context of strategic planning to enhance the effectiveness of management decision making.

It is my sincere hope that organizations will apply the methods described in this book as a strategic application of benchmarking. I believe that the lessons learned from Six Sigma will help managers undertake a serious assessment of their business assumptions, technological aptitudes, operational capabilities, and organizational competencies in the context of the skills, knowledge, and attitudes of their people to drive increased performance through a sound use of the scientific method. Best wishes on your journey!

—*Gregory H. Watson*
Espoo, Finland

Acknowledgments

After writing so many books, I have come to realize that no book is a unique inspiration from the gods! It is the product of a frustrated mind, stored ideas that are accumulated from many sources, and the sincere support of a circle of others who know that this birthing process is as painful and labor-intensive as the physical process that women know much better than I will ever know as a mere observer! So allow me to express my thanks to a few special people!

First, I would like to acknowledge Dr. Camille De Young, my teaching colleague at the Oklahoma State University Department of Industrial Engineering and Management who teaches a class in benchmarking. Camille allowed me to sit in on her class to gain insight into the problems that her students encounter with benchmarking in order to learn how to teach this course to such young, inquiring minds. This experience allowed me to develop a curriculum for a university-level class on benchmarking that uses this book for a text and supplements it with additional materials that are available by email for college and university instructors (greg@excellence.fi). Camille, I express my deepest thanks for granting me this experience!

Second, many thanks to my editor at Wiley—Laurie Harting—you are indeed a real professional who can inspire the confidence of an author and who is able to provide immense insightful guidance on how to direct a project so that its readers get the greatest value out of it. I think that we make a great team, and I am looking forward to collaborating with you again soon!

Third, my gratitude is also extended to my good friends—Bob King, Ken Case, Paul Borawski, Bill Tony, Risto Lintula, and Timo Hannukainen—thank you for your heartfelt personal and professional encouragement. Many times when writing my books seems like such a pressure, it is your kindness and words of support that lift my spirits and cause me to continue with these mammoth projects. I thank all of you for your willingness to listen when I have painted myself into a paragraph and need a bit of help to think differently about the space I am in!

Next, I thank my many colleagues of the International Academy for Quality that have given me personal and professional encouragement. You have entrusted to me the role of publisher for our books, and I deeply appreciate the faith that you have in me, and I pledge to do a "benchmark" job in executing this strategic process on our behalf!

Also, I really appreciate my long-term business partner, Jeff Martin, and his family—wife Michelle and daughters Alex and Jamie Martin—who provided me with hospitality and a haven for thinking and writing between consulting engagements and conferences in the United States. Thanks for letting me become a part of your days and for being such wonderful lifetime friends. To Jeff's Mom—thank you for sharing your love of life with both myself and Inessa. Your kind appreciation of my wife's singing of Russian romance has touched us both very deeply.

I am grateful also to Asya Belfer, *maya mamushka,* who watches me write and gives me confidence with her kind looks and caring smiles. Thank you for having such a gentle spirit and for opening your warm heart to embrace me in your family. Thank you also for having faith in me and appreciating what is my unique way of writing. Your gracious support encourages me with confidence.

All of my family is an inspiration to me: Crista, Andrew and Laura,

Acknowledgments

Dina, and Sasha—especially my big boy Alex and young, charming Sanya! Your youthful outlook on life reminds me to stay young and encourages me about the potential future of the world that will be inherited from the hands of my generation. You all make me more sensitive and feel more intensely about the urgent need to take positive action that preserves our ecosystem from the encroachment of global warming. You are the next generation for whom we must preserve the quality of life on this Earth that God has entrusted to us!

And finally to my wife Inessa, whose music has taught me about the dance of life and how to move my clumsy feet to a more invigorating beat. You are the true muse that ignites my creative side, and it is your love that frees my mind to gain inspirational insights. *Spasibo balshoy tibeah zhena maya!*

Introduction

Benchmarking: The First 25 Years (1979–2004)

Benchmarking is a management process that developed during the twentieth century. It has transitioned through four generations of development and now is in a fifth generation of maturity. This chapter expands on previous writings and clarifies the relationships in the transition of benchmarking that has brought it to its current level of global benchmarking through the ubiquitous access to data and information that is offered through the Internet.[1] The purpose of this chapter is to provide the historical context that defines what benchmarking is today, based upon an overview of how it developed. Let's begin this historical journey by gaining the perspective from the close of the nineteenth century to understand how the industrial revolution and its approach to interchangeable parts fostered the idea of interchangeable business processes and the application of the scientific method to study business became extended into the use of business measurements to define best practices.

1. Gregory H. Watson, *The Benchmarking Workbook* (Portland, OR: Productivity Press, 1992), xx–xxii and Gregory H. Watson, *Strategic Benchmarking* (New York: Wiley, 1993), 5–9.

THE DAWN BEFORE BENCHMARKING SCIENCE

In the late 1800s, the management science work of Frederick Taylor encouraged comparison of work processes through the application of the scientific method. Taylor's concept was that there was "one best way" to do work and that it could be discovered through the scientific study of the way that work was performed. When the best way was discovered, then this should be applied as the standard for work performance until a better way was discovered.

These technical studies of work practices were conducted by industrial psychologists and industrial engineers. During the Second World War, this practice of making comparisons extended so that it became commonplace for companies to check with other companies in order to develop standards for pay, working hours, safety regulations, and related business hygiene factors.

Perhaps the most interesting insight in this period leading up to the development of benchmarking comes from comments describing how comparative product analysis and reverse engineering were applied in Japanese industry. In his book describing the development of the Toyota Production System, Taiichi Ohno, former vice president of manufacturing and coarchitect of this system, with industrial engineer colleague Shigeo Shingo, described the visit that opened their eyes to the possibility of *lean manufacturing* as he talks about the observation of the stock replenishment system that allowed fruits and vegetables to be sold while fresh and reduce waste from spoilage. As he admits, "From the supermarket we got the idea of viewing the earlier process in the production process as a kind of a store." He further observed that the Japanese adopted many of these practices because of their innate "curiosity and fondness for imitation."[2]

Indeed, during the period of 1950 to 1975, many American businessmen felt that Japan was merely a copycat and therefore it did not present

2. Taiichi Ohno, *Toyota Production System: Beyond Large-Scale Production* (Portland, OR: Productivity Press, 1990), 25–26.

a serious business threat because it did not invent any new technologies. At the macroeconomic level this may be true, but what the Japanese did invent was the ability to produce products with minimum waste because they did not have a resource-rich environment that could tolerate the loss to society that came from indiscriminate use of its scarce materials or poor productivity practices. Indeed, during this time many Americans joked about the stereotype Japanese industrial tour where engineering visitors came gawking at the magnitude of American industry taking many photographs to illustrate its greatness. These pundits missed the point of the tours — to identify ideas that could be transitioned to Japanese industry and improved to assure congruence with their developing manufacturing practices that focused on lean operations. At the same time that its engineers toured American plants, others stripped down the products and looked for ways to deliver the same functions at lower prices — effectively value engineering the products by eliminating waste from the design and its production process simultaneously.

During this same period, American industry tended to internalize its efforts rather than look toward external influences as if they would somehow poison the miracle of the post-war industrial might that was transforming America into the world's greatest economy. In its arrogance, many leaders in American industry believed that Yankee ingenuity was the solution to everything and that they had no need to look elsewhere for creative ideas in either product or process technology. Given this internal focus, it is not surprising that in the 1950s, business leaders like Hewlett-Packard's Bill Hewlett and Dave Packard encouraged their engineers to develop "next bench syndrome"—the practice of checking with engineering colleagues to define those functions and designs to be developed and implemented. This commercial arrogance was prevalent in American products—engineering push of features into the marketplace without consulting customers about needs or desires. This led to a systemic vulnerability that could be exploited by Japanese companies if they could discover what it was that customers wanted and deliver it first. And exploit this vulnerability they did—as history shows!

Throughout this first 75 years of the last century, methods related to benchmarking could be best described as an art rather than a science. The development of benchmarking into a science was the contribution of the Xerox Corporation as it sought to fight an onslaught of Japanese businesses that were taking advantage of a court ruling that stripped Xerox of its patent protection for its copier business due to its monopolistic business practices. The largest beneficiary of this ruling were the Japanese firms that developed disruptive technology at the low end of the copier business and caused Xerox to lose market share drastically in the period from 1976 to 1979—with a subsequent drop in return on net assets from 25 percent to under 5 percent. How did Xerox respond to this crisis?

BENCHMARKING—AN OPPORTUNITY THAT EMERGED FROM A CRISIS

After Xerox was forced to put its patents into the public domain in 1975, a steady stream of foreign competitors entered its markets—lead by Canon of Japan and Savin from France. The manner in which they chose to enter into competition causes little concern among Xerox managers because they were producing personal copiers—low throughput devices that fit onto a manager's desktop or file cabinet and were only capable of reproducing a single page at a time and very slowly, compared to the large, big-speed copiers that Xerox sold for use in central copying locations. However, it became clear over a number of years that these small machines were taking work away from the larger machines, and the Xerox business model leased the machines but sold individual copies that they produced. Thus, Xerox was losing its business one page at a time!

Xerox CEO David Kearns turned to his Fuji-Xerox Japanese joint venture led by Tony Kobyashi to discover what could be done to stem the tide of lost sales and profitability. The Xerox benchmarking method was borne out of the business requirement to estimate their competitor's strength by triangulating from two known sets of performance results (Xerox, USA, and Fuji-Xerox) to learn about the unknown capability of their Japanese competitors.[3] This created a real wakeup call for the Xerox business leaders—not only were Xerox new products twice as long in development, but their manufacturing cost was equal to the sales price of the competing products. Thus, there was no way that Xerox could compete head to head on these disruptive technologies.[4] This provided the first indication that there was real trouble at Xerox—performance indicators that demonstrated that there was a gap in performance, but it didn't tell what the gap was, why it existed, or what to do about it! Competitive benchmarking proved its value by delivering this wake-up call, but it wasn't capable of providing a change agenda that would return Xerox to profitability. For this, Xerox had to learn from business leaders in each of the performance areas where they suffered from shortfalls against the competition, so they put together a team to create a process for learning, which they called *benchmarking.*[5]

3. The Xerox benchmarking story is told through three books: John Hillkirk, *Xerox: American Samurai* (New York: Macmillan, 1986); Robert C. Camp, *Benchmarking: The Search for Industry Best Practices That Lead to Superior Performance* (Milwaukee, WI: ASQ Quality Press, 1989); and Richard C. Palermo and Gregory H. Watson, eds., *A World of Quality: The Timeless Passport* (Milwaukee, WI: ASQ Quality Press, 1994).

4. Harvard Professor Michael Porter in his early book *Competitive Strategy* (New York: The Free Press, 1985) describes the competitive dynamic for a market entrant where the barrier to competition has been removed (patent protection) and the entrant has cost-differentiated itself from the market leader. Harvard Professor Clayton M. Christenson in his insightful books, *The Innovator's Dilemma* (New York: Harper Business, 2003) and *The Innovator's Solution* with Michael E. Raynor (Boston: Harvard Business School Pres, 2003), calls this approach to a competition "disruptive innovation" in which new market entrants fundamentally change the game of the competition by seeking a lower-profit, vulnerable market from which to attack the mainstream market. In this environment, the new market entrant is given freedom to operate in this market because it costs too much in terms of lost gross profit margin for the entrenched leader to defend a poor profit market. Over time, the market entrant earns the right to compete for the mainstream market. This is precisely what Canon and its Japanese competitive cohort did to Xerox.

5. In a 1992 interview with John Kelsch, then corporate director of benchmarking for Xerox, he described the history of the development of benchmarking and the roles of the various individuals. Several key people stand out in this process: Frank Pipp, the division vice president who served as the champion for benchmarking; Norm Ricard, Bob Strosser, and Steve Snow—the original team who did the first studies; Jules Cochoit and Bob Edwards who prepared their initial course on benchmarking; Jack Kelly and Art Tweet who introduced me to benchmarking in 1985; Dick Barchi, who authored the first internal description of "competitive benchmarking" (which is what

While the lessons learned from competitive benchmarking told what was wrong and estimated how far Xerox lagged behind the competition, it was the benchmarking of industry best practice that gave sparks to fuel what Xerox called the *creative imitation* of observed leading processes and practices that brought Xerox out of its crisis. Xerox turned to companies with successful practices in those areas where they had observed their own shortcomings—the retailer Sears provided insights into inventory management, while the mail order firm L. L. Bean contributed learning of warehouse operations. Learning was incorporated at a furious rate, and Xerox converted itself into a new company with the result that by 1985 Xerox had increased its return on net assets to over 10 percent.[6] However, benchmarking was restricted at this time to the few companies that Xerox studied and was largely held as an internal practice within the Xerox Benchmarking Network—about 100 middle managers who conducted these studies. It was only after Xerox put these methods into the public domain by opening sharing the practice after they won the Malcolm Baldrige National Quality Award in 1989 that the interest expanded and laid the groundwork for Bob Camp's best-selling book on the subject of benchmarking.

MEANWHILE, CORPORATE PARTNERSHIPS AND SHARING FLOURISHED

In 1981, a second event stimulated interest in business improvement. Dr. W. Edwards Deming was featured in the NBC television white paper titled "If Japan Can, Why Can't We?" A challenge was issued to American management. They could improve their business and survive

---

Xerox first called this process) and is referred to as "The Red Book" by management of that day; and, finally, Bob Camp, who reported on the version of benchmarking that was described in the company's application for the Malcolm Baldrige National Quality Award.

6. While Bob Camp's book doesn't fully describe the background history of this time, the introduction to my book *The Benchmarking Workbook* provides a comprehensive description of the first decade (1979 to 1989) of benchmarking prior to the time when Camp's book put the spotlight on this business practice.

or allow it to grow stagnate in the face of the Japanese competition and die! At this time, many American industries were under attack by Japanese firms — Xerox was not alone; however, the influence of Deming was just to focus management on the need to improve; his ideas and approach to management were not universally accepted. Indeed, Deming was not a big fan of benchmarking, as can be observed by a few of his quotations:

- "Adapt, don't adopt. It is error to copy."
- "I think that the people here [in America] expect miracles. American management thinks that they can just copy from Japan. But they don't know what to copy."
- "It is hazard to copy. It is necessary to understand the theory of what one wishes to do or make. Americans are great copiers. The fact is that the Japanese learn the theory of what they wish to make, [and] then improve on it."[7]

Deming believed that no number of examples of success or failure in the improvement of quality and productivity would indicate what success another company could enjoy in the application of a process. To him, success depends only upon the profound knowledge that you are able to gain about your own process. In comparing performance between two organizations, he observed that quite often neither company knows whether or why any procedure is right. Also, they don't know whether or why another procedure is wrong. Deming said, "The question is not whether a business is successful, but why? And why was it not more successful?"

However, Dr. Joseph M. Juran was the quality consultant who most influenced Xerox, and it is unclear if Dr. Deming ever really understood how the Xerox benchmarking methodology worked. Deming talked as if he felt that benchmarking was more art than the science it had become! But Deming always asked the question, "How do you know?" It is this question that is central to any effort at benchmarking and is the point where Deming's philosophy and benchmarking merge.

---

7. W. Edwards Deming, *Out of the Crisis* (Cambridge: MIT Center for Advanced Engineering Study, 1982), 128–129.

The effect of Deming's television white paper should not be diminished—it did stimulate both an active dialog among companies as well as the sharing of best practices (although these practices were often derived by Theory O and not by using a scientific method like Xerox encouraged in its benchmarking process). In the early 1980s, a number of companies engaged in cross-company sharing and studies, which were foundational as subsequent benchmarking networks. Some examples from my direct experience at Hewlett-Packard include the following:

- The General Motors Cross-Industry Study of quality best practice in quality and reliability is a 1983 study of business leaders in different industries to define which quality management practices led to improved business performance.
- The General Electric Best-Practice Network is a consortium of some 16 companies who met regularly to discuss best practice in noncompetitive areas. These companies were selected so that none competed against any other participant, thus creating an open environment for sharing sensitive information about business practices.
- Hewlett-Packard also had a wide variety of collaborative efforts with other businesses. For instance, HP helped Proctor & Gamble understand about policy deployment (*hoshin kanri* or the planning process that grew to maturity at HP's Yokagawa Hewlett-Packard subsidiary). The nature of this collaboration included inviting two P&G executives to work inside of HP for a six-month period to experience firsthand how this planning process worked. Another company that enjoyed a special relationship was Xerox, as it actively sought to learn from the leaders in product development, and HP had a strong reputation for effective new product development. Also, Ford and HP conducted business practice sharing on many different levels as the CEOs were on each other's boards of directors. Hewlett-Packard also was a founding member of the GOAL/QPC Research Committee, a consortium of some 30 or so companies established to study Japanese quality practices and translate

Japanese training and academic research material into English. Finally, HP joined with many other firms to give support to Florida Power & Light as they successfully challenged the Deming Prize of the Japanese Union of Scientists and Engineers (JUSE). Florida Power & Light and HP shared the same Japanese quality consultants, which facilitated this cross-company learning.[8]

- Another example of extensive corporate sharing during this period is the development of the criteria for the Malcolm Baldrige National Quality Award. These criteria were developed as areas to address by some 120 corporate quality executives from leading American businesses who agreed on the basics of best practice in business that lead to success as grouped into the seven categories of the criteria.
- The GOAL/QPC Research Committee was a consortium of some 35 companies that was established by Bob King in 1987 to study quality methods from Japan as well as breakthrough concepts from around the world. One committee established in 1990 was dedicated to the study of benchmarking. This committee documented its findings in a research that was published in 1991.[9]

The Diffusion of Benchmarking as a Practice

Another significant event that accelerated the spread of benchmarking as a recognized business best practice was the presentation of the Malcolm Baldrige National Quality Award to Xerox, which put a public spotlight on benchmarking as a practice that made a difference at Xerox. David

8. The most notable shared consultants were Dr. Hajime Makabe and Dr. Noriaki Kano.
9. Milt Boyd, George Murray, Glen Hoffherr, and Dona Hotopp, *Benchmarking*, GOAL/QPC Research Report 91-01. While this committee heard presentations from many companies, they settled on a best-practice benchmarking process to present in their paper, which was based on a briefing by the Compaq quality group (Gregory H. Watson, Director of Quality; Charlie Burke, Manager of Quality Processes; and Joseph M. Wexler, Benchmarking Manager). It should be noted that these individuals also worked with the International Benchmarking Clearinghouse at the APQC in Houston, Texas, to develop its benchmarking process, which has become a standard methodology used throughout this community.

Kearns, the Xerox CEO who led the company throughout its turnaround effort, decided to put all of its quality practices into the public domain (these included the benchmarking process, problem solving process, and quality improvement process) and Xerox also followed the practice of Baldrige Award Winners of offering seminars to explain what they did and how it was accomplished. Bob Camp's successful book reported on the work of "Team Xerox" to develop and deploy a common method for benchmarking throughout the company. Following these efforts, benchmarking gained more public attention as a number of books that were published in the 1992 to 1993 period that facilitated the diffusion of learning about the benchmarking process.[10]

INSTITUTIONALIZATION OF THE PRACTICE OF BENCHMARKING

However, it wasn't until the Houston-based American Productivity & Quality Center (APQC) established The Benchmarking Clearinghouse (IBC) in 1992 that a common methodology and approach for benchmarking was spread into a consortium of companies who purposefully gather to share and study their internal practices in common interest groups. The IBC was the brainchild of Dr. C. Jackson Grayson, the founder of the APQC and one of the drivers behind establishment of the Malcolm Baldrige National Quality Award. Grayson believed that benchmarking was not just a fad but that it was also an essential business practice. Grayson had been a dean of two graduate schools of business and administrator of the wage and price controls process put in place to

10. Benchmarking did not appear in the criteria for the Malcolm Baldrige National Quality Award criteria until after Xerox won the Award in 1989. In addition to the books cited in the previous footnotes, the following books on the subject of benchmarking were published during this time: Michael J. Spendolini, *The Benchmarking Book* (New York: AMACOM/The American Management Association, 1992); Gerald J. Balm, *Benchmarking: A Practitioner's Guide for Becoming and Staying the Best* (Schaumberg, IL: Quality and Productivity Management Association, 1992); Kathleen H. J. Leibfried and C. J. McNair, *Benchmarking: A Tool for Continuous Improvement* (New York: Harper-Collins, 1992); and Joseph M. Wexler and Gregory H. Watson, ed, *The Benchmarking Management Guide* (Portland, OR: Productivity Press, 1993).

control runaway inflation in the early 1970s under the Nixon administration. An endorsement about the business value of benchmarking coming from him was indeed high praise, but to have him actively engage in a process to broaden the scope of benchmarking through developing a forum that facilitated cross-company learning was truly indicative that benchmarking had transitioned from a company-specific quality improvement tool to an essential ingredient of management best practice.[11]

The contribution of the IBC that lead to the eventual mainstreaming the practice of benchmarking was fourfold:

- Creating a benchmarking network among a broad spectrum of industries and supported by an information database and library located at its Houston office
- Conducting benchmarking consortium studies on topics of common interest to members
- Standardizing training materials around a simple benchmarking process and development of generic business process taxonomy (in collaboration with Andersen Consulting) that could form a common process language and facilitate cross-company performance comparison
- Accelerating the diffusion of benchmarking as an accepted management practice through the propagation of the Benchmarking Code of Conduct that governs how companies collaborate with each other during the course of a study.

The final event that cemented the coming spread of benchmarking was its pervasive inclusion in the criteria for the 1991 version of the Malcolm Baldrige National Quality Award, which mentioned the use of benchmarking or competitive analysis in 12 of the 32 evaluation criteria sections. This level of reference surpassed all other quality tools and methods in

---

11. The first president of the IBC was Dr. Carla O'Dell; Gregory H. Watson served as Vice President for Benchmarking Services to design training programs, publish books, and establish a consultancy for members; and William Grundstrom was Vice President of Training Services for development and delivery of benchmarking courses (see www.aqpc.org).

terms of the number of mentions in the award criteria and indicates that benchmarking was fast-becoming a mainstream practice during this time.[12]

MAINSTREAMING BENCHMARKING INTO BUSINESS

By 1994, the IBC had directly reached over 1,000 companies in promulgating benchmarking; the Malcolm Baldrige Award criteria had been ordered by over 100,000 companies; and the combined sales of benchmarking books had surpassed 200,000 copies. Over the past 10 years (1994–2004), a number of channels have come available for diffusing the practice of benchmarking even further. Two channels for benchmarking are worthy of particular attention: the Internet and the Global Benchmarking Network (GBN).

It is clear that the advent of the Internet has changed many aspects of life by creation of an instant access to information and people. These are critical enablers of benchmarking and thus allow a much broader search for information and contact possibility than was previously obtainable through personal contacts and cross-organizational affiliations. The advent of the World Wide Web as a global communication resource strengthens the ability to gain access to data, but it also complicates the interpretation of information because there are no standards for analysis, and thus the web is inundated with a plethora of Theory Opinion that must be sorted and sifted to discover truth. In my opinion, the full impact of the Internet on benchmarking practices has yet to be felt.[13]

In 1993, discussions between the U.K. Benchmarking Centre, the Strategic Planning Institute (SPI) in the United States, the Swedish Institute for Quality (SIQ) in Sweden, the Informationszentrum Benchmarking (IZB) in Germany, and the Benchmarking Club of Italy came

12. Indeed, many of the earliest benchmarking authors were associated with the IBC in one way or another: Bob Camp, Gerald Balm, Mark Czarnecki, and Joe Wexler were all involved in the early development of the methods used by the IBC in defining its approach to the process of benchmarking, which is now defined as *collaborative benchmarking.*

13. In an earlier article, I described the potential for e-Benchmarking and other electronic tools: Gregory H. Watson, "Digital Hammers and Electronic Nails," *Quality Progress* 31 no. 7 (1998): 21–26.

together to evaluate the possibility of a cooperative network. In 1994, the Global Benchmarking Network (GBN) was officially established by these founding members as a community of legally independent benchmarking centers, with the objective to achieve a consistent understanding of benchmarking as a management method and to promote its worldwide spread and utilisation. I view the GBN as an extension of the Benchmarking Council of the Strategic Planning Institute, which preceded the founding of the APQC International Benchmarking Clearinghouse but focused on a few member companies following the model used by The Conference Board for cross-company sharing, thereby reducing its impact on diffusion of the benchmarking methods to a wider audience.[14] The GBN currently includes benchmarking centers of 17 nations. Together, they represent more than 25,000 businesses and government agencies. The President of GBN is Dr. Robert C. Camp of The Best Practice Institute in the United States and author of the first book on benchmarking.[15]

CHALLENGES OF THE COMING YEARS AND E-BENCHMARKING

At the beginning of this chapter, I proposed that the development of benchmarking could be viewed in a series of generations or stages in the maturing of this practice. This taxonomy of benchmarking is messy as the stages overlap, and some have no clear beginning or ending. The reason for this lack of clarity in the time line of benchmarking is that different organizations are at differing levels of maturity in their understanding and implementation of the methodology. But perhaps by documenting these distinctions, along with the logic that defines their boundary con-

14. The Strategic Planning Institute has returned to their original focus as provider of the PIMS database (Profit Impact of Market Strategy), which was first developed by General Electric and Harvard University and was later transitioned to the not-for-profit SPI for support to create broader access and a wider clientele of users (see the SPI web site at www.pimsonline.org).

15. Bob Camp may be contacted at either www.globalbenchmarking.com or rcampbpi@att.net. In addition to the IBC and GBN, there are a number of other operative benchmarking networks: The Benchmarking Network (www.benchmarkingnetwork.com), Best Practices LLC Global Benchmarking Council (www3.best-in-class.com/gbc), and The Benchmarking Exchange (www.benchnet.com).

ditions, managers will be able to clarify what exactly it is they are doing when they seek information to improve their business. What are these five generations of benchmarking development?

FIRST GENERATION—COMPETITIVE PRODUCT ANALYSIS AND REVERSE ENGINEERING

This first stage of benchmarking could also be labeled "natural curiosity and its natural extension." Even when production was done by craftsmen forming individual works with their own hands—artisans who saw each piece for its uniqueness—there was a tendency to compare your own work with that of others to determine which was the best of the best in your field.[16] Today, this practice is observed through the engineering teardown analysis used in reverse engineering to understand how competitive products have been designed, what materials have been used, and what technologies were employed in their production. Another focus is the competitive product analysis that can take one of two forms: marketing-based, comparing features or functional performance to customer perception,[17] and technology-focused, comparing degree of performance that is delivered against a standard (e.g., computer run speed for a benchmark software program). This form of benchmarking will probably continue ad infinitum.

SECOND GENERATION—INFORMAL VISITS AND PROCESS TOURING

In a paradoxical way, the second generation of benchmarking is once again more art than science in benchmarking. There is a syndrome among managers to seek the popular, adopt the new, and worship the popular without making a critical assessment of its validity or applicability. These

---

16. This concept of *best of the best* is described using the Japanese word *dantotsu,* which was the term Fuji-Xerox used to describe the object of their search for best practice.

17. Note that customer perception research is attempts to adjust the functionality of a product to the needs of the customer, while advertising is an attempt to adjust the customer need to the product functionality. What a difference this slight twist makes in terms of the objective of a research project!

are weaknesses that are inherent in many art-like benchmarking processes. Taking a walk in a factory does not constitute a benchmarking site visit—this is industrial tourism. Brief conversations with colleagues at a conference are not benchmarking—these are chats. Benchmarking must include three elements: definition of an object of study, performance measurement of the object, and comparison to other similar objects in order to determine which alternative has achieved the best capability and why. While these forms of benchmarking will probably also continue ad infinitum, they should be strongly discouraged, as they cannot produce profound knowledge of the process that allows your organization to drive improvement.[18]

THIRD GENERATION — COMPETITIVE BENCHMARKING (1976–PRESENT)

Science in benchmarking first started with competitive benchmarking as an extension of competitive intelligence and market research. Competitive benchmarking seeks to discover the specific actions that are being taken by competitors to gain advantage in the marketplace through their strategic choices and capital investments in products and processes. Because competition is the defining ingredient in a free market, this type of benchmarking is an essential ingredient in every informed company's portfolio of tools in their strategic business planning process.

FOURTH GENERATION — PROCESS BENCHMARKING (1992–PRESENT)

Process benchmarking can be either strategic or operational in its focus, depending on where it is focused. The importance of the subject and the

18. My initial involvement in benchmarking came from benchmarking with Xerox in 1985 followed by an assignment to define a benchmarking process for the Hewlett-Packard Corporate Quality Office, sponsoring the development of the Compaq Computer Corporation benchmarking process, then sharing this practice with other companies through the GOAL/QPC Research Committee in 1990.

breadth of its application distinguish between these types of studies. It is this type of benchmarking that forms the core of scientific studies. Process benchmarking will be the continuing focus of serious business investigations and will provide insights into the way businesses achieve flawless execution of their processes to achieve excellence in the perspective of their customers.

FIFTH GENERATION — GLOBAL BENCHMARKING (1996–PRESENT)

Global benchmarking extends the boundary of benchmarking geographically to encompass the best process that can be found in any location and in any analogous business. Thus, global benchmarking also includes the use of generic process comparisons and e-Benchmarking or the use of the Internet to screen for performance information, discover benchmarking partners, and share the results of studies. In this age, benchmarking will become easier and more accessible as a learning device.

CONCLUSION

We should all remember that like Sir Isaac Newton, benchmarking enables us to say, "If I have seen further, it is because I have stood on the shoulders of giants." We see more clearly and make better decisions because we are not replicating the mistakes of the past, but using the analysis of the past to sharpen our focus on the future! Discovering profound knowledge from history can help us understand the potential opportunities of the future with more perfect vision!

PART 1

The Business Context of Benchmarking

Stimulating Business Improvement by Benchmarking

Competitive innovation works on the premise that a successful competitor is likely to be wedded to a "recipe" for success. That's why the most effective weapon new competitors possess is a clean sheet of paper. And why an incumbent's greatest vulnerability is its belief in accepted practice.

—GARY HAMEL AND C. K. PRAHALAD

INTRODUCTION

Benchmarking is a process of comparing in order to learn how to improve. Motivation for a benchmarking study is the desire to improve and become more competitive. But benchmarking is not the silver bullet of performance improvement!

Ever since 1990 when Roger Milliken declared that "benchmarking is the art of stealing shamelessly," many executives have thought that the process of benchmarking is a "quick fix" for making business performance improvements. However, benchmarking is not a quick fix; it is a rigorous process that requires both *sweat equity*—learning about one's own processes and coordinating study missions to other organizations—and *analytical thoroughness*—measurement and analysis of work process performance as well as the detailed mapping of processes and side-by-side assessment of process differences.

Benchmarking uses the analytical information contained in a *benchmark*, a comparative measure of process or results performance, to establish which organization is candidate for a best practice in a specific business process. Then the business process must be thoroughly defined in order to understand how benchmark performance was achieved and to identify enablers of this successful performance. Finally, a cultural adaptation of the learning must be made in order to apply this new knowledge to your own organization. In order for benchmarking to be successful, it must heed the warning of Dr. W. Edwards Deming who said, "It is hazard to copy. One must understand the theory of what one wishes to do" (1982). Cultural adaptation and business model adaptation are necessary to assure that lessons observed from one place can be successfully transferred someplace else. As Deming also cautioned, "Adapt, don't adopt. It is error to copy" (1982). So how can we more carefully describe what is meant by benchmarking?

BENCHMARKING DEFINED ACCORDING TO CATEGORIES OF PRACTICE

Benchmarking has been described as a search for best practices—indeed, it is the process of comparing the performance and process characteristics between two or more organizations in order to learn how to improve. However, a problem that began early in the game of benchmarking was a lack of clarity in the meaning of the term. In Bob Camp's first book on benchmarking, he described four ways to approach the problem of data collection that were distinguished using the logic of where information was obtained. The way that he distinguished these categories was classified according to the source of the benchmarking data.[1] One problem with this breakdown of benchmarking is that it focuses too narrowly on where data is obtained, rather than on the objective of the study itself—in other words, the focus of the definition is on the process of benchmarking rather than on the lessons that must be learned. A different ap-

---

1. Robert C. Camp, *Benchmarking* (Milwaukee, WI: ASQ Quality Press, 1989).

4

proach is required to understand the context of benchmarking and how it fits into business. This was the approach that was initiated in my second book on the subject of benchmarking, and we will present a complete definition of benchmarking in this chapter.[2]

First, the starting point of benchmarking is measurement—the benchmark is after all a measurement. However, we must distinguish between the act of measuring performance and the process of benchmarking. A benchmarking process uses a common measurement standard to compare across organizations to determine where a best practice exists based on the results it produces. After the performance has been measured, then a further investigation is conducted to characterize the practices that lead to the observed performance and the root causes of the performance advantage are documented as a best practice. Thus, the first distinction that must be drawn is the difference between performance measurement and process benchmarking. Each of these ways to improve addresses a different set of questions (see Figure 1.1):

All benchmarking is process benchmarking. To understand the dynamic characteristics of a benchmarking study, the different terms that identify the choices that can be taken in the design of a study must be identified and defined. The first term that must be defined is *process benchmarking.*

- *Process benchmarking:* A method for studying work process performance between two unique or distinct implementations of the same fundamental activity. Process benchmarking includes internal inspection of an organization's own performance as well as the external study of another organization that is recognized for achieving superior performance as evidenced by an objective standard of comparison (the benchmark). The objective of process benchmarking is not to calculate a quantitative performance gap, but to identify best practices that may be adapted for improvement of organizational performance.

There are two categories of process benchmarking studies that may be differentiated according to their application as strategic or operational

---

2. Gregory H. Watson, *Strategic Benchmarking* (New York: Wiley, 1993).

Performance Measurement	Process Benchmarking
What is the level of performance that an organization has achieved?	Is the performance comparison between these two organizations a fair one?
What is the distinction between the lavel of performance of one organization and the rest of its industry?	How does the performance achieved relate to the potential performance capability of the organization?
What is the performance improvement trend of the organization?	How wide is the variation in the business practices of the organization; and does this variation relate to quantifiable performance differences (in average or variation)?
What is the current state of performance relative to the historical trend?	How consistently applied are performance enabler throughout the organization?
Is the organization improving in both the magnitude and direction it intended?	What is the progress of the organization toward its performance goal or objective?
How do the key performance indicators change as a function of time and effort?	What is the extent of improvement made in different parts of the organization? Is this a spot improvement or is it systematic?

FIGURE 1.1 Comparison of performance measurement and process benchmarking

studies. These two categories are further divisible into performance and perceptual benchmarking studies depending on the type of data that is being compared. The relationship among these distinctions is clarified in the following:

- *Strategic Benchmarking:* A benchmarking study whose objective is to discover ideas for improvement that will trigger breakthrough changes and may be leveraged across the business to enhance an organization's competitive advantage.

Strategic benchmarking studies challenge management to move from a current state to a desired state of business performance by identifying potential breakthrough opportunities that can generate significant profitability or productivity improvement. A strategic study focuses on critical business areas that must change to attain or maintain the competitive advantage of a business, including the validity of critical business assumptions, options for improving core competence areas, concepts for development of business processes, alternative ways to approach technology inflection points, or ways to strengthen business fundamentals that define the organization's operational strategy.

A strategic benchmarking study may change the total framework of an organization by assessing topics such as strategic direction; structure or governance of the business; decisions supporting capital acquisition or investments in research and design (R&D); decisions affecting management choices regarding either business or product line positioning; or change management strategies (e.g., pursuit of a specific strategy such as implementation of an enterprise software product or management's choice of an improvement methodology—for example, ISO9000, Total Quality Management [TQM], or Six Sigma) as a way to induce change in the organization. These types of benchmarking projects can act as triggers for greater change that may be leveraged across the entire organization.

Thus, strategic benchmarking studies tend to seek out business leverage opportunities and change trigger points that can cause an organization to make a breakthrough change that results in competitive advantage. A leverage opportunity is a business improvement concept that may be applied across the organization in a variety of areas and that will create a big performance difference. For instance, transformation of a core business process can achieve this result. A change trigger point is a single event that will create a sequence of changes—like a ripple effect as a pebble is thrown into a calm lake. These two different changes will become clearer in the context of a case study of a series of strategic benchmarking studies that is contained in Chapter 7.

Examples of strategic benchmarking studies include evaluation of options for the design of an organization's governance structure; assessment of approaches used to implement advanced technology (e.g., enterprise management software or paperless document handling); or strategic business issues that are faced by the organization (e.g., creating a web-based business capability; managing the technology transition across generations of advancement; or managing the routine work of the organization through management methods such as balanced scorecard, performance management, and business excellence assessments).

- *Operational Benchmarking:* A benchmarking study that is focused on the way that a specific work process is performed with an objective of improving the performance of that specific process (e.g., improving a sales process, printed circuit board production process, or distribution process).

Operational benchmarking will provide productivity improvement by concentrating on specific activities that will improve the effectiveness, efficiency, or economy of routine business operations. Operational benchmarking focuses on specific work activities that need to be improved and seeks to identify the work procedures, production equipment, skills or competence training, or analytical methods that result in sustained performance improvement as indicated by objective measures of process productivity (process throughput, cost per unit, defect opportunities, cycle time, etc.).

Examples of operational benchmarking studies include analysis of invoicing procedures to determine the most productive process; evaluation of production methods to determine the highest throughput methods that deliver lowest cost and least defects; and study of logistics distribution methods that result in both high delivery service performance and low levels of finished goods inventory.

Both strategic and operational benchmarking studies may focus on either performance or perceptions as the type of data that is being evaluated. Performance data consists of a set of measures about results or outcomes, while perceptual data comes from the feelings or reactions of an individual to the outcomes or results of the process. These two different focus areas for studies may be clarified further.

- *Performance Focus of Benchmarking:* At a strategic level of organization, a performance benchmark seeks to determine which organization performs best according to an objective standard that is typically financial, like return on capital employed (ROCE) or earnings before interest and taxes (EBIT). At an operational level, benchmarking product or service outcomes using a standard comparison or test under known operating conditions is also called *performance benchmarking.*

A performance benchmarking study seeks to answer the following question: Which organization, product, or service is better based upon rigorous assessment using objective performance criteria? Examples of performance benchmarking studies include consumer product analysis that evaluates products on a head-to-head basis using a fixed set of criteria for performance; the evaluation of product performance using a standard test, such as operating time, to run a specific application; or endurance tests that identify the ability of a product to perform over a fixed period of time under comparable operating conditions. What sets a performance-focused study apart from its opposite is the type of data that is used to make a comparison in the study.

- *Perceptual Focus of Benchmarking:* Perceptual benchmarking is a study using the process benchmarking approach but focused on feelings or attitudes about process, product, or service performance by the recipient of the process output. Perceptual benchmarking seeks to answer the following question: How do you perceive the delivery of service, performance of product, or execution of process by the people who are recipients of these outputs?

Perceptual benchmarking uses attribute or categorical data to quantify subjective feelings and establish relative performance rankings using criteria like timeliness of performance, goodness of knowledge transfer, soundness of information, courtesy of delivery agents, and so on. Examples of perceptual benchmarking include surveys of training satisfaction at the completion of a training event, employee satisfaction surveys

Category	Performance Study	Perceptual Study
Strategic Benchmarking	Focuses on the collection of performance information for key results indicators in the organization's balanced scorecard that are critical to satisfaction to customers.	Focuses on the market or finicial perceptions of the company's performance as a long-term indicator of its value (e.g., brand reputation or viability of strategy).
Operational Benchmarking	Focuses on the collection of process-level performance indicators such as productivity, efficiency, or cycle time.	Focuses on the feelings of a target audience about how the organizational activity affects them (e.g., employee or customer satisfaction).

FIGURE 1.2 Taxonomy of benchmarking studies

to determine either the work climate or structural issues regarding compensation and benefits, or customer satisfaction with the product or service delivery to the market place.

These different categories of benchmarking are related in Figure 1.2, which shows how strategic and operational studies map against performance or perceptual data.

The way to differentiate benchmarking studies is to consider the different ways that they seek our various sources of data.

BENCHMARKING DEFINED ACCORDING TO SOURCES OF DATA

This second group of terms to be defined is terminology that identifies the sources of data used in conducting a specific benchmarking study. This is an older and somewhat less helpful way to identify benchmarking studies that has its roots in the first set of studies that were conducted by Xerox.[3]

---

3. This distinction was made in Bob Camp's 1989 *Benchmarking* book and follows the original use of the Xerox Corporation.

- *Competitive Benchmarking:* An approach to benchmarking that targets specific product designs, process capabilities, or administrative methods used by one's direct competitors (e.g., the study of performance in the laptop computer industry that features only those companies that produce these products). The most stringent types of competitive studies will assess head-to-head competing organizations in the same industry and market.
- *Functional Benchmarking:* An approach to benchmarking that seeks information from a functional area in a particular application or industry (e.g., benchmarking the purchasing function must determine the most successful approach to manage a supplier base). In this type of study, information is compared for the same work process or business function either across industries or within the same industry, but the focus is always on the functional area.
- *Internal Benchmarking:* An approach to benchmarking where organizations learn from sister companies, divisions, or operating units that are part of the same operating group or company (e.g., the study of internal research and development groups to determine best practices that reduce time to market for the new product introduction process). In this type of study, performance information is compared for the same work process or business function within the same organization (perhaps looking at unique production lines, different plants, separate divisions, or distinct business units).
- *Generic Benchmarking:* An approach to benchmarking that seeks process performance information that is from outside one's own industry. Enablers are translated from one organization to another using an interpretation of their analogous relationships (e.g., learning about reducing cycle time in production operations by the study of inventory management methods used in stocking fresh vegetables in grocery stores). In this type of study, performance information is used through the development of an analogy that permits learning with broad comparisons for a specific process (e.g., studying distribution of food supplies to learn how to control automobile manufacturing logistics).

11

There is another refinement on this classification scheme that decomposes benchmarking studies into categories of data source. The second classification scheme distinguishes among the types of studies by the way a project is conducted: an internal study, industry study, benchmarking exchange study, or special interest group study.[4] This way of describing benchmarking studies adds two new perspectives to the sources of data approach. These categories may be defined as follows:

- *Internal Study:* Same definition as an internal benchmarking study.
- *Industry Study:* Same definition as a functional benchmarking study.
- *Benchmarking Exchange Study:* Benchmarking Exchange describes the activity in a benchmarking study where two or more companies exchange information about the way their processes perform — whether they are competitive organizations. In specifying the process for benchmarking, this is the step that follows identification of best practice (more details will be presented in Chapter 3 about the process of doing a benchmarking study).
- *Special Interest Group (SIG) or Collaborative Benchmarking:* In defining what is a benchmarking collaborative, the key ingredient is that it is a group of companies that have banded together in order to discover from their mutual experience what is the best practice in a particular subject area. The General Motors cross-industry study that was described in Watson's *Strategic Benchmarking* is precisely this kind of study.[5]

One concern about the collaborative or special interest group study is the usefulness of the data. Because companies self-select participation in the study based on their own needs, will the study of the group's own performance actually identify the peaks of performance and their related best

---

4. This distinction was made by Carl G. Thor in *Practical Benchmarking for Mutual Improvement* (Portland, OR: Productivity Press, 1995), p 2.

5. Collaborative benchmarking has been used in health care applications and is a model that is used for group studies by the International Benchmarking Clearinghouse. For more detail on this method, see Robert G. Gift and Doug Mosel, *Benchmarking in Healthcare* (Chicago: American Hospital Publishing, 1994).

practices, or will it merely identify a lowest common denominator that is observed from the self-nominated sample of firms? If truly excellent practices are not found within the participating organizations, then the sponsor of the study should not be complacent and settle for the best of what is found by chance and self-nomination, but should actively extend the study to seek out practices that will challenge the performance of all study participants.

No matter which scheme is used to identify the sources of data, it is clear that this way of describing a benchmarking study is incomplete without the two previous distinctions that define the focus of the study and the type of the data that is being used.

Examples of the way that strategic and operational benchmarking studies are pursued by using different sources of benchmarking data are described in Figure 1.3.

Source of Benchmarking Data ⟍ Types of Benchmarking	Competitive	Functional	Internal	Generic
Strategic	Analysis of a head-to-head competitor in terms of its strategic intent or its business strategy.	Analysis of a recognized leader in a specific function to determine future direction or developmental strategy.	Analysis of the internal business units to find the potential areas of synergy or leverage that exist across the organization.	Analysis of an analogous type of business to discover insights about relevance of technology or new operating systems.
Operational	Analysis of a specific process or functional area at a direct competitor to determine which company has the best practice.	Analysis of a specific practice of a functional leader in order to determine the key enablers of its sustained performance.	Analysis of a "sinister business unit" to discover why a process is able to perform at a higher level of effectiveness or efficency.	Analysis of a core business process in an unlike industry to determine the key enablers of its sustained performance.

FIGURE 1.3 Benchmarking studies versus sources of benchmarking study data

Source of Data	Advantages	Disadvantages
Competitive Benchmarking	Provides a strategic insight into marketplace competitiveness and a wake-up call to action.	• Legal issues regarding data sharing among competitors. • Study detail may not be good enough for process diagnosis.
Functional Benchmarking	Takes advantage of functional and professional networks to gain study participants.	• Functional concentration tends to support operational rather than strategic studies. • Does not challenge paradigm of functional thinking.
Internal Benchmarking	Provides highest degree of process detail and simplified access to process information.	The internal focus tends to be operational, rather than strategic, and reinforces the organization's cultural norms.
Generic Benchmarking	• Has the greatest opportunity for process breakthroughs. • Because organizations don't compete, reliable detailed information is usually available. • Provides incentive for strategic change initiatives.	• Difficulty in developing an analogy between dissimilar businesses. • Difficulty in identifying the companies to benchmark. • Difficulty in establishing the appropriate contact for a study.

FIGURE 1.4 Benefits analysis of benchmarking data sources

This way of categorizing benchmarking practice according to the source of data leads to conclusions about the relative usefulness of information (advantages and disadvantages) that is drawn from these different sources as presented in Figure 1.4.

So far our attention has been placed on defining those terms that specify the taxonomy of benchmarking: the types of benchmarking studies, the focus area of the study, and the sources of the data. In addition, there is another set of terms that describe the different component parts of a benchmarking study.

DEFINITIONS OF THE COMPONENTS OF A PROCESS BENCHMARKING STUDY

In order to be clear about how a benchmarking study is performed, it is important to learn some terminology that is commonly used to refer to the different parts of a benchmarking study. These terms include: *benchmark, best practice, critical success factor, enabler, process capability, entitlement, baseline analysis, gap analysis,* and *world class performance.*

- *Benchmark:* A measure of performance that is used to compare the products, services, or processes between two analogous organizations in order to establish superiority in sustained performance. Note that many of the benchmarks that are publicly promoted indicate only spot performance at a specific point in time and do not meet the criteria of enduring success by failing to establish the difference in performance between a *special cause event* and a *common cause* management process. A lack of statistical discipline in the use of benchmarks threatens to diminish the perceived value of the process of benchmarking.
- *Best Practice:* The set of activities, tasks, resources, training, and methods that created the observed benchmark level of performance in an observed work process. In a process benchmarking study, in order to qualify as a best practice, the performance must be observed and mapped to assure that the work performed is properly

identified and that process experts have validated and verified the distinctions between observed best practices and merely good practice. Without the objective assessment by work process experts, best practice becomes a subjective claim that is not verifiable.

- *Critical Success Factors:* These are quantifiable, measurable, and auditable indicators of process performance and process capability in key business processes. They indicate in basic business terms the performance level obtained in a comparative manner using such basic building blocks of processes to describe the performance of business effectiveness (quality), efficiency (cycle time), and economy (cost). Key critical success factors are universal and may be used for cross-organizational comparisons for the same process.

- *Enabler:* The specific activity, action, method, or technique that stimulated progress in one process over the comparative processes and led to identification of a best practice (e.g., the way quality function deployment or failure mode and effects analysis was used in a product design process; a process for data presentation that more clearly indicated the action to be taken by front-line operators; or an employee training and development system that delivers the appropriate skills and competence to process workers as they require these methods to perform their work in a changing technological environment).

- *Process Capability:* The analysis of the ability of a process to reliably produce a high quality output by evaluating the ratio of its customers' tolerance for performance quality to the ability of the process to control its variation. Process capability may be calculated as an ideal by comparing the total specification limit to six standard deviations of the variation for the same measure (Cp is the abbreviation used for the ideal form of process capability). Process capability may also be evaluated against average performance of the process by checking which side of the customer specification is closer to the process average. Here the process capability is calculated as the minimum between the difference in the ratio of the average to the lower and upper specifications divided by three standard deviations for the variation in the process. This real-world perspective of process capability is abbreviated Cpk and indicates the expected value of process performance as it is implemented.

- *Entitlement:* The set of work process lessons learned that are derived by examination of one's own processes and discovery of wasted activities, duplicated steps or non-value added work that can be eliminated or modified based solely on the self-analysis phase of benchmarking. An organization is entitled to make such process changes without relying on the lessons learned from external discovery. Such improvements permit the process to operate as intended and represent gap closure between original process design and current process performance. Entitlement also refers to the gap that may exist between the design process capability (Cp ratio) and the achieved process capability (Cpk ratio) as management is entitled to the performance which they purchased with their capital investment.
- *Baseline Analysis:* A comparison of performance baseline data across all benchmarked processes. A common scale is used for each comparison based on the variation observed in process performance. A best process is one that has both the highest average sustained performance and the lowest variation in the daily results. The performance baseline comprehends both of these factors using a standardized metric for process comparisons (e.g., process standard deviation as calculated using the defects per million opportunities as evaluated against a common customer requirement for targeted performance). The baseline analysis may be presented as an analysis of variance to illustrate the sampled performance across all of the different process locations.
- *Gap Analysis:* The evaluation of the performance difference between current internal performance and benchmark performance at the best-practice organization. To be effective, a gap analysis should include both the use of statistical confidence intervals and tests of difference (for both means and variance) to demonstrate that a real performance gap has been observed, not a gap due to chance observations.

17

- *World Class Performance:* A degree of performance achieved in a business practice that clearly sets it aside as exceptional — a unique performance level that is reserved for describing only the best of the best. The Japanese word for this degree of process performance is *dantotsu.*

The definition of world class performance requires a little more explanation.

While it may sound good to call an observed best practice "world class," some practical considerations should also be embedded in this label. For example, no organization is truly "perfect" or "flawless" or even "world class" — some are, however, much better than others. But we shouldn't make this judgment about "better" without basing it on scientific knowledge that has a statistical basis. All too often the judgment about superiority of an organization is based on reputation alone with a subjective leap of faith that their business practices (in all areas) must be somehow better and therefore are worthy of emulation! This is clearly not true! Another dimension that must be included in any systematic approach to benchmarking is the analytical element. This includes the establishment of a measure of comparison, a sampling plan to collect comparative data, a statistical method for observing comparisons that are significant, and a graphical means to present the comparison so it is understandable by decision makers. While it is intuitively clear that there is no "one world best performance" that exists at a particular point in time (the enormity of analysis to support such a claim would be unmanageable), it is possible to define a category of performance as "world class" using a rule of thumb; for instance, by using a standardized measurement process (e.g., the performance baseline analysis) and applying a decision criteria to determine which processes are observed in the top 5 percent of all organizations addressed in the study. This criteria indicates a high confidence level that the process is in a leader and worthy of further investigation as a potential best practice.

In addition, a caution should be added to the identification of a practice as world class. One should not fall into the trap of the "halo effect" — noting excellence in one business practice does not imply that all business

18

practices operate at the same exceptional level of performance. Just because one business process or management practice is evaluated as world class does not mean that the entire organization is world class!

Additionally, while observing the practices of a world class organization may lead to breakthrough process improvement and generate disruptive change, it may be possible to achieve significant gains through incremental, continuous improvement, or "sustaining" change that does not impact the organizational dynamics as strongly as the disruptive change does. This is the basic operating principle behind the Toyota Production System—the principle of bees gathering nectar from flowers—it is through many trips with small amounts of nectar that a community of bees creates its warehouse of honey!

AN OPERATIONAL DEFINITION OF WORLD CLASS PERFORMANCE

Benchmarking seeks to deliver performance that is best of the best (this is the Japanese word *dantotsu*) or world class performance. World class is an elusive performance level. To be the best of the best, it is necessary that you have both a high level of performance (typically in the top 5 percent of observed practices), and this level of performance must be sustainable across changes in product life cycle, underlying technology in both product and process, as well as successive generations of executive leadership. That is a tall order for any organization. What does it mean to be world class? In *Strategic Benchmarking*, I defined a *world class company* as one that is able to achieve and sustain a leadership performance level (or a Six Sigma level of performance), while at the same time exhibiting competitive considerations that are significant learning areas for a TQM-oriented organization. By definition, a world class organization does the following:

- Knows its processes better than its competitors know their processes
- Knows its industrial competitors business better than their competitors know their industrial competitors
- Knows its customers better than their competitors know their own customers

19

- Responds more rapidly to change in customer behavior than do its competitors
- Engages employees more effectively than do its competitors
- Competes for market share on a customer-by-customer basis

Clearly this definition of world class requires both an objective performance standard as well as the profound knowledge of its business and commercial environment in order to enjoy sustained performance at this level. Such an effort to develop knowledge at this level implies that organizations that use benchmarking must develop ways to mainstream this practice so it can be part of its regular business practices. Indeed, benchmarking is not an isolated business improvement tool—it was developed as part of an overall quality management program that Xerox called *Leadership through Quality.*

BENCHMARKING—A DISCIPLINE IN TOTAL QUALITY MANAGEMENT

Benchmarking has a unique place in TQM as both a tool to stimulate improvement and a management technique that aids in strategic positioning of an organization. Benchmarking provides opportunities for full organization-wide participation in business process improvement by engaging the management team in the architecture of change and choice of focus areas for study; involving the middle managers in self-assessment of the work processes that they own and in adapting the lessons learned from other organizations; and relying on the study of related processes by the organization's frontline process experts, who are charged with discovery of the significant differences that lead to performance gaps. Benchmarking is a tool that can engage the "Total" organization in "Quality Management."

The objective of benchmarking is to accelerate the process of strategic change that leads to breakthrough or continuous improvements in products, services, or processes, resulting in enhanced customer satisfaction, lower operating costs, and improved competitive advantage by adapting best practices and business process improvements of those organizations that are recognized for superior performance. Benchmarking is a method that forces organizations to look outside themselves in order to avoid myopic illusions of grandeur that come from reflecting on internal experience without external validation.

How is benchmarking used and what way is there to distinguish among the appropriate uses of this methodology and getting into traps that cause one to think incorrectly about the potential benefits of this methodology? Consider the juxtapositions that describe one way to identify the boundary conditions of benchmarking (see Figure 1.5).

Benchmarking is a structured approach for learning about process operations from other organizations and applying that knowledge gained in your own organization. It consists of dedicated work in measuring, comparing, and analyzing work processes among different organizations in order to identify causes for superior performance. Benchmarking is not complete with just the analysis, however. It must be adapted and implemented in order to have a complete cycle of learning.

Benchmarking is:	Benchmarking is not:
A discovery process	A cookbook process
An improvement methodology	A panacea for problem solutions
A source of breakthrough ideas	About business as usual
A learning opportunity	A management fashion of the day
An objective analysis of work	A subjective gut feeling or theory opinion
A process-based learning approach	Mere measurement of process performance
A means to generate improvement ideas	Just quantitative comparison of results

FIGURE 1.5 Benchmarking is–is not analysis

Benchmarking is not just a checklist or set of numbers that are used to make management feel better about their current performance. Benchmarking should make management uncomfortable due to the identification of gaps in business performance. Benchmarking should challenge management due to the discovery of performance enablers that could help them to improve.

When differentiating benchmarking by describing what it is and is not is helpful, it would be even more useful to understand more fully the logic by which a benchmarking study is conducted. What is the logic behind the conduct of a benchmarking study, and how is it distinguished from the logic of a benchmark—which is the typical mistake that is made in talking about this subject?

UNDERSTANDING THE LOGIC OF A BENCHMARKING STUDY

It is important to note that the logic of the benchmarking process does not fail the test that was issued by Dr. Deming in the early 1980s. He cautioned executives against deadly diseases in the management of business that were derived from setting arbitrary goals based solely on visible performance measures, without understanding the depth of profound (process-related) knowledge that lies underneath most high-level performance measures.

For instance, Deming would call *arbitrary* the use of benchmarking that followed the following logic:

- "Our competitor's cost is 15 percent lower than ours; therefore, we must lower our cost by 15 percent."

The logic of benchmarking is much more process oriented and requires the development of the type of profound knowledge that Deming advocated:

- "The leading companies have operations that are 20 percent more effective than our operations."
- "The reasons that their operations are more effective is because . . ."
- "The practices that they used to improve these operations include . . ."

- "The enhancements to our processes are appropriate for our business model and our culture and will improve our performance; these enhancements include . . ."
- "The estimate of performance gain due to using these enhancements is . . ."

The ability to apply this logic comes from developing an understanding of the root cause of process improvement at the benchmark organization and translation of their lessons learned into appropriate change for your own organization. By a process of conscientious learning and cautious adaptation, a company can learn the lessons needed to move its business results to the level of world class performance.

But how does one apply all of these taxonomies and differing benchmarking concepts into a coherent approach that allows an organization to gain useful knowledge that will encourage its improvement? Perhaps a summary will help make this chapter more useful.

SUMMARY OF EFFECTIVE BENCHMARKING PRACTICE

1. Benchmarking must be a systematic, structured process that follows a disciplined practice and applies the scientific method. The method may be applied to study the relative performance of key business processes, critical product functions, or service dimensions that differentiate the customer's experience.
2. The benchmarking process must be a constant pursuit—seeking lessons learned on a regular basis to assure continuous improvement in business performance. Perhaps most important is that benchmarking must become a process of continuous learning that encourages an organization to grow beyond its current capabilities.
3. The benchmarking process must be data driven—appropriately using data collection methods, sampling procedures, statistical analyses, and graphical comparisons in order to assure that appropriate comparisons are made and correct conclusions are drawn.
4. Benchmarking uncovers best practices—it doesn't stop after the

performance has been measured. The key is to identify leading practices or best practices that have enabled other organizations to make significant performance improvements.

5. The goal of benchmarking is to elevate an organization's performance beyond the degree of performance that is observed in benchmark organizations. Becoming the best of the best is a managerial aspiration and an objective for the study. Thus, in the final analysis, learning is not enough—doing is equally important. It is the discipline of execution that distinguishes between leading organizations and wishful thinkers!

The next chapter will focus on strategic benchmarking studies—in particular the linkage between strategic planning and benchmarking.

CHAPTER 2

Linking Six Sigma to Strategic Planning and Benchmarking

All learning is a continual process of discovering insights, inventing new possibilities, for action, producing the actions, and observing consequences leading to insights.

—JOHN DEWEY

APPLYING A SYSTEMS APPROACH

Russell Ackoff called the interdependent problems of a competitive business "a mess."[1] Indeed, quite often today's mess is the result of our solutions to yesterday's problems! In *Strategic Benchmarking*, I defined *strategy* as the "persistence of a vision" that occurs as an organization confronts its triggers for change in terms of technological and market disruptions that could signal strategic inflection points in the organization's rate of growth.[2] However, innovative organizations do not hold to a static vision in the face of contrary evidence. As the late Austrian economist Joseph Schumpeter pointed out in his theory of innovation, organizations must be prepared to "creatively destroy" their past—and "plan to abandon" their approaches in order to make way for the new dimensions that will define

---

1. Russell Ackoff, *Creating the Corporate Future* (New York: Wiley, 1981).
2. This was the definition of strategy that I introduced in *Strategic Benchmarking*, 26.

their future.[3] Thus, "persistence of a vision" contains a learning component by which organizations can adapt to their new future and avoid creating a mess. Indeed, if organizations hold blindly to a strategy, then they may well create chaos as they attempt to hold onto something that no longer is relevant. The real concern about living in this business chaos (or mess) comes from the potential for making the wrong choices in the face of the dynamic surprises and opportunities that are presented to an organization. In the face of all the uncertainty, fuzziness, and complexity of sorting out the issues that will become the future, how can an organization create dynamically adaptive systems for its management process that will permit it to be flexible while maintaining the momentum of business success?

Rigidity in visions, values or belief systems, strategies, operating methods, and procedures can indeed cripple an organization's ability to remain viable, and the words that should be inscribed on such an organization's tombstone would read, "But we always did it that way!" To participate in the future, an organization must be part of creating that future! How can organizations plan to abandon their past? This is the issue we will tackle in this chapter as we apply the systems approach to integration of benchmarking, strategic planning, and Six Sigma. The key for applying benchmarking is that it must become part of the organization's continual learning process—its way for observing and discovering new insights into what it can do and providing the theoretical foundation for adapting these new concepts into its core business processes.

STIMULUS: BEST PRACTICE OR THEORY OF OPERATIONS?

Economists Edith Wiarda and Daniel Luria of the Industrial Technology Institute in Ann Arbor, Michigan, make a pragmatic observation: "De-

---

3. Joseph A. Schumpeter, *Capitalism, Socialism and Democracy* (New York: Harper Torch, 1951, republished 1962, 1984); *The Theory of Economic Development* (New York: Transaction, 1983); *History of Economic Analysis* (London: Oxford University Press, 1996); and *Essays on Entrepreneurs, Innovations, Business Cycles and Capitalism* (New York: Transaction, 1989). Esben Sloth Andersen, "The Core of Schumpeter's Work: A Report from a Study on Schumpeter and the Analysis of Economic Evolution," *Smaskrift*, no. 68 (1991).

spite its hype, benchmarking remains a common sense proposition: Don't reinvent the wheel, learn what others do right, and look outside your firm for good ideas."[4] However, the size of the firm can make a difference in how benchmarking is applied. Wiarda and Luria observe that larger companies can begin their benchmarking process as part of their strategy process but that smaller companies have a need for help in managing the front end of a study in determining what to benchmark, defining appropriate measures, identifying appropriate partners, and interpreting and adapting the results. However, in both of these cases the unprocessed adoption of best practice can lead to poor results. This is because the best practice itself is based on a set of assumptions from the originating company, and, like the laws of science, generalities can only take a company so far in changing its own state. In order to develop a detailed engineering design, you must first understand the laws of physics that govern. What is the problem with best practice?

First, we must observe that what could be called a *best practice* in one context may lead to problems in a second case. Care must be taken in adapting best practices in order to assure that they are applicable in the *circumstances* where the practice is leveraged.[5] Clay Christensen of Harvard Business School warns that "early studies almost always sort observations into categories defined by the attributes of the phenomena themselves . . . assertions about the actions or events that lead to the results at this point can only be statements about correlation between attributes and results, not about causality."[6]

An excellent benchmarking researcher will first seek to discover the causal mechanism behind the phenomena of success (the enabler) and get beyond the copying mind-set that perceives that duplicating the at-

---

4. Edith A. Wiarda and Daniel D. Luria, "The Best-Practice Company and Other Benchmarking Myths," *Quality Progress* (1998): 91. As an overall performance measure to determine if a company is excellent, Wiarda and Luria recommend that a measure of value per employee be used. Here *value* is defined as revenue minus the cost of purchased materials, parts, or services. This is a helpful starting point in defining what is operationally meant by *excellence*.

5. This point is so important that in my first book on benchmarking. I singled out "Adapt" as its own step in the process (see Chapter 6 of *The Benchmarking Workbook*, Portland, OR: Productivity, 1992).

6. Christensen and Raynor, Op. Cit., 14.

tributes of a successful company is the solution to your own problems. The best insights occur from creative imitation when observations of causal mechanisms at a best-practice organization identify unique outcomes that in turn permit isolation of unique circumstances that can be successfully applied in other organizations.

Benchmarking *must* provide insight into the unique circumstances of each company that is participating in the study. Only when this knowledge can be collectively defined and the companies understood through a categorization process that identifies the mutually exclusive and completely exhaustive (MECE) categories can causality of activities to results become predictable.[7] Thus, the theories of causality for exceptional results must be built on the categories of circumstances that are easy to deploy operationally because business is conducted in the real-world circumstances of the work, not in attributes of the different organizations. Christensen observed, "We can trust a theory only when its statement of what actions will lead to success describes how this will vary as a company's circumstances change."[8] But how does best practice vary as a function of decisions of the implementing company—and its specific set of business circumstances as defined by its internal culture, business practices, and external environment? What can be learned from the complexity of the real world, and how can it be reduced to such a simple logic? What observations can lead to knowledge of the theory behind a practice? What experiments must be made to discover how this theory operates at the limit of its practice? How can a theory be developed that leads to leveragability in learning? Because benchmarking gains knowledge by observation, we must first understand the nature of what may be learned by observation. How does the scientific method create its profound knowledge by investigating the nature of the world?

7. The idea of MECE logic was referenced by Christensen and Raynor, but it refers to a thinking process that has been promoted by McKinsey Consulting Company for decades and was based on Aristotelian logic.
8. Ibid., 16.

INVESTIGATING THE NATURE OF CHANGE

This process of logical, scientific investigation begins with a simple state-ment, model, or notion of what is truth (called the *hypothesis*) to describe what is anticipated as the true explanation for observed performance over the long term (called the *theory*). Material clues—accepted facts that are either indisputable or, as Rene Descartes would say, "beyond rea-sonable doubt"—are the axioms or first principles from which the con-clusions about the theory must be drawn. From these axioms and hy-potheses, a logical progression follows of making observations, gathering facts, and then thinking up logical combinations of conjectures or pos-sible explanations that fit the facts, culminating with the attempt to prove these explanations correct by demonstration or experimentation.[9]

However, when a hypothesis about the real world is defined it inevi-tably introduces an irreversible element of action—as noted in the pre-ceding by Christensen. An action always has a consequence because it changes the system that is being acted upon. For instance, when you choose a solution, you stop looking for other alternatives. When you fol-low a possible path, you follow it in real time, and it may then be too late to find a different path. This is the logical trap of linear thinking; how-ever, we are living in a world that is only linear in its most simple expla-nations! The act of hypothesizing changes our underlying reality. We will

9. The process of data analysis is used to assess the evidence, and one must determine how much practical significance to attach to physical evidence and observations. It is also apparent that there may be a gap between that which is true and that which is provable. We tend to use the principle of Ockham's Razor, which states that as long as there's no physical evidence to the contrary, we would accept a simple hypothesis over a more complicated one. However, this rule can lead to errors as re-ality tends to become complicated when we examine it in detail. Because the logic of scientific rea-soning requires economy in the process of hypotheses development, we choose the most simple and reasonable explanation as there is no apparent reason to assume that something strange or extraor-dinary has occurred. Thus, we tend to observe what we expect to see. This thinking process can lead to oversimplification when we look into the definition of *best practice*. When people follow a strict pro-cedure, it is always possible to predict the way that they will operate and make their decisions. How-ever, in business, competitive thinking should leave the opponents guessing and create confusion be-cause the rationale of the underlying pattern is not in the visible world of open facts.

return to this concept as we consider the dynamic world and the impact of complexity later in this chapter.

Let's start at the very beginning—what do we mean by knowledge of something that is gained by observation of the state of nature? This section of the chapter will present a brief discussion of this philosophical topic. We begin with an insight from Karl Marx (1818–1883), who was both the thought leader behind the Communist movement and a member of the German ideology school of philosophy. Marx observed that "historically humanity has only asked itself the (logical) questions it can answer." Thus, people tend to only receive the answers that they seek! To discover the unique takes a lot more work!

How did the current thinking about knowledge come about? Consider the evolution of mankind's thinking about observations of nature and how this affects the pursuit and application of knowledge. For instance, the early Greeks believed that everything in the world evolved from four basic elements: earth, air, fire, and water. The principal reaction against this view was voiced by Heraclitus of Ephesus (circa 554–483 BC), whose theory of flux emphasized that the nature of things and existence is one of constant change and, therefore, that things are in a state of contradiction—that things can both be and not be at the same time.[10]

Aristotle (384–322 BC) reacted against Heraclitus's view and formally stated the law of contradiction as "one cannot say of something that it is and that it is not in the same respect and at the same time," which became a cornerstone of his logic. Aristotle was concrete and practical and relied on sensory observation as the starting point for understanding everything, and logic was his method for knowing based on sensory observation. Aristotle's logic was a formal set of rules or principles by which to develop correct reasons for relationships. This is the foundation of cate-

---

10. The following paragraphs draw on my initial studies in philosophy as a graduate assistant at American University where I studied logic, analytical philosophy, philosophy of language, and epistemology. At that time, I read Aristotle's *Logic*, Kant's *Critique of Pure Reason*, Wittgenstein's *Philosophical Investigations*, and Popper's *Philosophy of Science*.

gorical logic and the basis for asserting hypotheses for observation and testing according to the scientific method.

Aristotle's logic became the accepted style of thinking until it was challenged by the eighteenth century philosopher Immanuel Kant (1724–1804), who introduced the ideas of *a priori* and *a posteriori* knowledge. A priori knowledge comes from the mind that must understand its own experiences, and it can either be clearly proved or clearly refuted, while a posteriori knowledge is knowledge that is derived by logical rules and observations through methods of proof. Thus, a person's mind limits his or her ability to experience and constrains knowledge to mathematics and the natural, empirical world. Thus, a priori logic, first principles and axioms, cannot be offered for the speculative world of metaphysics, only in the world of mathematics and science. Kant defined four categories of a priori knowledge (with logical subcategories): quantity (unity, plurality, and totality), quality (reality, negation, and limitation), modality (possibility-impossibility, existence-nonexistence, and necessity-contingency), and relation (inherence and subsistence, causality and dependence, and community). From this set of a priori concepts, he believed that all judgments that create empirical knowledge possible can be made. Kant's structure of logical categories defines a framework for thinking about operational business theories.

Modern thinking has continued to cope with the concept of knowledge and the limits of what can be known. For instance, Werner Heisenberg's (1901–1976) uncertainty principle (or indeterminacy principle) says that it is impossible to know both the exact position and the *exact* velocity of an object at the same time—we can only approximate truth by applying probability theory. Now it is generally accepted that no treatment of any scientific subject, experiment, or measurement can be called *accurate* without defining the nature of its underlying probability distribution (or error) in its measurement. Thus, uncertainty characterizes the relative narrowness or broadness of the data distribution that identifies a physical observation. Thus, we can understand that an organization is in flux, but we can't determine if it is precisely at an inflection point that signals a shift in its direction of movement or growth.

Indeed, Kurt Gödel's (1906–1978) incompleteness theorem made a similar type of observation that all too often there isn't enough evidence to prove a hypothesis as guilty or innocent. One historical process of logic, called the *axiomatic method*—with its formal proof mechanism that starts with true statements (irrefutable first principles), and progresses in distinct logical steps toward the thesis of its conclusion—goes all the way back to the work of Aristotle and Euclid. However, this process is often inadequate to achieve the desired process. Why? Gödel's theorem demonstrated that there are, at the most elementary levels of arithmetic, logical statements that cannot be proved or refuted—they are beyond an axiomatic process.[11] Why did it take so long for this problem to be discovered? Why didn't the earliest Greeks confront Euclid with this problem? We must remember the observation of Marx: We only ask the questions that we can answer—it is part of human nature.

According to scientific theory, if a concept is provable, then it must have a proof. It we cannot prove the concept, then we must bow to the logic of analytical philosopher Ludwig Wittgenstein (1889–1951), who stated that problems arise from the misunderstanding of language, and he would advise us to "remain silent" on the question, not to talk about the subject because it is beyond the level of what is known or knowable, and therefore any type of statement about this subject would be subjective and based upon conjecture, rather than on analytical fact. Therefore, it is a question that cannot be answered within the context of our knowledge base built on empirical observation. Our ways of thinking are related to our experience with proving that something is true. If we have any weakness in our concept of proof, then we have a weakness in our ability to perceive and answer the question, What is reality?

---

11. Mathematically, Gödel's theorem deals with the limits of axiomatic systems. An axiomatic system describes the propositions that are derivable from a set of elements and axioms. The system is defined by its axioms, which are semantic rules for combining chosen elements. The system is reusable because we can apply the same axioms to different elements. Using the axioms, we can derive propositions about the axioms. Gödel's theorem states that for any given axiomatic system, there exists propositions that cannot be decided, or else the axiomatic system is incomplete. It took me by surprise to see these early studies combine with my graduate study of systems engineering to produce these paragraphs in this book! This is itself a wonder of systems thinking!

Both Heisenberg's principle of uncertainty and Gödel's theorem illustrate the same basic difficulty in our thinking processes for uncovering knowledge that is outside the realm of our experience. Logical paradoxes arise when the clear, crisp descriptions of physical phenomenon that exist on a large scale are translated into a subatomic world of such infinitesimal detail that everything becomes so much more complex. Exactly the same kind of relationship exists in the mathematical world where everything is also a question of scale. Thus, the indeterminable propositions of Gödel correspond to the subatomic world, to the minute magnitudes that are invisible in normal mathematics. Thus, if a mathematic question can be formulated within the same scale as the axioms, it must belong to the mathematician's usual world and be possible to prove or refute. But if it requires a different scale, then it risks belonging to the world — submerged, infinitesimal, but latent in everything — of what can neither be proved nor refuted. This is what W. Edwards Deming referred to as the "unknown and unknowable."

There is a difference between truth and that part of life that can be proved. This is the essence of Alfred Tarski's (1902–1983) corollary to Gödel's theorem. Karl Popper (1902–1994) contributed to this point by adding the requirement of the ability to falsify a theory in order to consider it scientific. Popper asserted that no empirical hypothesis, proposition, or theory can be considered scientific if it does not admit the possibility of a contrary case, that is, if you can't come up with counterexamples. For example, the proposition "all elephants are grey" would be falsified by observing a pink elephant, which would require a pink elephant to exist. A falsifiable theory must define what would counter the theory. For example, in this case the existence of a pink elephant is forbidden by the proposition in question. The possibility in principle of observing a pink elephant as a counterexample to the general proposition is enough to qualify it as falsifiable.

The defining characteristic of scientific theory is the fact it is falsifiable or people have an ability to test its predictions about things that have not yet been observed. The relevance and specificity of those predictions determine how potentially useful the theory is. Thus, any proposed theory that makes no predictions that can be observed is not a useful theory. Also, predictions that are not sufficiently specific to be tested are similarly not useful. In either case, best-practice theory that is not testable or able to be falsified is equally not useful—thus the need for the theory of profound knowledge that comes from the observation of process dynamics over time and their measurement using statistical tools to permit scientific prediction about their future behavior. What is the criteria by which a theory should be judged?

THE THEORY OF THEORIES

What does it take to make a good theory, say, about process improvement? In common usage, most people use the word *theory* to mean a conjecture, an opinion, or a speculation. In this usage, a theory is not necessarily based on facts; in other words, it is not necessary that the theory is consistent with a true description of reality. True descriptions of reality are what would be true independently of what people think about them.

In a scientific application, theory describes, explains, or models the interaction of natural phenomena. A theory is capable of predicting future observations of a similar experience and is also capable of being tested by experiment or verified by observation. Thus, theory and fact are closely related. For example, the fact is that an apple dropped to the ground and was observed to fall toward the center of the Earth. The theory that explains why the apple behaves in this way is the theory of gravity. Thus, theories generalize from a specific observation and are extended to other circumstances in order to explain other relationships (e.g., the theory of gravity is extended from Newton's apple to also explain the influence of the moon on the behavior of tides in the Earth's oceans).

Scientific researchers propose specific hypotheses as explanations of natural phenomena and design experimental studies that test these predictions for accuracy. These steps are repeated in order to make increasingly dependable predictions of future results. Theories that encompass whole domains of inquiry serve to bind more specific hypotheses together into logically coherent wholes. This in turn aids in the formation of new hypotheses, as well as in placing groups of specific hypotheses into a broader context of understanding. This is the same method that is applied in Six Sigma to investigate and understand how the phenomena of business processes operate.

One key to this inquiry process is the conviction that it must be objective so that the investigator does not bias the interpretation of the results. Another basic expectation is that the complete documentation of data and methodology are made available for careful scrutiny by other investigators, thereby allowing others the opportunity to verify results by reproducing them. This also establishes a statistical measure of the results' reliability. The scientific method also involves attempts, if possible and appropriate, to achieve control over the factors involved in the area of inquiry, which may in turn be manipulated to test new hypotheses in order to gain further knowledge.

In practice a body of knowledge is called a *theory* when it has met a minimum empirical standard. That is, the proposed theory must be determined to meet several criteria. It must be consistent with prior theories that have been experimentally verified, and it must also be supported by considerable evidence rather than a single piece of data. This ensures that the proposed theory represents a good approximation of reality, even if it is not totally correct. Additionally, a theory is generally taken seriously if it is tentative, correctable, and dynamic and allows for changes to be made as new data is discovered, rather than asserting complete certainty. A final element is the aesthetic of a theory; that is, it provides the most parsimonious explanation of the observations, or it passes Ockham's razor test for simplicity of explanation.

Theories do not have to be perfectly accurate to be scientifically useful. The predictions made by classical mechanics are known to be inaccurate, but they are sufficiently good approximations in most circumstances in that they are still very useful and widely used in place of more accurate but mathematically difficult theories. Another criterion that is often applied to define a *good theory* is the degree of testability or ability to refute the truth of the theory. Because people tend to frame questions for which we have answers, it is easy to discover the confirmation, or verification, for almost any theory—if we look for confirmations. What separates the scientific approach is the ability to test or refute it. Testability is the ability to demonstrate that the theory is false. However, there are degrees of testability. Some theories are more testable, more exposed to refutation, than others; they take, as it were, greater risks. Thus, a theory that is not refutable by any conceivable event is nonscientific, and the inability to refute a theory is not a virtue of a theory but actually the sign of a weak supposition, rather than a theory.

The proof of a theory comes from observation and experimentation. The most valuable time in a scientist's or mathematician's thinking process about such a proof comes at the moment when he or she has his first solitary intuition about a problem. This is the eureka moment—an "ah-ha" time in which discovery of the concept transitions it from the realm of tacit knowledge to explicit knowledge. How is such an observation made? How can this new knowledge be applied for competitive advantage? Consider the approach that Colonel John R. Boyd, USAF (1927–1997) developed to instruct fighter pilots as an insight into methods to leverage insight into competitive knowledge for business—what is called the *Boyd Cycle*.

LEVERAGING CHANGE FOR COMPETITIVE ADVANTAGE

Application of the Boyd Cycle allows an organization to leverage change to enhance its own competitive advantage. Colonel Boyd taught tactical engagement to USAF pilots, and he developed his cycle into a general theory of war that can be applied to competition.[12] Colonel Boyd was

12. The original writings of Colonel John R. Boyd, USAF, such as his brief essay "Destruction and Creation" and his briefing slides on "Patterns of Conflict" are included for free downloading from the web site www.d-n-i.net/second_level/boyd_military.htm. OODA is cited without reference to its originator in Joseph L. Bauer and Thomas M. Hout, "Fast-Cycle Capability for Competitive Power," *Harvard Business Review* (1988). Other books and articles that reference Boyd's work include William S. Lind, *Maneuver Warfare Handbook* (New York: Perseus, 1985); Grant T. Hamond, *The Mind of War: John Boyd and American Security* (Washington, DC: The Smithsonian Institution Press, 2001; Keith H. Hammonds, "The Strategy of the Fighter Pilot," *Fast Company* no. 59, (2002), 98; Chester W. Richards, *A Swift and Elusive Sword* (Washington, DC: Center for Defense Informa-

nicknamed "40-second Boyd" because he bet he could shoot down any opponent in just 40 seconds, and in some 3,000 hours of aerial fighter combat training at the USAF Top Gun school he did just that! What is the key to this method? The Boyd Cycle dictates flexibility and speed as the key effective ingredients in maneuver warfare.

Two key ideas expounded by Boyd were his definition of *cycle time* and idea of "getting inside the adversary's decision cycle." Boyd believed that, "He who handles the quickest rate of change survives"—the competitor who acts fastest wins! What is the Boyd Cycle, and how does it operate? Business competition takes place in time, and success in business, as in any real-time competitive rivalry, depends on the ability to perform a series of steps or a cycle faster than your opponent. The Boyd Cycle is a looped decision system that accepts and processes feedback from the environment and the cumulative effect of your prior actions. It allows a competitor to better understand cause-and-effect relationships by reducing the time between observations of caused events and their outcome. This performance feedback is processed and used to recalibrate activities for adaptation in the next cycle. The Boyd Cycle is often called the *OODA Cycle* for its four steps of Observation, Orientation, Decision, and Action. What happens in these steps?

- *Observation:* Sense yourself and the operational environment, and develop actionable intelligence to identify differences (the gap) between your original understanding of the circumstances and the changed reality in its current state. Observation seeks to discover the mismatches that define opportunities that give the potential for gaining competitive advantage. Rivals should begin the competitive process by observing their positions, the environment, and their opponents.
- *Orientation:* Interpreting the situation based on experience, culture, education, and data is the core process as it guides decisions and

---

tion, 2003); Robert Coram, *Boyd: The Fighter Pilot Who Changed the Art of War* (New York: Little, Brown, 2004); and Chester W. Richards, *Certain to Win: The Strategy of John R. Boyd Applied to Business* (Philadelphia: Random House, 2004).

also shapes action as well as establishes a perspective from which observations can be made. This mental snapshot of the current situation orients the implications of the tactical intelligence to their specific situations.

- *Decision:* The Decision step processes the learning from the observation and orientation steps, formulates hypotheses about the way that this information could affect the outcome of the current situation, and then makes rapid decisions about courses of action based on this understanding of the competitive environment.

- *Action:* All decisions are tested by taking action: "Decisions without actions are pointless and actions without decisions are reckless!" Action allocates the resources to execute tactical plans and checks to see if its action has changed the situation, causing the Boyd Cycle to start anew with the next observation round. Note that former AlliedSignal CEO Larry Bossidy would approve highly of this process as it is parallel to his idea of "execution" as the Achilles heel of business![13]

What is the purpose of strategy according to Boyd? He says strategy is used to, "improve our ability to shape and adapt to unfolding circumstances, so that we (as individuals or as groups or as a culture or as a nation-state) can survive on our own terms." The secret of moving faster than your opponent lies in the continuous reduction of friction, things that hold back an organization, through simple, reliable administrative structures and the use of flexible tools that can be adapted rapidly in response to changing tactics. The foundation for a flexible plan is astute observation of the moves of the market and decision making based on knowledge gained in the increment—the difference that occurs with each decision as it changes the dynamic of the market relationships. Living at the edge of this difference requires a pragmatic understanding of probability and also a continual learning process.

13. Larry Bossidy and Ram Charan, *Execution: The Discipline of Getting Things Done* (New York: Crown, 2002).

MANAGING YOUR ABILITY TO KNOW AND LEARN

Note how this philosophical discussion transitioned in thinking from a simplistic level (witness the atomic model of the universe) to the more complete, comprehensive, and complex level (e.g., description of the universe offered by quantum mechanics) as the understanding of researchers and the needs for new circumstances evolved and matured. The movement in knowledge growth is from simplicity to complexity. Thus, developing an understanding of underlying theory is necessary to gain profound knowledge. What is a theory? What is learning? What is the imperative for adaptation?

We must remember that the external environment of a business represents its true reality. The internal environment of the business has only been artificially created as an adaptive system to help the organization to cope better with this external reality and to aid in its ability to sustain itself and its growth. Consider the challenges that life presents to the simple amoeba.

The amoeba is perhaps the most simple of living organisms. Every part of it exists in direct contact with its external environment, so it is able to sense and thereby to respond to the externalities that support its life. The amoeba doesn't require sophisticated support systems in order to sense its environment, or hold its parts together, or control the communication among its parts. Complexity comes with growth beyond a simple state. As organisms become more mature, they become more complex—indeed, the surface area of the organism expands roughly by the square of its radius, while the internal mass grows at the cubic rate. The internal mass is dedicated to the support functions—muscle and skeleton to keep the organism together, nervous system to help it communicate with itself, and so on. With growth comes complexity—the purpose of which is to support the life system, and these components act in isolation from the external environment.[14] In a simpler environment, learning comes by mere observation; however, in a more complex environment, learning must be managed more adroitly.

14. Peter F. Drucker, *The Effective Executive* (New York: HarperBusiness, 1985) 15.

How does the learning process benefit organizations? First, learning exposes them to the mistakes of the past and enables organizations to avoid repeating them! Second, it builds sensitivity to the forces of change and enables the adaptation of business theory into the evolving dynamic of its business environment. Finally, learning permits enhancement of operations by exposing weaknesses and identifying opportunities for improvement from the more profound understanding of the way things work that has evolved through the learning process.

However, in order to encourage learning, we must challenge our causal mind-set and transition to a scientific mind-set. This transition entails a move from merely copying what is done in other environments to developing a theory of what operates generally and then adapting it to our specific circumstances—this is the theory of profound knowledge (which comes from understanding processes) applied to the work that we do. Mistake avoidance comes from the establishment of the theory that lies *behind* the best practice and its adaptation for your own organization's operating system, then its standardization and appropriate integration into your entire business system. As I described in *Strategic Benchmarking:*

> Another piece of advice from Deming also applies: "Adapt, don't adopt." Process enablers are developed to meet a specific business need within a particular business environment and company culture. No two businesses are exactly alike in these areas, and practices from one business are not directly transferable to another without rigorous examination of areas that need to be translated to fit a different environment and culture. Thus, stealing shamelessly can cause trouble if the business practices of one organization don't translate to those of another.[15]

Thus, the sequence of influence in this process is that learning leads to knowledge, and knowledge leads to innovation, and innovation stimulates improvement. However, only when the knowledge can be established

15. Watson, *Strategic Benchmarking,* 3.

within the context of a general theory as part of the learning process can this transformation process actually occur. The Six Sigma analysis process enables learning about the way work is done. Each of the steps in the process should lead to new knowledge about what is important for the long-term success of the process. The rigorous definition of investigation steps and fixed sequence of probing questions and analytical tools lead to gaining profound knowledge about the root cause(s) of problems and help identify opportunities for improvement. One saying in the culture of Six Sigma is that "We don't know what we don't know!" In order to fill in the missing knowledge and learn about the process, it is necessary to get data about its performance. In this search, some questions help uncover what is most important about the process operation:

- What do you want to know?
- How do you want to graphically display what you need to know?
- What tool will generate what it is that you need to see?
- What type of data is required to use this tool?
- Where can you get the required type of data?
- How much data is required to convince you?
- How will a random sampling of data be assured?

Aristotle said that "the beginning is half of everything." For learning to occur, we must "staple ourselves to the process"—open our eyes, observe, and then use probability theory to generalize what will happen over the long term. Observation starts with OODA!

ESTIMATING THE PREDICTABILITY OF PERFORMANCE

When I speak of the predictability of performance as required by a properly operating theory, it is because probability is the language by which we must interpret activity. No event or business activity is likely to be perfectly predictable for a number of reasons. One reason is that competition will not permit prediction as most business games are opposed! If your company is perfectly predictable, then it is easier to defeat. Thus, it is in the best interest of most organizations to behave in ambiguous or unpredictable ways as Boyd pointed out. A second reason for the lack of perfect prediction is that it presents a logical and computational challenge due to the large number of possible outcomes from all of the possible combinations and permutations of the business variables. Thus, there remains a challenge, even if all the factors are known because putting them together in a logical equation is a daunting task. A third reason for lack of predictability is suggested by complexity theory: Fully determined systems can generate random outcomes as they are part of an adaptive process. Thus, determining the extent to which outcomes can be predicted and assessing the significance of any residual uncertainty or unpredictability is a profound theoretical challenge with important practical implications for a business. It is precisely this challenge that is taken in a microscopic way on each Six Sigma project as the team seeks to logically determine the predictability of a process by generating its transfer function $Y = f(X)$ — the result or outcome (Y) is a function of the set of specified inputs (Xs) as demonstrated by the use of statistics to generate a probabilistic model of the process that operates in theory and is proven by experimentation.

A theory can confidently be employed in prediction only when the categories that define its contingencies are clear. Thus, Six Sigma projects (and benchmarking studies, too) must seek anomalies that cause their theory to break down. These anomalies will define what difference in circumstances make a difference in the outcomes for application of the methods, and this in turn leads to successful application of the observed practices.

The anomalies that influence an organization's implementation of a best practice are defined by the circumstances that motivate it to do things differently. These are either the functional, emotional, or social dimensions of the organization's operating philosophy or culture that defines how the best practice will be applied. Christensen and Raynor observe that "the readily available data actually obfuscate the paths to growth." The solution is not to use data that are collected for historical performance measurement purposes in the act of transforming one's business or developing new products. "Keep such data quarantined: they are the wrong data for the job. The size and nature of job-based or circumstance-based market categories actually can be quantified, but this entails a different research process and statistical methodology than is typically employed in most market quantification efforts."[16] This leads back to the necessity of experimentation and the use of variation and probability theory to express results in terms of their uncertainties.

What happens as a business is in the state of change? It reaches what Andy Grove and Robert Bugelman call a "strategic inflection point" that changes the dynamic of its environment significantly and causes it to change its circumstances. Business seeks to manage these opportunities or challenges by using strategic plans to manage change. Strategy is the persistence of a vision. Strategy is the ability to see where one wants to go and to do those things necessary to stay on track to get there. Strategy must look forward and sideways. It must clearly see the end-state, but it must also continually observe, learn, and adapt in order to provide in-course guidance that allows it to stay on target or redefine a target of opportunity that presents even greater interest.

The key to Boyd's observation process is noting the rate of change that follows the formula $\delta y / \delta t$ and is a partial differential equation (PDE). The partial differential equation notes that the rate of change in a performance indicator (difference in result or δy) can change in a variable way over time (or δt). Thus, at the point of observation of data defined by a PDE, one does not know if the *next* point will represent the observed trend in the slope of the data. This is the point of uncertainty where many people will yield to a linear assumption—tomorrow will be pretty much like today. However, the content of the observation made *at* that point must be closely examined to determine if it contains any hint of movement toward the next observation. Miyamoto Musashi observed in his *Book of Five Rings*, "the principle of strategy is having one thing, to know ten thousand things." The question evolves into a new form: What is the one thing that we need to know to make sense of our knowledge and discover the pathway forward? Thus, in order to understand the change required, one must understand the transition—the fact that it is occurring, what triggers it, and how this knowledge can be leveraged with the ca-

16. Christensen and Raynor, 89.

pability that the organization has previously developed in order to create its future or effectively to abandon its past in order to adapt to the stimulus of change. What is the *one thing* that the organization needs to know in order to discover the ten thousand?

This observation implies that organizations must live in the present and rigorously assess their performance observations for meaning in a systematic way to assure that their critical business assumptions have not been violated and that disruptions in their market are not evolving. How should these observations be conducted? The answer is strategic benchmarking!

EVALUATING YOUR BUSINESS AS A SYSTEM

Strategic benchmarking provides information input for making enterprise-level strategic business decisions and supports the strategic policy-setting obligation of the board of directors and executive management team. Strategic benchmarking should be integrated into the process of management for the organization and occupy a *driver* position in the planning process. To understand how strategic benchmarking fits business architecture, examine the most simple, generic model of a business system. This model represents the activities that almost any organization conducts to plan and execute its work.[17] How does this model work?

The architecture of the organization is simple—there are only three levels of decision making and action: The enterprise level is where policy is developed and corporate governance is initiated. The responsibility of this top tier of the organization is to choose the business that will be conducted and to study and develop the strategic intent or direction of the organization. Typically in the annual planning process this level of the organization takes the longest range perspective of the business environment and makes choices about what to do based on the world of possibilities available as well as its core competence and available resources. These planning activities are typically conducted by the board of di-

---

17. This model was developed during the production of my earlier book, *Business Systems Engineering* (New York: Wiley, 1994).

rectors, the top management team, and the professional planning staff members. The output of this planning activity is the organization's vision, values for its way of working, strategic intent, business goals, and long-range plan (typically a minimum of three to five years).

The second tier of the generic business systems model focuses on developing the plan for a specific business area or product line for the next short-term period in the organization's planning calendar (typically the coming one to three years of the organization's future). This plan describes the set of objectives to be achieved in order to deliver the strategic intent and business goals. The plan also describes how the corporate resources and staff competence will be coordinated in order to make the most effective use of core capabilities in achieving the business imperatives—actions that must be accomplished in order to deliver the strategic direction. Also, this level of the organization is where the measurement system of a balanced scorecard is consolidated for reporting performance and monitoring progress achieved toward the corporate goals. This balanced scorecard is cascaded into the organization using dashboards of actionable measures that are deployed to the frontline activities that comprise the third tier of the organization. Indeed, these two top tiers of the business system provide a number of linkages that connect the organization: vision, values, strategic intent, business goals, business imperatives (strategic change projects), reporting measurements, and annual objectives. These planning activities are typically conducted by the business team that manages a product or service that is delivered to the market (this could be an operating unit or a product line of a business or, in a small business, it could be the same group that developed the planning architecture in the top tier of the model). The output of this planning activity is the annual plan, objectives, and targeted performance to be achieved as well as strategic change projects that have been commissioned by the management team to facilitate the transition of its infrastructure to the requirements of the foreseen future state.

The third tier of the systems model engages the entire organization in the planning and execution of the operational work of the business and defines an annual planning horizon. The third tier of the organization converts the objectives to be achieved and planning targets for performance into the routine work of the organization and the set of improvement projects that must be accomplished to achieve the incremental improvement that is required by the plan. The focus of this level is on the operational activities or routine work that the organization accomplishes. The planning process at this level has four main objectives — to align the work objectives of individuals to the objectives that must be achieved in the plan; to budget for activities that support accomplishment of the plan; to define improvement projects that will create constant gains in performance; and to review actions and define countermeasures, corrective actions, and preventive actions that will keep the plan on track.

Recognizing the Levers of Change

How does this three-tiered systems model of a business deal with change? Each level has a different responsibility as highlighted in a Six Sigma project — the *enterprise level* is the one responsible for recognizing the need to address critical subjects as change projects, the *business level* is responsible for defining the project to be accomplished within the context of its own operating systems, while the *operations level* is responsible for the execution of the project and the presentation of the findings for standardization and integration into the organization's business control system for process management.

What are the triggers for change that can be observed at the instant in an organization's PDE of its results? What levers of change can be manipulated to manage this position? At what point is there a tipping point (a point in the S-curve of the organization's growth function according to former Intel CEO Andy Grove and Stanford University professor Robert Burgelman[18]) that signals a critical change in this function, beyond which

18. For more on strategic inflection points and S-curves, see Andrew S. Grove, *Only the Paranoid Survive: How to Exploit the Crisis Points That Challenge Every Company* (New York: Doubleday Currency, 1996); Robert A. Burgelman and Andrew S. Grove, *Strategy Is Destiny: How Strategy-Making Shapes a Company's Future* (New York: Free Press, 2002); and Nicholas Imparato and Oren Harari, *Jumping the Curve: Innovations and Strategic Choice in an Age of Transition* (San Francisco: Jossey-Bass, 1993).

return to the prior circumstances is no longer possible? These questions indicate a business imperative—the requirement to *observe* and execute Colonel Boyd's OODA logic!

Thus, we return to the question of how strategic benchmarking, business planning, and Six Sigma contribute to managing this point of inflection to address an organization's most critical change initiatives. Change management is the job of strategy—recognizing a need and opportunity for change is the job of strategic benchmarking—defining and executing the strategic change management projects is a job for Six Sigma! But how can the Six Sigma approach take all of this theory and make it practical?

LEARNING TO SEE DIFFERENTLY—SIX SIGMA RECOGNIZE

While Six Sigma organizations conduct statistical problem solving using Define-Measure-Analyze-Improve-Control (DMAIC), it is the principal responsibility of management to establish the business context for the Six Sigma change management process. To maximize the business benefits derived from Six Sigma projects, management should begin by initiating Six Sigma projects in concert with its strategic planning and implementation processes using the methods of policy deployment to define the highest priority business process improvement projects that require the degree of diagnostic sophistication that is available from a Black Belt analyst. Only when management chooses projects that improve the infrastructure of their business processes—typically work processes whose performance contributes the most to the common cause variation in the business performance—can the most significant gains be realized from a comprehensive Six Sigma improvement effort. Note that Bob Camp calls this same concept *Step Zero* or determining what to benchmark—while this is the job tackled by the *Recognize* activity that precedes the Six Sigma DMAIC process.[19]

---

19. Robert C. Camp, *Business Process Benchmarking* (Milwaukee: ASQ Quality Press, 1996), 24–29. Camp's first book was published in 1989, and in between his two books we worked together at the IBC to establish its benchmarking program. At the midpoint between these books, I published my book *Strategic Benchmarking*, which Camp called "a useful contribution to the field of bench-

RECOGNIZE

The term *recognize* combines the prefix *re*, meaning "again" with the noun *cognition*, meaning "the act of knowing including both awareness and judgment" or, in layman's terms, "to think."[20] Thus, to recognize means "to think again"— a reflective act in which one contemplates what has gone before (building awareness) in order to formulate either a decision or a judgment about what to do in the future.

The preliminary step that precedes all Six Sigma projects has been called the *Recognize* step—executives involved to recognize the critical issues that most affect current business performance (from such business factors as technological discontinuities, business growth inflection points, or ineffective use of capital resources). In this step, management's work is to assess the current state of the business, diagnose current and prospective business vulnerabilities, determine what are the best technologies and product innovations along with their potential sales market opportunities, and determine the adequacy of the current strategic intent and allocate the resources of the organization to achieve its objectives for both short-term profit and long-term strength. Once such a current state analysis has been completed, then leaders must make the strategic choices that are imperative for identifying the best direction to follow.

This Recognize step follows two stages for change implementation: Strategic choice and follow-up action are the real objectives of business measurement and strategic planning. In the last analysis, excellence comes from execution, not from the effort of business analysis. Business analysis must lead to timely and proper decisions or else it is worthless, and no sophisticated set of analytical tools and methods can overcome the problems of a nonresponsive leadership team. Business leaders must know what they should do in order to gain all of the benefits of a Six Sigma implementation.

How does management focus on what it must study in order to determine its theory for change management? The short answer is that management must put in place the methods to "recognize" their priority busi-

---

marking through its linkage with corporate strategy"—which is precisely what happens in Step Zero of the revised benchmarking process that he introduces in his second book.

20. *Webster's Ninth Collegiate Dictionary* (Springfield, MA: Merriam-Webster, 1987), 287.

ness improvement needs as an information gathering step in it search for triggers of change that may be leveraged for growth.

One sound business practice that leading Six Sigma organizations use is to choose Six Sigma projects in a way that also implements their most significant business change strategies. By identifying the direction that the organization needs to move and then decomposing this plan into manageable projects, leaders of these businesses were able to focus their Six Sigma resources on driving strategic change. In other organizations that were not as successful, projects could be initiated anywhere, and there was no mechanism to prioritize among the projects from a business perspective—in many cases the Black Belt had to decide which project to tackle next. But these highly motivated individuals often lack the strategic business perspective to choose projects that will provide the organization with the biggest long-term benefit and meet its strategic objectives. The best practice in a Six Sigma company is to identify strategic change projects using a *hoshin kanri* process and then deploying these projects as Six Sigma Black Belt projects once they have been appropriately scoped for successful completion.

IMPROVING BY ADAPTATION—COMPLEXITY IS REALITY

Ideas evolve over time, and their acceptance follows the same general type of S-curve as Andy Grove described, and they also follow the general principles of systems dynamics:[21]

- All systems are composed of activities and feedback loops, and feedback loops contain all decisions in the system.
- Performance of systems may be described using either a rate of change in process or the levels of achieved change—thus, rates are incremental activities that attain levels, while levels are accumulations from the actions of rates.

21. These systems principles are summarized from the "Roadmaps to Systems Dynamics" created by the MIT System Dynamics in Education Project. For more information, see http://sysdyn .clexchange.org/.

- First-order processes, those with only one level and feedback loop, behave exponentially over time as they approach their limit condition —
  either as a growth or decay function. In addition, exponential behavior is the only stable behavior of higher-order positive feedback loops.
- Levels describe the current state of the system performance, and
  they change smoothly but not instantaneously as there may be a delay in their response to a rate change.

Indeed, reality is often a complexity that cannot be observed in both its
current state and rate of change simultaneously. Thus, observations of
benchmarking studies must take a conscientious approach to observation
of both the level of change and its historical rate of change, noting that
there is no assurance that the rate of change can be extrapolated in order
to predict a future level of performance. However, by observing the actions within the process and their effect on the circumstances of producing the best practice, a more pragmatic judgment may be made of projected performance based on the assumption that the organization will
persist in implementation of its strategy. These judgments must be made
within the context of the organization's will to change and its savoir faire
or self-knowledge about how it operates and performs its work — its ability to self-regulate its performance (change its rate) based on observation
of the level achieved and degree of effectiveness of the actions taken to
achieve that level. When this behavior is seen by an external observer,
then it may be used to formulate an estimate of future results. Thus, the
process of benchmarking is an organic process of discovery.

How does an organization change its behavior? Figure 2.1 summarizes
a model for organizational change that begins by observing the current
level of performance (called the *status quo*), which is being influenced by
a vision of the desired state of performance). Then by observation of the
process, a potential state may be defined as the achievable level of performance that could be accomplished by taking certain actions that have been
interpreted as drivers of results. These actions result in both intended results as well as unintended consequences that both generate a reaction in
the system (either positive or negative) and define the new current state

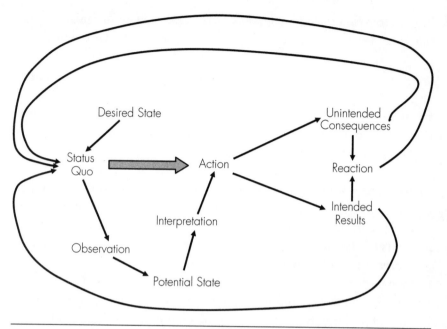

FIGURE 2.1 Organizational change model

of performance. By this process, a rate of change is generated that then is accumulated as a level of change that is observed in a new status quo.

This organizational change model underlies the operation of the DMAIC process in a Six Sigma project. One good question to ask in a Six Sigma project review is, Are we doing this Six Sigma business process improvement on the Xs or on the Ys of the process? There is a big difference to organizations! Strategic benchmarking tends to focus on the Ys in order to determine which Xs could be the disruptors of the process performance, while operational benchmarking focuses on the Xs to define the drivers of the rate of change that most influences the level of the Y.[22]

---

22. The interpretation of this discussion also applies to a design for Six Sigma project where the fuzzy front end of the design process is tasked with refining the rate of change to deliver a logical, rational operations process as a resultant level of change—a predictable factory in a reliable organization that always delivers the service level expected by its customers. Well, design is ideal, even though the reality may differ a bit!

The bottom line is that complexity is the reality of an organization and that to understand a specific reality we must cope with its complexity.

LEARNING FROM COMPLEXITY THEORY

Complexity theory provides a unique perspective to understand the way that processes operate as well as insights into the requirement for adaptation of benchmarking results.[23]

One observation of complexity theory is that a process evolution — essentially adaptation to the environment — gives rise to a kind of complexity that greatly hinders our attempts to solve some of the most important problems currently posed by our world. The issue that complexity theory attempts to explain is there is coherence under the influence of change. The answer proposed by this theory is that the system is able to adapt because it has a learning system composed of feedback loops that make decisions that in turn will influence the rate of change and thus, eventually, its level of performance. The very word *adapt* comes from the Latin root meaning "to fit" or alter circumstances.

Some would call this type of adaptation *spontaneous self-organization* — or the ability of an organism to learn from its environment and to create an operating mode that suits the change in circumstances that it is experiencing. However, there is also a cohesiveness in the act of many parts of the organism that are learning together and working together to achieve the end of survival of its whole. This coherence is the enigma that is studied at the Sante Fe Institute, a think tank on the leading edge of science that was founded by George Cowan to "create the sciences of the twenty-first century," which has sought to develop such concepts as neural networks and chaos theory.[24]

Some observations from this emerging science of complexity theory

---

23. For an entry-level discussion of complexity theory, see John H. Holland, *Hidden Order: How Adaptation Builds Complexity* (San Francisco: Addison-Wesley, 1995).

24. The story of the Sante Fe Institute is told by M. Michael Waldrop in *Complexity Theory: The Emerging Science at the Edge of Order and Chaos* (New York: Touchstone, 1992).

have migrated into the world of computational mathematics and have significant implications also for the world of business. One of the foundations of complexity theory is the fact that the behavior of a complex adaptive system (CAS) is more than the sum of its parts as the interactions between the parts create new knowledge, and that allows the organism to adaptation to external change. Thus, a simple trend analysis of the past will not be able to reproduce the nonlinearities that are created by the adaptation process because it is the result of many individual decisions at the level of the microcosm, and a holistic model cannot predict the new vector of change that comes as an organism makes many small independent choices in a complex mechanism to produce a new rate of change ($\delta x/\delta t$) vector that will drive it toward a new level of performance in the direction that the parts mutually desire to assure their joint survival.

How does such a complex system operate? A good example is the human immune system, which is coherent enough to provide a scientific definition of a person's unique identity. In fact, the human immune system is so good at distinguishing you from the rest of the world that it will reject cells from any other human. Thus, identity is learned at the level of cellular operations and is not just a mental construct. The same is true in business life as corporate culture will often reject noncultural behavior as well as the proponent of such asymmetrical change! Thus, learning behavior depends on interactions, not just the cognitive and kinesthetic activity of the body. These interactions are modified by the ability to anticipate consequences by modeling the external behavior to determine what behavior or action should be undertaken.

In such a complex system, there may be lever points where a small input or change can produce a major predictable, directed change. In other words, it is a point where an action has an amplifier effect on the performance of the whole. It is precisely these lever points that must be discovered in a strategic benchmarking study. What will create the change that drives systemic evolution? To understand the lever points of an organism or the collection of organisms into an organization, one must build a systems model that defines the rules and relationships by which the agents operate together to preserve the identity of the whole.

Each model that is built about a reality provides a unique opportunity to learn because it offers its own perspective of the way a system operates. Different representations or views will emphasize different functionalities and will produce different learning about how a system can operate. Truth is not so much a case of a correct or incorrect model as it is about the questions that are being investigated. Thus, Six Sigma studies both how a system operates as well as how it can fail and attempts to understand the probabilistic logic behind both of these alternatives in the face of myriad potential causes. One observation of such modeling is clear—the complex behaviors of the whole emerge from the aggregate interactions of the parts that are significantly less complex. However, the response of the whole to an external stimuli is based on the ability of the network of individual parts (called *agents* in complexity theory) to learn how to respond. By just studying the building blocks, it is impossible to understand how the entire system as a whole will operate. One must learn the theory behind the interactions in order to build a model that is predictive of the system behavior. Thus, Six Sigma studies multivariable relationships, not just simple linear models, in order to characterize the performance of a system as a whole.

In business, there is rarely one problem that must be attacked at a time, rather there are interdependent sets of problems that exist in a complex system (Ackoff's "mess") of interwoven processes. These processes also extend outside the business and involve customers and suppliers as well as regulatory bodies and other external observers. Thus, to understand how a business takes on the external world, one must first understand how its internal world operates and how it seeks to change itself based by learning how to respond to stimuli—its action orientation.

EXPLORATION VERSUS EXPLOITATION

Modeling a business system quickly demonstrates a fundamental duality that exists between two seemingly contrary action orientations. One orientation seeks to explore new directions, to design, to innovate, and to integrate external learning. The other orientation seeks to exploit the current capability and improve or refine the internal capability to an optimal performance. This is a duality of business management—the challenge to simultaneously find the future and fund the future! Organizations must simultaneously create a product design and design the process that delivers the product. This duality is expressed using such alternative concepts as the following:

- Evolutionary change versus revolutionary change
- Continuous improvement versus breakthrough improvement
- Sustainable innovation versus disruptive innovation

However, following the principle discovered by Jim Collins in his book *Built to Last*, this is not a question of either/or logic—it is a proposition that requires *and* logic—both of these change dimensions must be integrated into an organization in order for it to learn. Remember the way an amoeba functions—how adaptive is your ability to relate to change? As your organization grows, do you focus differently on the internal and external elements of change? How do you assure that the internal elements get stimulated by the environment as much as the external elements that are more directly sensing and experiencing how the environment is changing? In an adaptive organization, this mechanism can either grow informally or it can be encouraged by managerial action. Benchmarking, strategic planning, and Six Sigma unite to help create exactly this type of learning. The purpose of an operational benchmarking study is to observe and study specific behaviors at the work-process level in order to discover the theory of change and the lever points to apply it in order to influence the directional shift required for the general system change. This link requires benchmarking to operate as a stimulus for planning, which then creates change projects that can be directed using Six Sigma methods. By taking this approach, the duality of change will be resolved as the complex system seeks the appropriate level of change for each of the three levels of the organization.

MANAGING YOUR CORE BUSINESS PROCESSES

When I worked at Hewlett-Packard, the company created a daily management system by building a work-process measurement system that they called "Business Fundamentals Tables." Similarly, other companies refer to the set of measures that translate strategic goals into operational measures of work (in units such as quality, cost, and time) as either a customer dashboard or a balanced scorecard. These systems are used to monitor the daily operations of a business and to report to management on the progress in the process for developing and delivering value to customers. This measurement process monitors the pulse of the organism to provide a feedback loop that allows the management to stimulate action and drive performance in its desired direction. Such a system must have minimal delays in gathering and processing information and must have close to real-time operations to permit process owners to take appropriate corrective action that will limit the escapes of defects, errors, or mistakes to external customers. These measures of core work processes are called *business fundamentals* because they must operate under control for the business to achieve its fundamental performance objectives.

Thus, a daily management system defines the details of an organization's operations, and the measurement and the point at which it is both monitored and controlled are parts of this daily management system. In the language of Six Sigma, a "Business Y" (such as profitable growth) that must be achieved is the strategic goal of the organization that provides the mutually-agreed direction of the organization, while a "Process X" (such as creditworthy customers) delivers this performance in the transfer function $Y = f(X)$ and is therefore a business fundamentals measure in the daily management system. In an adaptive (agile or flexible) organization, the information presented at this X point of measurement must allow decisions to be made that will ultimately influence the Y—in a positive direction. Thus, the organization operates according to the principles of chaos found in complexity theory. The actions of agents, measured by performance Xs will be accumulated into the behavior of the whole through a complex interrelationship or a network of interactions that does not exactly follow the process of consolidation found in a standard cost accounting practice. Changes must be made to both the *X*s and the *Y*s in order to drive change systemically.

Collins and Porras have stated that most leading companies will stimulate results through *evolutionary progress* as well as through *revolutionary progress,* where the word *evolutionary* describes progress that resembles how organic species evolve and adapt to their natural environments. Evolutionary progress differs from the revolutionary progress of strategic progress in two ways. First, whereas revolutionary progress involves clear and unambiguous goals ("We are going to climb *that* mountain"), evolutionary progress involves ambiguity ("By trying lots of different approaches, we're bound to stumble onto something that works; we just don't know ahead of time what it will be.") Second, whereas a Big Hairy Audacious Goal (BHAG) involves bold *discontinuous* leaps, evolutionary progress begins with small *incremental* steps or mutations, often in the form of quickly seizing unexpected opportunities that eventually grow into major — and often unanticipated — strategic shifts. Evolutionary progress represents a means to take advantage of unplanned opportunities for improvement that are observed at the point of application — the daily management system. The accumulation of many evolutionary improvements results in what looks like part of a brilliant overall strategic plan.[25]

Both types of change are needed to stimulate the organic growth of an enterprise. If an organization can make improvements in the right *X*s, then it will improve its performance on the critical Business *Y*. However, this means that the organization must first learn which *X*s influence the *Y*s and create a probability model that demonstrates how the interaction effects operate synergistically.

Thus, Six Sigma is required to make complexity theory become operational reality. Benchmarking provides the strategic insight that stimulates the learning of leverage points of change and strategic planning coordinates the activity of the business system to produce the desired result

---

25. Collins and Porras, 146.

that is achieved one project at a time through the sweat equity of many individual agents, who act both uniquely and conjointly.

Thus, like the amoeba, the larger an organization gets, the more complex it becomes—defying the ability for simplistic solutions to be applied and also defying the ability to coordinate change across all of its independently operating agents of change!

INTEGRATING BENCHMARKING WITH STRATEGIC PLANNING

Benchmarking improves performance of organizations by providing a methodology to learn and challenge critical business assumptions and encouraging management to think differently about their strategic direction. Applying benchmarking as a tool of business strategy is an effective way to evaluate options and perform an assessment of alternatives by considering the strategic implications that may be observed in other analogous situations. Such lessons reduce the likelihood of repeating the mistakes of others.

At its core, benchmarking represents nothing more than a comparison between two organizations. This is a natural act and has occurred ever since man has observed that there are differences to be observed! What makes benchmarking different than basic observations (e.g., we could heat our house better if our fireplace worked like the one our neighbors built, etc.) is that it is a systematic process with a scientific basis in order to draw statistically valid comparisons. In a scientific approach, we develop hypotheses and test their validity in small experiments. Thus, objective measurement is an essential ingredient in any benchmarking study. While performance measurement is a key ingredient in business process benchmarking, benchmarking goes beyond the activity of performance measurement. Benchmarking also has as its aim not just the observation of differences, but also the desire to understand and *adapt* the best practices that created the difference in order to improve the organization's performance.

Figure 2.2 illustrates the essential logic of benchmarking. It begins by

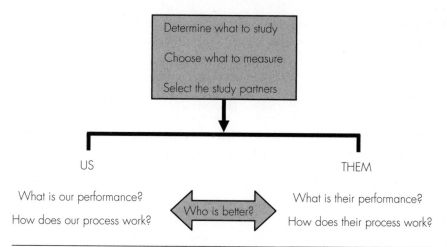

FIGURE 2.2 The essence of benchmarking

choosing a topic to study—what will make a difference to the future of our organization? What is so very important that it *commands* management's attention? In a comparative study of this topic, management generates ideas about what is *imperative* for them to change. However, the specific lessons about how to adapt these lessons about what to change and ideas about change must be delegated to the organization's experts to define the mechanisms that will produce the desired results in their own business system and management culture.

There are different ways to understand how benchmarking is applied. It is a poor misconception that an organization must compare itself against its commercial rivals in order to benchmark. Competitors have no motivation to help your organization learn to become a better competitor against them. In fact, in many instances there are legal injunctions against collaboration among competitors! While gaining information about competitors is an important aspect of any organization's strategic planning process, this information is typically not scientific in terms of the degree of confidence that may be placed in the results. What competing organizations are really doing is kept close and not disclosed in advertising or public announcements. Indeed, one tactic organizations employ is to only release information about new technology or products when they are available to the market. This strategy helps to create an additional buffer of time in the market through the exercise of the Boyd Cycle.[26]

DOING BENCHMARKING — BEING *DANTOTSU!*

The Japanese use the world *dantotsu* — becoming better than the best — to represent the strategic goal for breakthrough improvement.

- What knowledge must you obtain to beat your competition? How will you get it?
- What is *common sense* — how to distinguish? Better use of statistics to demonstrate that a difference really does exist?
- How does the best practice apply in theory? What will happen as it approaches the limits of its application?
- What information should we be willing to barter in order to gain access for potential performance improvement?

To discover how strategic benchmarking can make a difference in companies, we must examine the transition from the strategic illumination that occurs at the discovery of the leverage points of change, to the creative imitation that comes from adaptation of these lessons to your own organization, and then the flawless execution that implements the change in your daily management practices. This journey of discovery and action will generate success for a benchmarking study. But first we must understand the process of conducting a study.

---

26. This application of the Boyd Cycle was discussed in my book *Design for Six Sigma: Innovation for Enhanced Competitiveness* (Salem, NH: GOAL/QPC, 2005), 126–128.

PART 2
The Process of Benchmarking

CHAPTER 3

Understanding the Essence of Process Benchmarking

Learning is not something that requires time out from being engaged in productive activity; learning is the heart of productive activity. To put it simply, learning is the new form of labor.

—SHOSHANNA ZUBOFF

INTRODUCTION

In the first part of this book, we have described where benchmarking came from, what benchmarking is, and the importance of benchmarking for business improvement. Now in this second part of the book, we will turn our attention to how to conduct a benchmarking study of a business process, how to analyze the information that is gathered using statistical methods that have been incorporated from Six Sigma methods, and how to use benchmarking in the process of management. The first two chapters develop the theory of benchmarking, while the three chapters in Part 2 define the practice of benchmarking.

BUSINESS IMPROVEMENT AS A PROCESS

A general principle of TQM is that all work may be described as a process—benchmarking and Six Sigma are not exceptions. Rather than define all of the alternative process designs for benchmarking, this book will focus on presenting a best practice for benchmarking that integrates the Six Sigma statistical methods in order to strengthen the quality of the comparisons that are made in the studies. The general model for all business improvement is based on the Shewhart Cycle, which is typically referred to as the Deming Plan-Do-Study-Act model.[1] The process for business improvement follows four phases of work: developing an understanding of the situation and defining the work; measuring and analyzing the process to determine the opportunities to make it better; experimenting with change to see what works best; and implementing the changes to the process in order to achieve the projected benefits. Thus, the proper way to think about the inclusion of Six Sigma in the model for process benchmarking is that the most general model for continuous improvement is the Deming PDCA model that has been developed by a more rigorous statement and sequence of analysis tools in the Six Sigma Define-Measure-Analyze-Improve-Control (DMAIC) model. In the next phase of development, the DMAIC model is being embedded (or loaded) into the process benchmarking model. This final step is described in this chapter. What all of these models share in common is that they are a logical structure to help facilitate discovery in a learning process. As the detail in these models moves from the most generic (PDCA) to the most specific (process benchmarking), the abstraction level of the process decreases, and the steps involved become more concrete and specific. The linkage in the logic between these models may be observed when a logical transition from PDCA to DMAIC is mapped in Figure 3.1.

1. Dr. Walter A. Shewhart proposed the model in his early work on statistical process control, and one of his colleagues was Dr. W. Edward Deming who took this idea to Japan. As Deming delivered his lectures in Japan over a number of years, the engineers that he briefed simplified the model to make it easier to use and to improve on its operation. Colleagues of Dr. Kaoru Ishikawa actually developed the Plan-Do-Check-Act (PDCA) model as a revision of Deming's work, which he then accepted. In Deming's later years, he changed his presentation of the model to the final version—Plan-Do-Study-Act—because he believed there was confusion over the word *Check*, and he wanted to assure more clarity in the model's description. A definitive history of the PDCA transition is being developed by Dr. Noriaki Kano of Tokyo Science University and will be published later this year. PDCA is also the intellectual parent of the Six Sigma DMAIC model.

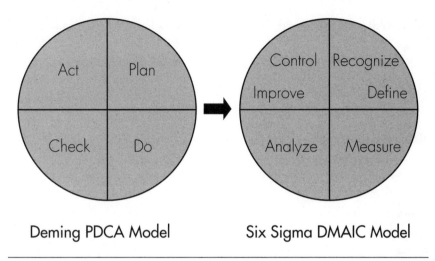

Deming PDCA Model   Six Sigma DMAIC Model

FIGURE 3.1 Comparison of PDCA and DMAIC process models

As described in the previous chapter, Six Sigma begins with the linkage into strategy of an organization through the implementation of a precursor stage to the DMAIC model, which is usually called the *Recognize phase* of benchmarking. Recognize is the starting point of DMAIC because it focuses selection of projects into areas of critical or strategic importance to the organization. The Recognize prelude to the DMAIC process is analogous to strategic benchmarking and the process of operational benchmarking. In addition, operational benchmarking closely follows the logic of the Measure-Analyze-Improve-Control (MAIC) portion of the Six Sigma DMAIC model.

Thus, the Six Sigma analysis model and the benchmarking process model have the same fundamental logical structure, and when the Six Sigma content is added to the model for process benchmarking, then it forms a very powerful approach for stimulating business improvement. To understand the contribution of Six Sigma and its analysis toolkit to benchmarking, we will characterize the nature of this transition in development of process benchmarking by describing it as a transition from art to science. In the next chapter we will describe the statistical elements of DMAIC that are used to strengthen the science of the benchmarking process.

BENCHMARKING WAS DEVELOPED AS AN ART AND IS TRANSITIONING TO A SCIENCE

Reflecting on the early history of benchmarking, it would be fair to characterize the initial intellectual development as more of an art than a science. In the early manifestations of benchmarking, it was conducted by specialists who sought evidence that performance was better at one organization. They looked at the processes and made judgments about what drove the performance difference they observed. As benchmarking matured as a business practice, it developed a more objective approach to defining best practice and identifying the enablers of performance. The transition that benchmarking is currently undergoing will complete the transition from an artlike framework to a more scientific basis. What characterizes a science? Figure 3.2 presents two sets of characteristics that distinguish the end points on a scale that juxtaposes the features of art and science.

Art depends on people and related investments in training and development, reward systems, and retention. Science depends on processes and tools and their related investments in equipment purchases, training and development, and system maintenance. Science should be emphasized when there is a need for performance improvement and process consistency that can be best achieved through measurement and control. On the other hand, art should be emphasized when there is a need for the craftsman's touch or an understanding of a situation, and creative energies need to be "juiced" in order to discover a different way of dealing with a situation. (Note that this artistic pathway can also be supplemented with thinking tools to encourage increased creative expression.)[2]

2. Bob King and Helmut Schlicksupp, *The Idea Edge* (Salem, NH: GOAL/QPC, 1999).

Characteristics of an Art	Characteristics of a Science
Subjective	Objective
Abstract/Vague	Concrete/Measurable
Organic/Unpredictable	Defined/Predictable
Never the same choice twice	Repeatable judgments
Creative/Freethinking	Documented/Dogmatic
Flexible/Flowing	Rigid/Rules
Personal process	Organizational process

FIGURE 3.2 Comparison of the characteristics of art and science

LOADING SIX SIGMA INTO PROCESS BENCHMARKING

Integration of Six Sigma methods into benchmarking converts benchmarking from an art into a science. In order to qualify as a science, a discipline must have a distinct body of knowledge consisting of a sound theory, a process model, and demonstration of results where that theory has been practiced. How does Six Sigma become loaded into these three components of the benchmarking science, and what is the contribution of the Six Sigma methods to converting benchmarking from an art into a science?

The acquisition and application of the methods of Six Sigma combined with a continuous pursuit of strategic insights into business knowledge sets the foundation for successful benchmarking.[3] The initial steps in the-

---

3. These comments draw upon the work of Clayton M. Christensen, Paul Carlile, and David M. Sundahl in "The Process of Theory Building," an unpublished paper provided by Professor Christensen for academic use in my courses in engineering and technology management at Oklahoma State University.

ory building begin with a careful examination of the history of the subject and understanding the contributions of the previous work on the subject (the history of benchmarking is presented in the introduction to this book). The next phase — *theory creation* — carefully observes and characterizes phenomena into categories (this decomposition of the benchmarking science was presented in the first chapter of this book). The final phase of theory building is the creation of a model to explain the way that these elements of these observations operate to create observable phenomena. The purpose of such a model is to explain how the categories work together and to provide a systematic linkage of the concepts in a way that produces replicable results. This focus on the creation of the benchmarking process model is the concentration of this chapter.

Theory is useful because it has predictive power — thus, the addition of statistical tools and methods to benchmarking theory by "reloading it with Six Sigma methods" is not just an impractical extension of knowledge. This integration represents a step forward in drawing more confident conclusions from benchmarking studies about the utility of the study observations, precisely because this predictive capability has been embedded into the methodology! Thus, implementing the findings of benchmarking studies should more closely predict the achievement of demonstrated results because a more careful characterization and projection methodology has been used to draw conclusions.

This present chapter will extend the initial benchmarking process model presented in *Strategic Benchmarking* by integrating the methods of the Six Sigma DMAIC process. Thus, this chapter concentrates on the model of the benchmarking process, while the next chapter focuses on the statistical methods of comparison that are applied throughout the benchmarking process. The case study chapters following this will illustrate how results can be demonstrated and made practical.

WHAT IS THE SIX SIGMA DMAIC PROCESS?

How does the Six Sigma methodology relate to process benchmarking? First, we must remind ourselves that we are considering two categories

DMAIC Step	Step Focus and Activites
Define	Plan the project and obtain commitment of resources.
Measure	Document the process and measure the performance baseline.
Analyze	Determine drivers of change—shifting the mean or reducing variation.
Improve	Identify the critical control parameters and their operating envelope.
Control	Put the revised process into a state of business and statistical control.

FIGURE 3.3 The Six Sigma DMAIC analysis process

of benchmarking studies as process benchmarking—strategic and operational. Strategic benchmarking studies relate to the Recognize phase that precedes DMAIC and focuses the attention of the entire organization on strategic business change, while the DMAIC process is the engine for defining and creating the change necessary to achieve management's business objectives. How does DMAIC work?

The DMAIC process changes in focus areas and activities conducted as progress is made through the five phases of its statistical problem solving process. These phases may be summarized as in Figure 3.3.[4]

In Six Sigma, the DMAIC model merges project management with the analysis process to form a comprehensive approach for stimulating improvements. There are three Six Sigma DMAIC activities where senior management has an obligation of participation—project selection, business review, and performance leveraging.

The DMAIC process is executed following management's decision to approve a project for improvement using the Six Sigma methodology.

4. For more information about the DMAIC process, see my book on the subject for managers: Gregory H. Watson, *Six Sigma for Business Leaders* (Salem, NH: GOAL/QPC, 2004).

The project selection process should be tightly coupled with the strategic planning process of the organization to assure the relevance of the study as well as its potential to impact the organization in a positive way. Thus, choosing a study topic should be part of the ongoing strategic examination that senior management makes of its business environment and operating assumptions—this should be true of both Six Sigma projects and benchmarking studies.

The second area is the business review of projects. In a DMAIC project, management is responsible for reviewing projects to assure their business focus and delivery of bottom line results. In benchmarking, the decisions of selecting long-term partners and establishing alliances for sharing of business practices and performance enablers must not be relegated to chance—business leaders must be involved in the identification and solicitation of these relationships so that appropriate support and collaboration between the organizations can occur. For both Six Sigma and benchmarking, business leaders must decide how they will integrate competitive information with technology forecasts, market intelligence, and managerial judgment in order to develop an insightful picture of options available for defining its future. In all external relationships, business leaders must also exercise oversight to assure that the business secrets and core intellectual property that provide its competitive differentiation are not inadvertently disclosed through these cross-company business alliances.

The final area of required participation is the need for leadership attention to the principle of "leverage-in, leverage-out" for both Six Sigma and benchmarking projects. This is the principle that lessons should be learned from the history of prior work before starting any study or improvement project and that the lessons learned during that project must be shared and implemented across the organization after its completion. To achieve this requires cross-functional leadership and a broader span of control than is found at the lower levels of an organization.

These are just some of the similarities between benchmarking and Six Sigma—other aspects of their focus indicate the true strength in their symbiotic relationship.

THE PROCESS OF BENCHMARKING

Like Six Sigma, Benchmarking also follows the basic principle of statistical thinking that all work can be described as a process. Thus, we should not be surprised to discover that benchmarking also has a process model that describes the sequence of activities that are taken to conduct a study. Many different organizations have illustrated benchmarking processes with levels of detail from 4 to 42 steps; however, the process that we will use has 7 steps that highlight the work that must be done in a benchmarking study and that also follow a four-phase process that is generic to all benchmarking models:

1. *Identify Subject:* Choose what to benchmark.
2. *Plan Study:* Identify your partners and plan your data collection.
3. *Collect Information:* Actively collect the data and visit partners.
4. *Analyze Data:* Analyze the data for performance trends and consistency over time.
5. *Compare Performance:* Compare results to test differences for statistical significance.
6. *Adapt Applications:* Prepare the lessons learned for transition to your own culture.
7. *Improve Performance:* Implement projects to improve your processes.

A higher-order set of four generic phases that describes these steps roughly follows Deming's PDCA cycle for process management and improvement. These four phases of process benchmarking may be summarized as follows (also see Figure 3.4):

- *Plan:* Design the study and evaluate the baseline performance.
- *Collect:* Collect internal and external data about the process.
- *Analyze:* Conduct a gap analysis and determine enablers of success.
- *Improve:* Adapt the recommendations and implement the process improvements.

It is important to note that this model describes activities of both strategic and operational benchmarking, although it is more concretely fol-

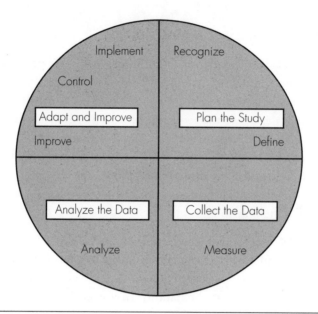

FIGURE 3.4 DMAIC related to the phases of process benchmarking

lowed in an operational benchmarking study. Why is operational benchmarking less abstract in its method?

Strategic benchmarking is defined as a "systematic process for evaluating
alternatives, implementing strategies, and improving performance by understanding and adapting successful strategies . . ." and it differs from
operational benchmarking in terms of the scope and depth of its implications for the core business model. Strategic benchmarking has the potential to fundamentally change a business, not just incrementally improve
its operating process performance.[5] Operational benchmarking seeks
"significantly better practices" as a means to leverage improvements by
adapting lessons learned from the experience of other organizations.
Thus, operational benchmarking learns its lessons by observing the actual practices of the organization, while strategic benchmarking learns its
lessons from the environment, philosophy, decisions, and choices that

5. Watson, *Strategic Benchmarking*, 8.

motivate the action of another organization. Thus, it is the practice of operational benchmarking that is most directly linked to the steps of DMAIC as it more closely follows the model for process benchmarking.

Rather than focus on the process model for Six Sigma problem solving, the approach that we will take is to "load the logic" and methods of Six Sigma into the benchmarking model that was presented in *Strategic Benchmarking.* The four phases of this reloaded model for process benchmarking are described in the following sections. Each of these four phases will be described in terms of the steps taken to complete the process, questions that guide progress through these steps, and Six Sigma DMAIC methods and tools that can help accelerate progress toward a more scientific knowledge base in the approach. So let us turn our attention to the process of benchmarking and its planning phase.

THE BENCHMARKING PROCESS: PLAN PHASE

The objective of the planning phase of a benchmarking study is to establish the basis for a comparison with external organizations—to set a frame of reference from which to make comparisons.

The steps involved in planning a benchmarking study include the following:

- Select process
- Gain owner's participation
- Select leader and team
- Identify customer expectations
- Analyze process flow and measures
- Define process inputs and outputs
- Document the process
- Identify process critical success factors
- Determine data collection elements
- Develop preliminary questionnaire

These steps can be framed using a set of questions to guide the progress through the activities required to complete this phase:

73

- What process should we benchmark?
- What is our process, and how does it work?
- How do we measure it?
- How well is it performing today?
- Who are the customers of our process?
- What products and services do we deliver to our customers?
- What do our customers expect from our process?
- What are the critical success factors for this process?
- What is our process performance goal?
- How did we establish that goal?
- What data should we collect for comparisons?

The steps of this process phase are expressed as a flow chart in Figure 3.5.

Notice that many of these questions that are addressed throughout these phases of process benchmarking are similar to the basic questions that one confronts in any TQM improvement project. These initial questions are focused on learning about the current state of internal process performance and seeking insight into the system of performance that has been developed for use by our own employees. Subsequent questions shift to the external organization and the comparisons that may be drawn between the data sets.

Six Sigma DMAIC tools and methods that are appropriate for application in this phase of a benchmarking study include the following:

- Process mapping
- Operational definitions
- Attribute agreement analysis
- Measurement systems analysis
- Failure analysis
- Exploratory data analysis
- Parametric analysis and matrix plots
- Pareto charts
- Capability analysis
- Tests of difference
- Regression analysis

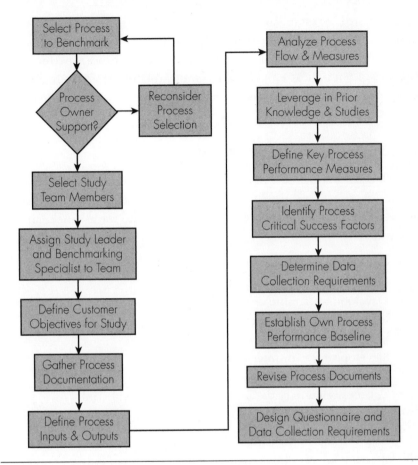

FIGURE 3.5 The plan phase of process benchmarking

- Multi-vari charts
- Analysis of variance
- Control charting
- Lean process analysis
- Standardized work procedures

After own-process performance has been measured to establish your baseline capability, the next step is to turn to the external view of performance in order to establish the comparison. Measurements taken of own-process performance should include key indicators of the efficiency of operations (time-based indicators), effectiveness of the process performance (quality-based indicators), as well as indicators of the economic impact of the process (financial measures of cost and return on investment).

THE BENCHMARKING PROCESS: COLLECT PHASE

The objective of the data collection phase of benchmarking is to gather the information that is used for comparison against your internal performance. Thus, the steps involved in collecting data for a benchmarking study include the following:

- Collect internal data.
- Perform secondary research.
- Develop partnership criteria.
- Identify benchmark partners.
- Plan data collection.
- Develop survey or interview guide.
- Solicit participation of partners.
- Collect preliminary data.
- Define site visit protocol.
- Conduct site visits.

The following are questions that guide the conduct of information gathering activities in this phase:

- What companies perform this process better?
- Which company is best at performing this process?
- What can we learn from that company?
- Who should we contact to participate as our partners?
- What is their process?
- How representative is the process across different areas of their organization?
- How do they measure process performance?

- What is their performance goal, and how was it set?
- How well does their process perform over time?
- Is there a performance gap between locations or any change observable over time?
- What business practices, methods, or tasks contribute to the process performance?
- What factors could inhibit the adaptation of their process into our company?

The sequence of activities that are performed during the data collection process are expressed as a flow diagram in Figure 3.6.

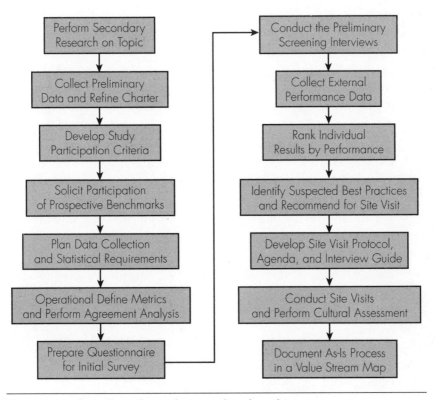

FIGURE 3.6 The collect phase of process benchmarking

Six Sigma DMAIC tools and methods that are appropriate for application in this phase of a benchmarking study are the same set of tools that are used for assessing own company performance.

Now that data has been collected to indicate your performance and that of comparative organizations, it is time to turn the study focus to the analysis of the comparisons. This subject will be described in more detail in Chapter 4; however, a summary is presented in the following.

THE BENCHMARKING PROCESS: ANALYZE PHASE

The objective of the analyze phase of the benchmarking study is to make comparisons, determine significant differences, and identify practices that caused these differences.

The steps involved in analyzing benchmarking study data using Six Sigma tools include the following:

- Aggregate the data across business units within each comparative organization, but be careful to preserve subgroup relationships.
- Normalize performance to a common performance base (e.g., using the sigma scale for a standardized customer requirement).
- Compare current performance to historical data.
- Test performance for difference in both trend of performance average and variation.
- Test differences for statistical significance and practical significance.
- Identify performance gaps and investigate to root-cause level any major differences.
- Identify entitlement opportunities for improvement of own-process capability.
- Forecast performance observations to the business planning horizon.
- Isolate process enablers.
- Assess adaptability of process enablers.
- Develop case studies of best practice.

The following are questions that guide performance of the analysis phase of process benchmarking:

- What is the basis for comparing our process measurements?
- How does their process performance compare with our process performance?
- What is the magnitude of the performance gap?
- What is the nature or root cause of the performance gap?
- How much will their process continue to improve?
- What characteristics distinguish their process as superior?
- What activities within our process are candidates for improvement?

The sequence of activities that are performed during the analysis process can be expressed as in Figure 3.7 as a set of process steps that embeds a sequence of the application of Six Sigma tools:

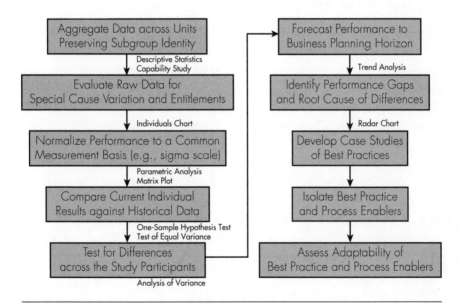

FIGURE 3.7 The analyze phase of process benchmarking

Six Sigma DMAIC tools and methods that are appropriate for application in this phase of a benchmarking study include the following:

- Descriptive statistics
- Process capability studies
- Statistical process control charts
- Hypothesis tests of means and variance
- Analysis of variance
- Trend analysis and moving averages
- Pareto charts and radar charts

Now that relative performance is understood and potential best practices have been identified, it is time to work on process improvement. The study is not done until the findings have been approved *and* implemented!

THE BENCHMARKING PROCESS: IMPROVE PHASE

The objective of the improve phase of benchmarking is to adapt the discoveries of the study for implementation in your organization and to transition the organization to a new level of performance by effectively executing the recommended changes.

The final steps to implement the lessons learned from a benchmarking study include the following:

- Set goals to close, meet, exceed the gap.
- Modify enablers for implementation so they fit the culture and business model.
- Gain support for change among all involved parties by sharing benchmark data and the study findings.
- Develop the action plan.
- Communicate the plan.
- Commit resources to achieve the plan.
- Implement the improvement plan and document the changes.

- Monitor and report progress on targeted schedule.
- Identify opportunities for further process improvement.
- Recalibrate the benchmark measure after implementation.

Some of the questions addressed during this phase of a benchmarking study include the following:

- What is the difference in performance between the benchmarked organizations?
- Is this difference consistent from location to location, over time?
- What is the gap from achieved performance to process-designed performance?
- How does our knowledge of their process help us to improve our process?
- How should we forecast the future effectiveness of their process performance?
- Should we redesign our process or reset our performance goals based on this benchmark?
- What activities in their process need to be modified to adapt it into our business model?
- What have we learned during this study that will allow us to improve on best practice?
- What goals should we set for our own process improvement?
- How can we implement the changes in our process?
- How will other companies continue to improve this process?

Note that many of the questions addressed in the preceding are the same as would be addressed in managing implementation in any project improvement process.

The sequence of process activities in this final phase of the benchmarking process is shown in Figure 3.8.

The tools and method used to implement the last phase of the benchmarking process are not unique to Six Sigma, rather they are the meth-

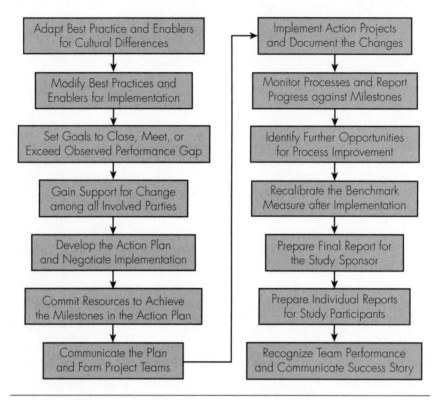

FIGURE 3.8 The improve phase of process benchmarking

ods of change management and project management that focus on collaboration, participation, involvement, and guided action. In the case of DMAIC projects, these same tools must be brought to bear in order to have successful transition of change to a state of business control.

APPLYING THE BENCHMARKING PROCESS TO CONDUCT A STUDY

While this fundamental benchmarking process model appears to be simple and direct, several amplifications can be added to enrich our understanding and provide for a more effective implementation of the entire process. The following paragraphs contain some tips for more effective application of the benchmarking process.

COLLABORATIVE OR GROUP STUDY

A distinction in the process of benchmarking may be drawn between an individual study and a group or collaborative study in terms of the way the process of benchmarking is engaging the participants. An individual study is conducted by a single organization in order to meet its own objectives. A collaborative study will modify the benchmarking process to focus upon a shared objective so that each individual company that participates in the study must develop its own comparative assessment using a standardized process template. In this case, the basic approach to benchmarking is modified to fit a slightly different process model:

1. Define the study topic and establish a common objective.
2. Identify the cohort to form the collaborative study.
3. Develop a standard process specification and data collection template.
4. Conduct internal studies using the standardized information request.
5. Conduct a cross-participant study of the contributed benchmarking information.
6. Report results and draw conclusions and document best practices.
7. Adapt and apply results at each of the individual participating organizations.

There are many different ways to approach benchmarking; however, none can truly compete with the creation of a society of firms—a collaborative in which mutual trust is built among non-competing firms that results in an openness to share the operational detail of their processes. In such an environment, firms can truly learn what clicks in their own business—what makes a significant difference. By developing long-term collaboration for benchmarking and best practice sharing, organizations gain a multiplier result in terms of learning effectiveness. Thus, over the past 10 years a variety of different networks have evolved as vehicles for interorganizational sharing of best practice (for more details of this evolution, see the introduction to this book).

MANAGING A BENCHMARKING STUDY

Given all of the variants of process benchmarking, how is it made practical for use in organizations? The process benchmarking model describes how a study is conducted at the level of analysis; however, it does not fully describe a management process for doing benchmarking. The process diagram shown in Figure 3.9 assigns this sequence of benchmarking steps into a series of five project management stages to execute a detailed benchmarking process model.

This overall process for conducting a benchmarking study combines the analysis method with project management in the following detailed steps:

1. *Identify the Topic:* The topic will be assigned by the operating committee based on an initial assessment of opportunities for organizational development or improvement.

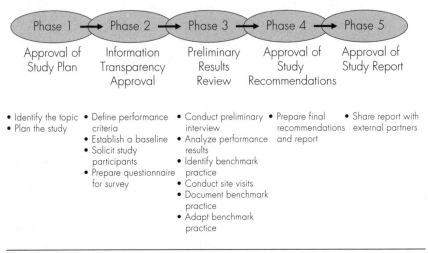

FIGURE 3.9 The five phases of a benchmarking study

2. *Plan the Study:* The study plan will be developed jointly by the benchmarking project sponsor and the benchmarking process owner. A formal study plan will be issued to the benchmarking project team that they assign to conduct the study. The director of quality will assign a benchmarking specialist to facilitate the study.

3. *Define Performance Criteria:* The performance criteria for the benchmarking study will be established during a preliminary process characterization study that uses the Six Sigma Define-Measure-Analyze (DMA) process to baseline the performance and establish the theoretical base case performance of the business focus area.

4. *Establish a Baseline:* The baseline performance of the study subject will be defined in the preliminary Six Sigma DMA study. The baseline will include the historical trend of data, process capability calculations, customer specification of tolerance in process variation, and operational definitions of key terms used to describe the measurements.

5. *Solicit Study Participants:* The benchmarking project sponsor will establish a study advisory team to define the criteria for soliciting study partners and approve the set of organizations that will be contacted for participation. This study advisory team will execute managerial oversight for the benchmarking project team.

6. *Prepare Questionnaire for Survey:* The benchmarking specialist will facilitate the benchmarking study team in developing a questionnaire for initial screening of the potential study partners. This questionnaire should be reviewed by a specialist to assure the questions are objective and are phrased so their meaning is not ambiguous.

7. *Conduct Preliminary Interviews:* The benchmarking specialist will conduct all of the preliminary interviews (via e-mail or telephone) and will prepare a summary report for the team. The team will identify those organizations that they wish to pursue for data analysis.

8. *Collect Performance Data:* The benchmarking specialist will coordinate all external data collection with partner organizations and

will evaluate this information to assure it is feasible to make meaningful cross-comparisons among the partner organizations.

9. *Analyze Performance Results:* The benchmarking specialist will analyze submitted performance results and establish performance envelopes for each organization as well as performing appropriate statistical comparisons to assure that the results have been sustained over time.

10. *Identify Benchmark Practice:* The team will apply the company's decision criteria to the analysis of the performance results in order to determine which study partners are benchmark practices. Permission for a site visit will be requested from these partners.

11. *Conduct Site Visits:* The benchmarking specialist will lead a subgroup of the total benchmarking study team in conducting a site visit at the identified best practice for the purpose of developing an understanding of the practice in operational detail.

12. *Document Benchmark Practice:* At the completion of each site visit conducted, the team will document the benchmark practice as soon as possible to assure that they capture all the necessary lessons to be learned.

13. *Adapt Benchmark Practice:* The benchmarking study team will meet with the study advisory team to adapt learning from the study into a recommendation for internal change. This joint team recommendation will be presented to both the benchmarking project sponsor and the operating committee for final approval and implementation.

14. *Prepare Final Recommendations and Report:* The benchmarking study team will prepare two final reports—a comprehensive report for internal distribution and a final report for sharing with external partners.

15. *Share Report with External Partners:* The report that is shared with benchmarking partners should include the following items: the performance survey results with participant identity blinded, statistical analysis of best-practice performance, documentation of

best practice (performance indexed value stream map), and operational definitions of the critical process enablers.

The benchmarking standard operating procedure that is provided as a reference in the Appendix to this book can be used as a starting point for developing your own company approach to managing and conducting benchmarking studies.

METHODS OF DATA COLLECTION

In conducting a benchmarking study, there are several different approaches to collecting data that can be pursued by a benchmarking team. Figures 3.10 and 3.11 illustrate several data collection schemes and identify when to use each approach as well as the advantages and disadvantages associated with each of the methods.

Method	Existing Data Review	Questionnaire/Survey	Telephone Survey
Definition	Analysis and interpretation of data that already exists in-house or in public domain.	Written questions sent directly to benchmarking partner; can contain any type of question: multiple choice, open-ended, forced choice, or scaled answer.	A written script of questions used to solicit data or information over the telephone.
When to Use	Before conducting original research to establish what is the historical baseline.	When you need to gather information from a wide number of sources.	When information is needed quickly or to rapidly screen potential sources.
Advantage	A large number of sources of information is available.	Permits extensive data gathering over time, can be analyzed by computer, and data is easy to compile.	Can cover a wide range of respondents quickly; people are more candid over the telephone.
Disadvantage	Gathering the appropriate information can be very time consuming.	Response rates are low: the interpretation of questions is sometimes subjective, creative ideas rarely surface, difficult to probe for how-to answers.	Locating the right person to answer your questions; no exchange of process information requires multiple calls.

FIGURE 3.10 Data collection method summary—Part 1

Method	Interview	Focus Group	Site Visit
Definition	A face-to-face meeting with a benchmarking partner using questions that are prepared and distributed in advance.	A panel discussion between benchmarking partners with a third party facilitator at a neutral location.	An on-premise meeting at a benchmarking partner facility that combines the interview with work process observation.
When to Use	When you need one-on-one interaction to probe and drive data collection to a specific objective or level of detail.	When you want to gather information from more than one source or perspective at the same time; when there are diverse opinions or ways to approach the objective.	When you need to observe specific work practices; when interpersonal or face-to-face interaction is needed to evaluate human aspect of a process.
Advantage	Encourages interaction, in-depth discussion, and open-ended questions; a flexible style can provide unexpected information.	Direct sharing of information on best practice; brings the partners together to discuss a mutually established agenda.	Can observe actual practice and verify process, enablers, and measurement systems.
Disadvantage	Takes time; interviewees may be reluctant to talk about sensitive issues.	Logistics must be managed; result may be the lowest common denominator.	Requires careful planning and preparation; who asks what of whom?

FIGURE 3.11 Data collection method summary — Part 2

PRESENTING BENCHMARKING RESULTS

A few additional points should be made about the process of bench-marking relative to the analysis and presentation of benchmarking data. Care must be taken in the data analysis efforts to assure that bench-marks are representative of real-world performance. Specific cautions include the following statistical problems observed in some benchmark-ing studies:

- Single data point measurements that are passed off as "benchmarks"
- Measurement systems not validated for sensitivity of observation or calibration
- Averages used to represent performance benchmarks
- Missing variation data in process characterization
- Components of variance not identified according to their source
- Comparative charts not indicating *both* mean and variance
- Process changes not related to performance shifts

- Interaction effects not identified among the different process variables

Clearly, there can be many issues that create problems in the measurement and analysis of results from benchmarking studies. Careful planning and solid data collection and analysis efforts can eliminate opportunities for introducing errors into benchmarking. Thus, whenever possible, analysts conducting benchmarking projects should have the same education as Six Sigma Black Belts in statistical analysis to assure the analytical soundness of study results.

COMPARATIVE ANALYSIS AND COMPETITIVE ADVANTAGE

What does an organization gain in terms of competitive advantage from benchmarking? In the long run, competitive advantage comes from out-thinking and outperforming the competition. When an organization uses benchmarking effectively, it is able to think ahead of its industry and to act efficiently by adapting lessons learned from cross-industry studies to permit it to creatively imitate the best performing processes in the world. Over the long haul, this can establish them as the thought leader within their own industry. In the final analysis, it is not out-thinking or prior knowledge that results in competitive advantage; it is the excellence of execution of such new knowledge and the creative application of break-through insights that win in the long term. To achieve a dominant position in a market, a company must *both* know and execute better than its most aggressive competitors. Benchmarking can develop the competence to achieve this position, but benchmarking must be supplemented by management will, commitment, and self-discipline in order to drive sustained success.

BENEFITS AND PITFALLS OF BENCHMARKING

Benchmarking is a business change process that encourages managed change by making an external and objective assessment of its own per-

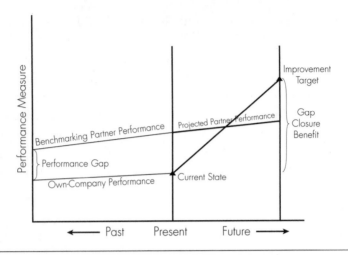

FIGURE 3.12 Performance gap illustration

formance. It is the discovery of the performance gap that provides a wake-up call that causes alarm in an organization and develops a state of urgency and dissatisfaction with the way things have been done. (See Figure 3.12.)

The benefit of benchmarking comes from three specific actions:

- The gap between internal and external practices creates the need for change.
- Understanding the benchmarked best practices identifies what must change.
- Externally benchmarked practices provide a picture of the potential result from change.

However, lest benchmarking appear to be a panacea for management, a few potential pitfalls in conducting benchmarking studies must also be highlighted. Studies can have difficulty when the following occur:

- Selecting benchmarking partners that do not convince management (not respected)

- Choosing benchmarking partners to meet popularity tests with no performance substance
- Accepting public relations claims as process performance benchmarks
- Assuming that measurements are the same in different organizations (without checking)
- Identifying process measures that are not traceable from strategic to operational levels
- Conducting statistical analyses that represent surface observations, not root causality
- Failure to validate performance with on-site inspection to verify benchmark claims
- Enforcing implementation of a benchmarking lesson across a cultural barrier
- Use of benchmarks for management decisions without recalibration over time

SUMMARY

Process benchmarking is an important management tool, and it can help improve both strategic direction and operational process performance. It is a discovery methodology that is used to stimulate learning and help organizations to think about creative options for the design and implementation of its business processes. Coupled with solid statistical data analysis, best-practice identification and cultural adaptation, benchmarking can help organizations to both learn and do the work of their business processes more effectively, efficiently, and economically.

Making Statistical Comparisons in Benchmarking

Not many executives are information-literate. They know how to get data.
But, most still have yet to learn how to use data.

—Peter F. Drucker

Introduction

The essence of benchmarking is making comparisons based on facts and then using these facts to discover knowledge that leads to enhanced performance. Thus, the efficacy of the benchmarking process depends decisively on how well we can make a numerical comparison. However, the quality of the comparisons made in many benchmarking studies is highly questionable. For instance, some common errors are prevalent:

- Comparing measurements from two organizations without first validating that the factors that are used to calculate these measures are indeed operationally defined in the same way (indeed, where does delivery time begin and end?).
- Taking a single data point representing the "best performance claim" of an organization at face value without validating that the performance was indeed sustainable or understanding what it rep-

resented (e.g., best-ever achievement in the process, average achievement in the process, top fifth percentile, etc.?).

- Using performance indixes that confound the performance of the fundamental terms in the metric (e.g., return on capital confounds the revenue flow with the level of capital employed. Either can change and affect the ratio's outcome).
- Failure to determine causation between the performance result and a practice that is offered as the explanation of that improvement (causation is more than mere statistical correlation—one goes up and so does the other. This behavior can also be explained by colinearity, confounded variables, and plain chance!).
- Presenting information in a graphical format that confuses the underlying set of measures (e.g., most common is representing performance results using a bar chart to illustrate the maximum level or the result of an index calculation, rather than showing the statistical distribution of performance of the factor over time to communicate a sense of the measurement's variation).

It is in the correction of such problems where use of Six Sigma methods has created an ability to develop much stronger benchmarking studies and assure that the focus for knowledge transfer is placed firmly on those business practices that will, indeed, make a performance difference. So what is it that Six Sigma does that can be so helpful?

CONTRIBUTION OF THE SIX SIGMA MOVEMENT

Six Sigma uses of data in business decision-making processes are much more explicit than occur in conventional applications where comparisons are made for performance against plan and across reporting periods (e.g., looking at cost of goods sold [COGS], actual versus planned, and then comparing Q3 this year to Q3 last year). In a company doing Six Sigma, there is an expectation that the organization will communicate more effectively using data to properly describe the facts of the situation. For example, consider the way a Six Sigma company would look at the same reporting information:

- The measure of cost of goods sold would be subdivided into elements that are either controllable or noncontrollable by management (within the short-term performance period and the long-term performance period, e.g., during the term of the contract).
- The sources of variation in the controllable elements of COGS would first be identified, and then a strategy for managing this variation would be developed.
- Process capability for the cost control system would be determined, and then the cost drivers in this system would be monitored to assure they remain in a state of statistical control.

In a standard approach to measurement, we only get after-the-fact explanations for any observed changes to the original plan based on a hindsight look at actual achievements. In a Six Sigma approach, the deviation events that drive the cost differences are known, and these specific events are monitored to assure that management can take action as the change is in the process of occurring. Six Sigma measurement makes performance much more controllable by paying attention to known drivers of change by managing sources of variation.

In the next chapter, we will focus on how Six Sigma companies can use data more effectively in their management reporting and decision-making processes. In this chapter, we will focus on the specific tools and methods that can be used to create a measurement system that is the foundation of the strategic benchmarking process, as well as a key enabler of business process improvement by its use for operational benchmarking.

THE NATURE OF COMPARISON

We often make loose statements to compare performance, claiming things like, "Brand X is fifty percent better than brand Y" or "Today's cars get two hundred percent more gas mileage than they did ten years ago." However, most such claims are meaningless as the statement itself does not describe the basis for the comparison. Such simple errors can become compounded as a more sophisticated approach to analysis is taken. Thus, a well-trained Six Sigma professional will follow the KISS principle, or, as Dr. Steve Schmidt would say, "Keep it statistically simple." This principle follows the guidelines of Ockham's Razor: "What can be done with less is done in vain with more." In order to understand how Six Sigma uses statistics in a simple manner, it is necessary to review some of the basics that lie behind the act of making a comparison:

- What is the nature of the performance measure being used?
- What is the type of data being compared?
- How is the data being collected?
- Is the measurement system good enough to accurately observe the performance?

Once these foundations are established, then it is possible to look into the issues of the statistical methods to make comparisons and the graphical and verbal expressions that should be used to explain these statistical observations.

THE NATURE OF PERFORMANCE MEASUREMENT

What is performance measurement? Performance measurement is a series of actions that result in an accurate and useful observation and description of the facts that influence the results of work activity. This is the activity of performance measurement is initiated by an observation of what is important to be measured? After all, as Bill Hewlett, one of the cofounders of Hewlett-Packard, is quoted, "What gets measured gets managed." Perhaps the best way to establish what must be measured is to do a thorough process analysis to determine what the performance drivers are in the system. For instance, is the yield of a process dependent on an initial event, or is it controlled at a bottleneck in the operational flow of process steps? Such observations can lead to a profound knowledge of what is required to manage this process effectively.

Six Sigma uncovers performance drivers in the first three phases of the DMAIC analysis methodology—define, measure, and analyze. In the define step of DMAIC, the focus is on identifying the business factors that make a performance difference. In the measure step of DMAIC, the focus is on assuring the integrity of the measurement system and also establishing the performance baseline so that improvement may be judged relative to this standard. In the DMAIC analyze step, the magnitude of the contribution to variation for each of the key factors is calculated so their effect may be prioritized based on impact on the process. Taken together these first three steps of DMAIC (DMA) are collectively referred to as the *characterize phase* of statistical problem solving, and they result in both identification of all key performance drivers and prioritization of their impact on performance results.

The DMAIC process applies the principles of statistical thinking to create performance-improving opportunities. Statistical thinking is a way of observing and learning about process performance to enable action to be taken that improves the results. This way of thinking is based on three principles:

- All work occurs in a system of processes that are interconnected. This work will combine to create a successful outcome when a process is operating effectively.
- Variation exists in all processes that can inhibit the process from performing as it is expected to perform (at the nominal, target, or average level). Taking data about process performance can help to identify the inefficiencies of process activities.
- Understanding and acting upon unwanted variation in a process is the learning key to making business and process improvement.

Given the importance of choosing the right measures for estimating the outcomes of the process performance, what are the criteria for good performance measures? Here is a set of criteria by which to judge if your measures are appropriate:

- Measures must be operationally defined. Operational definitions eliminate the potential for misunderstanding or misinterpretation of measurements. An operational definition specifies the meaning of each component of a measurement definition and indicates how it may be factually observed (more information about this topic will be coming in this chapter).
- Measures must be actionable. When a performance measure is also a performance driver, then process changes will predictably result in changes to the magnitude of the measure. In other words, when a worker makes a process change by taking an action, the measure that observes the process also changes, and the performance of the process becomes acceptable.
- Measures must be auditable. It must be possible for a third party (either from the accounting organization or an external benchmarking partner) to be able to verify the performance results indicated by the measure.
- Measures must be standardized across operating units. All organizations that are involved in this same process should measure it in exactly the same way. This is a key principle that should also be applied for sharing with external benchmarking partners. Only when all organizations are using exactly the same measures and have verified their measurement capability can any comparison be assured valid!
- Measures must be reliable and indicate desired results. This criteria means that the measures should be consistent predictors of the desired results or outcome of the process being observed. Satisfaction of the conditions of a root cause under the DMAIC analysis methodology will assure that selected measures consistently predict process performance.
- Measures must be timely indicators of performance. Delays in data collection, analysis, and presentation reduce the value of the information it generates for making appropriate business decisions. When real-time data is monitored and used for decision making, then losses are minimized when performance drifts from its desired op-

erating envelope. Thus, delays must be removed from the entire measurement process to assure that management can make the best use of the information to guide its business performance.

- Measures must be capable of validation against external systems. Measures that only reflect internal performance do not assure continuing competitiveness as they do not allow for an assessment of performance against market conditions. Thus, it is important that the structure of the management accounting system *anticipate* its own external validation through benchmarking at the point of its initial design!

- Measures must report performance regarding defects, cost, and cycle time. At the atomic level of work, all activities can be expressed in terms of their successful (or unsuccessful) accomplishment, the time it takes to perform the activity, and the cost for the transaction of the activity. Thus, the core measures of a management system must reflect all three ingredients from the base level to the top tier of the organization. At the basic process level, performance indicators of defects (those transactions that do not meet the output performance criteria), value (the cost it takes to accomplish the desired output), and time (the time required for processing a transaction from beginning to end) must be measured. These measures must be consolidated into a performance system at the higher level that defines the impact of the defects on the customer, the productivity of the organization, and the margin of value (benefit beyond cost) that is produced for shareholders. Six Sigma takes the measure of the core events and creates a transfer function that predicts the higher-order business performance factors.

- Measures must be owned by process managers and team members. The idea of measurement ownership conveys the importance of accountability for applying the performance indicators that reflect process activity. The measures must be owned by both the managers of the process who use them to assure achievement of results and by the team members who use them to manage to deliver the results.

- Measures must reflect the expectations of all stakeholders. Process performance must indicate that it is effectively delivering the output desired by its customers in a manner that is cost-effective for the organization's owners. Likewise, it is also important to monitor compliance with external regulations, laws, and mandates and also assure that the working environment supports employees so that they are able to self-regulate the quality and productivity of their own work.

Once measures have been identified and operationally defined, then the focus must turn to the data that will be collected to express these measures.

TYPES OF DATA USED FOR COMPARISON

There are two types of data that are used in performance indicators. One type of data is called *attribute data,* which represents discrete data that can be counted and plotted as unique events or transactions (e.g., the number of purchase orders, complaints, people, units produced, etc.). Attribute data is used to describe the presence or absence of relationships between observations. The second type of data is called *variables data,* which describes numerical data that is expressed using a continuous measurement scale. Variables data can be used to describe the fact of association and also the strength of the association between observations. Why is this difference between the claims that can be made based on the type of data that is collected so important?

Consider an example. You are building a house, and all you know is that your client is taller than you are. If you are medium height and your client is considered tall, then what does that mean in terms of decisions about counter top, door, and ceiling heights? That is an example of attribute data—we know into which category an individual event has been assigned, but we don't know the relative strength of that assignment. For instance, we could describe the category of people who are of medium height as including those individuals who are over five foot six inches but less than six feet tall. Thus, we have no information at which end of this spectrum the builder's height is or how far above the lower end of the tall limit the client is. There could be no significant difference in these measurements using variables data (e.g., the difference between five feet eleven inches tall and six feet tall), but the strength of the difference is not known using attribute type measures — just that the two observations are in different categories.

A second advantage comes from the use of variables data over attribute data — most of the important statistical tools were designed to operate on variable data. While analogous methods do exist for most techniques for application to attribute data, the results do not provide insight into strength of association between the factors. This is one of the most important findings that can be derived from performance measurement. Thus, in almost all cases, variables data is preferable to attribute data.

What variables data can be collected? All processes, whether business or commercial, can be measured using basic continuous variables such as time and productivity. For instance, cycle time is a continuous measure of the time it takes to perform a transaction. Cycle time may be also categorized according to the type of activity being performed and the relative value of this activity to the paying customer. Productivity implies production of acceptable results — thus, it includes the effect of quality as unacceptable results are not counted in the tally of produced outcomes. Cost can be assigned for the produced outcome based on a calculation of the total expense involved in its production (this is the job of the organization's cost accounting system). Thus, all three measurement types can be expressed using variable data, even when attribute data is used to judge performance quality.

When is attribute data preferable to variables data? There is a general case when attribute data is more useful than variable data — when operators are asked to compare their work process output against a standard of performance. They are answering a question that has a discrete yes or no response: Does the output of this task meet the requirement for its performance? A simple and easy-to-apply rule can be developed to make a comparison that is meaningful. The analogy in benchmarking would be to ask a question: Is group A better than Group B? However, the answer to this particular question is not so useful, unless you can describe how much better and why!

How should attribute or variables data be collected in order to assure that the information learned is appropriate to the observations made and that the comparisons are meaningful?

COLLECTING DATA TO EVALUATE PERFORMANCE

One cannot overstress the importance of formulating the questions to be answered before beginning to design a data analysis procedure. We must determine which questions we need to answer in order to determine what data needs to be collected in the first place. In the case of ongoing process analysis, or *process monitoring* as it is also called, a question that is continually being asked is, "Has the process changed in any way that is important to the customer?" Actually, this is perhaps the most fundamental question for all process analyses. To answer this, one must be able to observe baseline performance—how does this observation represent a change from what? Elements of the first principles of work process knowledge include the following:

- Description of the standard process from which changes to work is evaluated.
- Documentation of the work performance indicator by which the change in work is measured.
- Definition of the customer requirement that defines the limits of acceptable work process performance.
- Identification of the individuals involved in the work and knowledge of their specific contributions to the successful accomplishment of the tasks at hand.

Once the opening question is posed, then the next step is to observe process performance and take measurements of its key characteristics. There are a number of different ways to observe data in the context of process operations:

- *Single Data Point:* The observation of one fact and calling it representative of the operation of the process. Clearly, this will lead to errors in management judgment and application.
- *Distribution Data:* Distribution data summarizes the history of observations, and it provides summary statistics of the results in terms of the central tendency of the data and the distribution of the data over the time of the observations. This way of looking at the data beats the single data point by providing an expected value for the process experience. However, this summary does not describe the way the data history was experienced at the workplace. The time component of the work experience has been concatenated by observing the distribution perspective.
- *Trend Data:* Alternatively to the distribution view, a trend analysis can be used to illustrate a time-sequenced history of experience as observed by measurements of the process. This viewpoint has the advantage that it corresponds to the memory of the people working in the process, but the pure trend data is without statistical summary of the entire observation period.
- *Statistical Process Control (SPC) Data:* An SPC perspective blends a distribution view of the entire data set with the trend data view of the historical experience to present a comprehensive insight into the process that is able to generate profound understanding of the process operation.

Now that we understand the type of data that provides the most knowledge about the process (variables data presented using an SPC chart), we must face some specific issues regarding the collection of process data. Data collection involves the determination of a number of factors:

- *Choosing what data to collect:* For most applications, the performance data that you will want to choose to determine benchmark performance will be data that describes the process performance for quality, cost, or time. Typically, measures of cycle time and productivity will be adequate for continuous measures of the performance with cost per unit produced used as a way to rank the relative levels of operational performance.

- *Calculating how much data to collect:* It is typically desirable to strike a balance between the amount of data produced and the risk involved in making a wrong because not enough data was collected. As a general rule of thumb, at least 30 data points should be observed in a data set, but a calculation should also be made to determine the risk of such a decision point and the power of the test for making correct analyses. These calculations may be easily made in a software package like Minitab or JMP.

- *Determining how to collect this data:* The process for collecting data must also be specified to assure that the data collectors gather the data randomly and do not destroy the analysis assumption of independence in the observations of the data. There is a strong human tendency to collect data in a convenient way, rather than in a random way.

- *Deciding how to store and retrieve this data:* Data availability and data access are important when attempting to create information to guide real-world process improvement decisions. Thus, the methods used for data storage and retrieval, as well as availability of information for performing real world analysis and making decisions, are critical success ingredients.

The set of all potential data that could be collected for a predefined logical condition is called a *population* (e.g., the entire production history of a product, when it is made to the same specification on a production line that remains in the same configuration with the same suppliers). When data is collected from this observation in small subsets that are observed from a relatively short period of time when the process is operating under a stable set of conditions, then these observations are called a *sample.*

Samples represent their population to the degree that they are taken using a plan that assures the individual observations are random and independent (that all potential observations are equally likely for selection and that the selection of one observation does not relate to the selection of other observations, e.g., don't take five samples in a row). In addition to sample size, the degree of a sample's representation of its population is also a function of the following factors:

- *Sampling Method:* The procedure by which samples are taken by operators.
- *Capability of the Measurement System:* The ability of the measurement system to detect change or process variation whose magnitude is important to a customer's perceived level of process performance.
- *Capability of the Observer:* The training level of the observer as well as the sum of their physical capabilities for making accurate observations.

In addition to these guidelines, there is another pragmatic factor in getting good data—do not take grab samples or use convenient data! What does this mean? A grab sample is exactly what it sounds like—you are looking at a process and decide you need to do some analysis, so you "grab" a sample of the data and analyze it! Grab samples are not random and are not independent; thus, they destroy both of the assumptions that constitute sound statistical data analysis! Convenient data is also at least one step removed from all good data analysis practices. Taking convenient data means that you take data that is collected based on prior decisions about what data to collect. Sometimes, this occurs because of the way a process has been designed (automated data collection pick-off points on a piece of production equipment or the data collection specified in a standard software package). The problem with convenient data is that it may not be sufficient to answer the questions that are most pressing on your management system. Only by thoughtful planning to find the right questions and determine what data should be collected, and then collecting it in a rigorous, scientific manner, can proper information be generated to resolve problems in your business operations. These considerations also assume that the measurement system is appropriately designed.

But how do we assure that the measurement system is any good? Is your measurement system able to detect differences in process performance that would transfer to concerns from your customers about the quality of performance that they receive? Testing the way your measurement operates and determining its adequacy is another primary contribution of the Six Sigma way of thinking to advancing benchmarking analysis methods.

JUDGING THE GOODNESS OF A MEASUREMENT SYSTEM

One of the biggest contributions of the Six Sigma movement has been to popularize the methods of measurement system analysis as a means to assure that the variation that is observed in measurements comes from the objective of the measurement rather than from variation that is induced by the elements of the measurement system. There are four types of studies that are involved in evaluating the goodness of a measurement system:

- *Operational Definitions:* An operational definition is an explicit explanation of each of the key elements of a term that is important in making a quality judgment. If, for instance, you are asking people to judge the type of an error that is reported as an attribute of *quality,* then it is important that each person making an observation about this quality share the same definition in order to make a common judgment about the object observed. The operational definition precisely describes the quality characteristic that you are trying to measure so you can ascribe an objective value to it. The two elements of an operational definition are identification of the logical sub-groups included in the object of measurement and identification of the boundary conditions that set the limit on the method of measurement.
- *Attribute Agreement Analysis:* The second step toward clarity in the measurement system is to conduct a small experiment to assess the ability of the observers to make the same judgment about the quality of an item based on using a common operational definition as their criteria of goodness.
- *Variable Measurement Studies:* Variable measurement studies are called *Gage Repeatability and Reproducibility* (R&R) studies. These studies are conducted as small experiments in which multiple operators use

106

the same procedure and instruments to measure the same set of parts multiple times. The objectives of the study are to quantify the consistency of each operator's measurements; determine the amount of variation between operator measurements; and determine the degree of measurement variation that is due to the operator, due to the measuring system, or due to the parts (this last category is the variation that is of true interest).

- *Attribute Measurement Studies:* Attribute Gage R&R studies are also conducted as small experiments. The objective of these experiments is to determine how well the characteristics of the quality judgment made (good or bad, success or failure, go or no-go) represent the variation that occurs in an associated variables measure for that quality characteristic.[1]

All measurement system studies will benefit from the first two of these techniques — the operational definition and attribute agreement analysis. These analyses indicate the level of consistency in the human element of the measurement system to make interpretations. If problems exist in this area, then the rest of the measurement studies are meaningless. The variables measurement study builds upon this first judgment to determine if the basic measurement system is capable of detecting changes in the physical world that are critical to the satisfaction of the customer of this quality characteristic. This measurement study will typically be performed on measurements taken at process control points — a point where measurements may be taken in real time and the direct observation of the measure can be used to adjust the system quality performance or throughput. Finally, the attribute measurement study is needed at the point where an operator is making a self-diagnosis of the quality of the process throughput — is it good or bad? Here the basis of the judgment

1. The specific analysis techniques used for these methods are found in either the Minitab software package (www.minitab.com) or the JMP software offered by SAS Institute (www.jmp.com) and are worthy of being the subject of an entire textbook chapter in themselves. For more information on all the statistical methods in this book, see Forest W. Breyfogle, *Implementing Six Sigma* (New York: Wiley, 1999).

validation is the relationship of the operator's judgment to the variable measure of that quality. This does not require that the variable data measurement be taken directly by the operator. Attribute measurement studies can be performed on data using off-line devices or third-party analyses. What is important here is to demonstrate that the operator judgment is consistent with the variable measure that is related to the same quality characteristic (e.g., a colorimeter may be used to measure color in angstroms, while the operator may make a judgment about color using a pantone color panel).

After determining the goodness of the measurement system, we are now in a position to conduct a statistical analysis and make comparisons between alternative processes as to which has the better performance.

STATISTICAL ANALYSIS FUNDAMENTALS

When we wish to analyze data, the first consideration after determining what to analyze is to ask how much data is needed. The answer to this depends upon the type of question that we need to resolve with the data. For instance, are we asking if a process is performing differently than it did in the past or if it is currently performing to quality specifications that have been set? If so, then we would need to compare a sample that is representative of the current performance against the past history (population) of prior data or against the point estimate of the specification limits. Stating the comparison in this way illustrates two statistical concepts that we must understand: What is a sample, and what is a population? First, let's define a *population*.

A population is the totality of all units or members in a group of similar items from which a sample is drawn. It is often referred to as the "universe" or the entire group from which data may be observed (or from which a sample may be drawn for observation). The set of information derived from a population represents the ideal characteristics that may be achieved by sampled data. Thus, tests are performed to see how close sampled data is to the population data. Any gap between a sample and its population thus represents a gap between surface knowledge and profound knowledge—or knowledge about truth about how the process performs over time. Note that a population may represent either the past (historical) or the future (desired) performance.

Samples are observations that have been drawn from a larger collection of observations (the population). A sample is selected from a subgroup of a population that is used to gain information or to predict a trend about a population. A sample may represent either the overall population performance or a subgroup of the population. Samples that only represent subgroup performance are called *nonrepresentative samples* because they have been taken in a way that induces a bias that results in drawing incorrect inferences about population's total performance. Samples of recent information can also be used to indicate changes from the past performance of a population (e.g., the historical trend in process performance).

What may be different between a population and a sample?

- The population reflects a distribution of activities over time, while the sample may be drawn from a specific set of activities in time—populations describe what has happened over a long term, while samples are taken in the short term.
- Different functions operating on a population may have different effects over time (e.g., long-term effects on a process like inflation or corrosion may not be evident in the short-term data).
- Samples reflect the current state of a process, while a population reflects historical performance.

Populations are described mathematically as distributions of data, and distributions are characterized by two primary factors:

- Location on their measurement scale (central tendency or average)
- Dispersion across their measurement scale (dispersion or spread)

When observing the accumulation of data about a process over time, we observe that the data tend to cluster around a central tendency or value. Measures of central tendency are numerical indicators of location for the data using the scale of their measurement for either a sample or population. Thus, central tendency is one way to characterize data—location of the total mass of the data, which in turn leads to using this indicator as a means for summarizing the expected value of the process performance. The measures of central tendency include the mean, median, mode, proportion, and percentile. However, central tendency does not accurately describe the performance of each particular event in a sequence of individual process steps. However, central tendency is a good guess at the expected value of the performance, given no further information. However, more information is usually available in a distribution of information.

The second piece of data we can derive from a distribution comes from the observation that process data tend to be spread around the central tendency as a way to illustrate the consistency in performance of process operations. Measures of dispersion are numerical indicators of the spread, or distribution, of data across a sample or population. These measures indicate the span of the distribution, and this dispersion of data is a good way in which to illustrate how processes differ from each other. The measures of dispersion are range, standard deviation, variance, percentile span, and interquartile range.

Taken together, measures of central tendency and dispersion define a relative magnitude of performance between two alternatives and also establish their performance consistency over time. The empirical rule links these two measures of distribution density together: This rule states that in distributions that behave like the normal distribution (the so-called bell-shaped curve), then 68 percent of all the observations will fall within 1 standard deviation of the average; 95 percent of all the data will be within 2 standard deviations of the average, and about 99 percent of all data will be contained within 3 standard deviations of the average. These indicators are also expressed using descriptive or inferential statistics.

Descriptive statistics are measures used to tabulate, depict, or describe a collection of data from factual observations (however, the data from a sample can also be used to establish a probability judgment about its population using inferential statistics). Inferential methods of statistics infer properties of a large collection of data (long-term, general trends that could include an entire population) from the analysis of a sample of data. These methods apply probability concepts and typically express their results using confidence intervals to define the probability linking the sample to the population (e.g., we are 95 percent confident that the population mean lies in an interval between these two points that are estimated using sample data).

Because we wish to draw conclusions about the data, it is essential that we move beyond the simple observation of data and establish causality—this activity actually cause the degree of performance that separates two separate instances of the process under study. In order to understand causation, we must first define what is meant by two phrases: *passive* and *active data analysis.*

Passive data analysis is also called an *observational statistical study.* In this type of study the data may be historical data that has been collected for other purposes or data may be collected expressly for the purpose of this analysis, but no intervention is made to change a process while the data is being collected. A passive study would be conducted in the following way:

- The process or phenomenon is watched, and data are recorded as the process is operating under normal circumstances (no warning or special training of the operators, and no special attention is taken to the condition of either the materials or the equipment involved in the process).
- There are no interventions on the part of the person conducting the study to adjust things that may be observed that are not proper in the system—no corrections of poor procedures or issues about operational discipline in following procedures.
- The objective of this study is to estimate population characteristics (e.g., determine how much or how many) based on the analysis of the sampled data.
- Conclusions drawn from the statistical analysis can apply to the target population to the degree to which the sample is *representative* of the entire target population.

- Any conclusion regarding cause and effect relationships is tentative at best and represents only a sound theory to be tested using active data analysis methods.

The second type of study is called active data analysis. Active data analysis experiments through either hypothesis testing methods or structured experimental designs to move the factors that are believed to create performance differences to demonstrate the effect of the movement of these process factors on the process output variable. During an active data analysis, the focus is on the study of the cause and effect relationship (e.g., the why and when of the performance), and the analyst develops a strategy for manipulating process variables in a random order over a fixed range of performance in order to determine their effect on the output of the process results while regulating the operating environment of the process during the term of the study. An active data analysis is typically associated with the scientific method of discovery.

Note that only when an active statistical study is performed can causation be effectively demonstrated (e.g., when we move this causal process factor, we observe that it has this specific effect in the results—always!). Causation requires that the following basic set of conditions be met for an event to be called a root cause of a subsequent event. Potential causes must do the following:

- The preceding event (potential cause) must have a logical or physical relationship to the subsequent event (the effect).
- The first event must precede the subsequent event in time sequence of the process activity.
- The two events must also have a strong statistical correlation (it may be either a positive or negative correlation).
- No other explanation should be available for the creation of this effect.

Typically, early process data analyses are passive—based on historical data—as they explore the relationships that exist in past process performance. However, only by conducting an active data analysis can you determine if a symptomatically linked event is really a root cause of the effect observed. Statistical methods used for active data analysis are either hypothesis testing or experimental data analysis. When one can characterize and predict the behavior of a system of causation in a process, then one has generated what is called *profound knowledge* about the process. Elements of profound knowledge include the following:

- Profound knowledge is found by characterizing process variation to determine the degree of consistency, reliability, or repeatability in making the process outcomes.
- Profound knowledge is only achieved when the root cause of process outcomes is understood, and this knowledge may be used to control the process performance.
- To achieve profound knowledge, one must know the process factors that influence both its central tendency and dispersion in process results as well as how to use manipulation of the process inputs to create the desired output performance.
- Discovery of profound knowledge is achieved through scientific investigation of the sources of process variation.

THE SUPERIORITY OF STATISTICAL COMPARISONS

By this time, you may be asking yourself, "Why don't we just compare the two numbers that we are given? We can trust each company to do their data analysis correctly." It would certainly be simpler to just use information that is available from each company rather than to go to all this trouble of developing operational definitions followed by the statistical sampling and analysis of the data! The reason that we need to be careful to specify statistically derived information as a means to determine which process is superior is threefold:

- First, using a statistical comparison assures process objectivity and eliminates any subjective judgment that could bias the decision about relative process superiority. It is natural for a company to bias its performance as it is sharing data just because it wants to put its best foot forward—show itself in the best light as it is exposing its inner working to external observation. Thus, the statistical data assures that the treatment of data will be objective and meet a rigorous criterion that eliminates any halo effect from subjective observation.

- Second, using a statistical comparison is superior to head-to-head metric comparison because the rigorous process that has been used to create profound knowledge about the process and reported performance is based on statistical understanding (not data or measures that are grabbed from a periodic management report without any analytic scrutiny). The statistical comparison is based on an understanding of both the distribution data (summary over time) and the trend data (a summary in time sequence) as the means to properly describe process performance. The analytical method to report this joint perspective of performance is the SPC chart. An SPC chart links historical activity in a process to the distribution of performance information over time and acts as a continuing hypothesis test each time that the data is taken and asks whether this new sample comes from the same population as the previous history of this process information. For this reason, the SPC chart is sometimes called the *voice of the process*. Because it is linked to time sequence information about the process activity, the statistical comparison of process performance using this type of information can point out process superiority as well as be used to identify and diagnose those operating conditions that truly represent critical success factors that enable the best practice.
- Finally, statistical comparisons are superior to point observations of process data because they have a potential to be extended to other processes and provide the basis for applying the lessons learned more broadly than a subjective judgment or measure that is too closely tracked to a single process instance.

Now that the need for statistical observations has been established and the means for their development has been outlined, we should consider the types of statistical comparisons that may be used in benchmarking studies.

TYPES OF BENCHMARKING COMPARISONS

Two types of statistical comparisons for individual performance measures (or benchmarks) can be made. First, comparisons made head to head (or between two different organizations). These comparisons address the question of which organization has the superior performance. The second type of comparison asks the same question across an industry or set of participating companies where the performance of the entire group is queried to determine which organization is best at a specified practice. This logic is the logic of statistical hypothesis testing. Is the average performance of group A statistically different from the average of group B (this difference may be assessed as an equality or as a greater-than or less-than relationship).

At this time, an illustration of these differences will be instructive. In Figure 4.1, we can see a typical presentation of benchmarking data across a number of companies. Note that in this chart we must take each data point at face value—not knowing which is really best or how changes will affect this performance over time. In this case, the information presented is for the process averages.

Clearly from this graphical presentation we are inclined to describe company C as the process performance leader and thus as setting the benchmark for this process. But this judgment takes into account just this point data. More inquisitive analysts will want to know how this data stands up over time and what can be done to understand more deeply the process performance that these data represent.

In order to gain a deeper insight into this process, the data can be collected over a period of time and displayed as box plots as shown in Figure 4.2, instead of using the point estimate approach shown in Figure 4.1. At this time, analytical insight into the relative performance raises more questions than it answers! Examine these two figures to see what differences you would highlight. Now which process appears to be the best?

Note that in the first chart the superiority of process C was much more evident. However, in the second chart, a more interesting observation can be found in company B. The level of process consistency is much

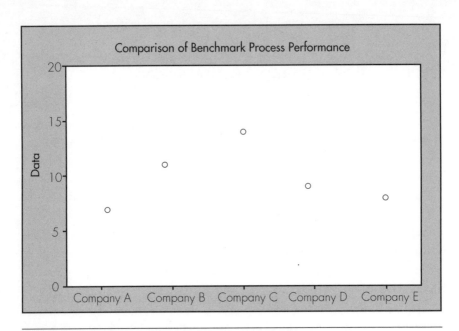

FIGURE 4.1 Comparison of benchmark process performance at five companies

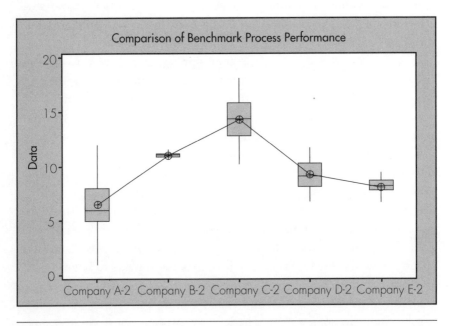

FIGURE 4.2 Sample data comparisons of five benchmark participants

higher than the rest of the industry. It seems that this one company has found a means to decrease process variation in order to provide much more consistent outputs! Note that company E is also better than the other three companies if process variation is the performance indicator! In this case, if you are company C, you should not rest upon your laurels as having the best performing process as, statistically speaking, the best is the one with the lowest variation. If company B could find a way to increase its output while at the same time maintaining its lead in process reliability, then it could become the benchmark! The question for company C then becomes: What can we learn from company B that will make our process more consistent? The lesson is clear: Biggest is not always best!

How can this type of graphical comparison be presented using statistical information? Well, first of all, one cannot make a statistical comparison of a single data point. However, because the data points in Figure 4.1 are actually the average performance levels found in Figure 4.2, we have some options for presenting the comparisons using statistical methods.

Hypothesis tests may be used to evaluate the statistical equality of averages, proportions, or variances. These tests may be used to compare a single sample against a population (or specification limit) using a one-sample hypothesis test, compare relative performance of two samples using a two-sample test, or compare the relative performance of a number of samples using a one-way Analysis of Variance (ANOVA). We will illustrate the simpler version of this analysis in the following.[2]

When conducting a hypothesis test to evaluate the performance of these two processes, it is essential that two comparisons be made to answer the questions: (1) Is there a difference in performance level (average output)? and (2) Is there any observable difference in the relative process reliability (variation of the output)? This requires conducting two different tests of hypothesis — one is a test of the hypothesis of equal means (central tendency), and the other is a test of the hypothesis of

.

2. For instructors desiring to use this book as a university-level text or for those who simply want the full statistical explanation of these methods, a teaching supplement to this book is available from the publisher.

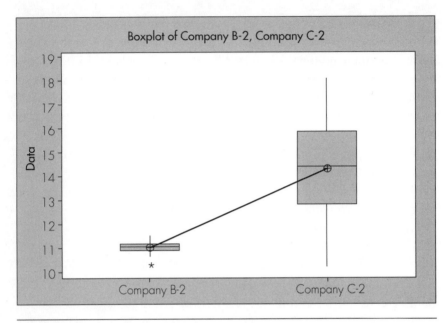

FIGURE 4.3 Statistical comparison of equal means for company B and C performance

equal variances (dispersion). These hypothesis tests are presented in the following for this data set (Figure 4.3).

When the data sets do not overlap, then the calculations will always indicate that there is a statistical difference (when the sample size is large enough to discern a difference). The interpretation of this graph is clear when one is looking at the combination of the average data and its distribution. Almost all of the data from process C is superior to the level of performance of process B! Indeed, this distinction is valid at above a 95 percent confidence level when the probability of the difference is evaluated in Minitab! However, a big question is also raised by looking at this graphical presentation of the data: Why is the operation of process B so much more consistent than the operation of process C? This brings into question the clear value of process C as a benchmark in all potential areas of learning. There may be something of value to learn about the relative consistency of process B. Is this graphical observation statistically significant? Consider the following test of equal variance for these groups that clearly indicates the difference between the two processes in terms of consistency—the tighter the confidence interval and the smaller the magnitude of the standard deviation, the more consistently a process performs. Thus, process B is indeed more consistent in a way that is statistically significant. This is clear on the graphical output of a test of equal variance between these two processes (at a 95 percent confidence level), as shown in Figure 4.4.

Two other types of benchmarking comparisons can be made to illustrate the difference between the processes. First, an SPC individuals chart (it is also called an *I-chart*) can be interpreted as continuous hypothesis testing as it is used to compare the performance of the data stream from a single process against its historical performance (which represents ap-

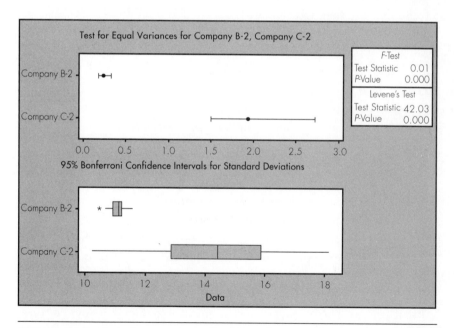

FIGURE 4.4 Statistical comparison of equal variances in company B and C performance

proximately a 95 percent confidence interval). When this analysis is done in Minitab, a set of tests can be used to supplement the chart and evaluate the patterns of variation to determine if there are any low-probability patterns that are occurring in the data. These patterns define events that are rare in normal data and should be investigated to determine if there is any special cause for their occurrence. This is one of the cues that a Six Sigma Black Belt will use to drill into a specific process area and performance interval in order to seek out improvement opportunities. The two I-charts of these two processes are presented in Figure 4.5, and it is clear by examining the chart patterns Process C appears to be more consistent over time. But a clear conclusion cannot be drawn using this data alone.

The SPC chart has been called *the voice of its process* — a way for the process to talk or describe how well it is doing. Other types of the SPC chart (the X-Bar R and X-Bar S charts) operate as an application of the central limit theorem to summarize small samples of the data as point data on a trend line and then to calculate the distribution of these points as control limits that are set at plus or minus 3 standard deviations. The central limit theorem states that the means of means are normally distributed. Thus, the distribution of any control chart that is structured using sampled data in this way will have a bell-shaped distribution around the average that is indicative of the normal distribution for data that is collected over time. By sampling data from the distribution found in the history, the underlying distribution is converted into a normal distribution, despite the distribution that the data appears in naturally. Oversimplifying this point, this approach to sampling allows the use of standard statistical methods without adjustment or transformation of data — a great advantage in helping teams to understand the application of the data analysis.

The last type of benchmarking comparison that may be helpful uses ANOVA to compare performance between different logical subgroups for different performance factors — this is called an *N-Way ANOVA* (where *n* equals the number of factors used to compare for difference in the results measures). The N-Way is more sophisticated than the previous types of comparison and does not have a graphical output, so it requires more knowledge of statistical comparisons to interpret — thus, its application

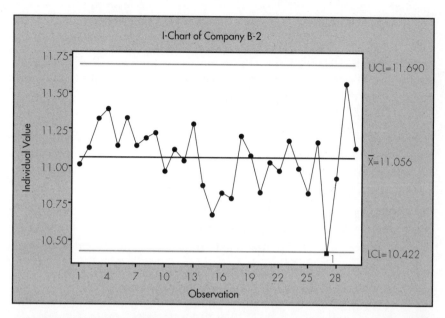

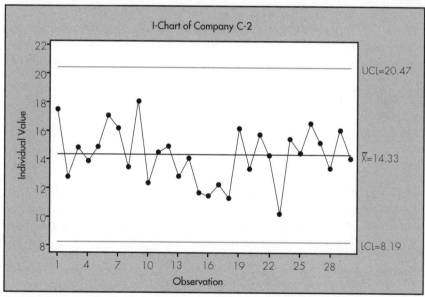

FIGURE 4.5 Individuals charts comparing processes B and C

will be left to on-the-job coaching by a Six Sigma Black Belt or statistician when this tool is used for making more complex comparisons between alternative process designs. However, the complexity of the method should not distract from its utility. This is a most powerful method, and the use of it is the foundation for most scientific experiments.

One final comment must be made before leaving this subject. So far the analysis that has been described has not fully developed the support for a root-cause determination. To have a root cause, there must be a sequential relationship between the factors as well as high statistical correlation between the events. However, the final element has not been determined — does changing the cause reliably produce the effect? In order to make this judgment, active data analysis must be conducted as a follow-up to these statistical tests. Is the practice that presents a statistical difference in performance actually the root cause of that observed difference? Only by conducting a dedicated statistical experiment using the methods of design of experiments (DOE) can causation be finally proved. Again, this application will be part of the on-the-job training for management![3]

GRAPHICAL PRESENTATION OF BENCHMARKING STUDY RESULTS

As baseball legend Yogi Berra said, "It's surprising what you can see by just looking!" The use of graphical analysis for discussing output of individual data analyses has been illustrated several times in this chapter. The clarity of the conclusions that may be drawn using graphical methods makes them ideal for management presentations of comparative differences. Graphical methods may also be used to summarize the results of process benchmarking studies. These methods fall into two categories: methods that are useful for single-factor comparisons and those that are useful for multifactor comparisons. A short discussion of the output

---

3. For a relatively unsophisticated yet valuable introduction to DOE, see the paperback book written by Mark J. Anderson and Patrick J. Whitcomb, *DOE Simplified* (Portland: Productivity Press, 2000).

graphics that can prove useful for report summaries is presented in the following and supplemented with illustrations of their graphical formats.

SINGLE-FACTOR COMPARATIVE DATA ANALYSIS

Z-Chart

This is the classic two-organization comparison chart that was documented in Bob Camp's original book on benchmarking. It shows performance for a single factor but illustrates the historical trend for both organizations in an exchange type of benchmarking situation. The top and bottom lines in the letter *Z* illustrate the historical trend in performance of the two organizations, while the crossing of these lines (the slash that connects the top and bottom part of the *Z* character) is an indication of the gap between these performances. Note that the Z-chart can be extended to multiple trend analyses, but the interpretation of the gap is more difficult. The Z-chart is illustrated in Figure 4.6.

B versus C Pareto

Another way to look at a comparison is to look at the "Before versus Current (B vs. C)" performance difference using two Pareto charts that sum-

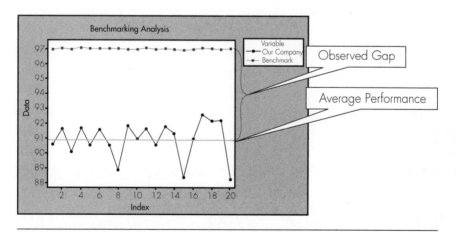

FIGURE 4.6 Illustration of a Z-chart for benchmarking performance comparison

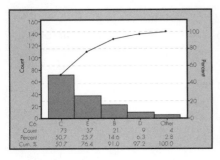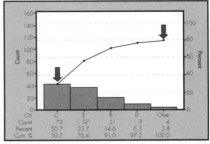

FIGURE 4.7 Illustration of a B versus C Pareto chart for benchmarking comparison

marize the count information about performance (e.g., number of defects by failure code). Using this chart, the scale for the two charts must remain the same (the 100 percent performance of the before chart is used for the second chart so that the cumulative defect line shows the magnitude of improvement in the current state [after change performance]). Also, in this chart the order of the factors remains the same between the two charts, so it is clear what caused the overall observed performance improvement. Figure 4.7 shows the construction of the B versus C Pareto chart.

MULTIFACTOR COMPARATIVE GRAPHICAL ANALYSIS

Matrix Plot

A matrix plot shows in matrix format the relationship between the designated factors in an analysis. Using Minitab, it is possible to cross-plot all of the factors (this is also called a *parametric analysis*) or to select a subset of factors to be plotted against a specific Y-variable. While there is no calculation of the strength of the relationship (however, this analysis may be supplemented by Minitab correlation analysis for the same factors), it is possible to select a regression line that indicates the best data fit among the paired comparisons. Figure 4.8 illustrates a pairwise comparison of company performance for a given process output factor using a matrix plot from Minitab. Note that most of the relationships are flat (the flatter

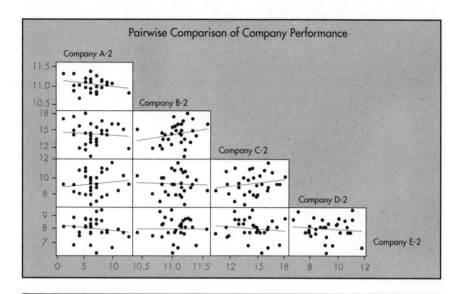

FIGURE 4.8 Illustration of a matrix plot for benchmarking factor comparison

the line in this plot, the closer to a zero correlation). The strongest potential comparison that is illustrated is between company B and company C (as judged by the positive slope to the regression line and the fact that it has the steepest ascent as the line is shown).

Data Fishbone
A data fishbone diagram is an adaptation of the Ishikawa diagram, which replaces the word phrases on the "bones" of the fish with charts that summarize performance of the key process variables. Instead of a problem statement, the "head" of the fish becomes the performance history for the key process output variable. This presentation helps to graphically illustrate the $Y = f(X)$ relationship among critical performance parameters. (See Figure 4.9.)

Radar Diagram
A radar diagram compares the performance of multiple variables in several dimensions of interest (for example, cost, cycle time, quality, or pro-

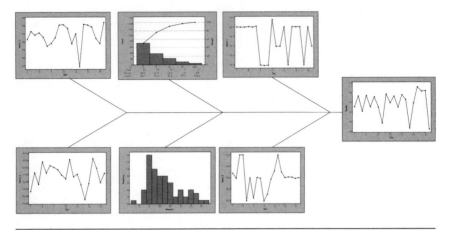

FIGURE 4.9 Illustration of a data fishbone for benchmarking factor comparison
Note: Graphic edited from Minitab output of various graphs.

ductivity). These dimensions are displayed on a single chart as spokes from the center where each measure has its own unique scale, but all indicators are shown on the same graphic to illustrate a performance profile for a specific process or a summary of its performance within a specific time period. A radar diagram provides a more complete picture of the benchmarking results than does a single-point measure of performance comparison. (See Figure 4.10.)

VERBAL REPRESENTATIONS OF THE STUDY RESULTS

It is said that people think with both sides of their head—one side being highly rational and the other side being more artistic. Numbers and graphs appeal to the rational side of the brain, while words and pictures appeal to the artistic side of the brain. When graphs are interesting pictures and supplemented by both numbers and words, then the analyst has made a more complete communication to their intended audience. What would this look like? Consider the illustration in Figure 4.11.

A word of warning should also be made about how data should be supported by verbal claims about improvement. Perhaps we have all seen

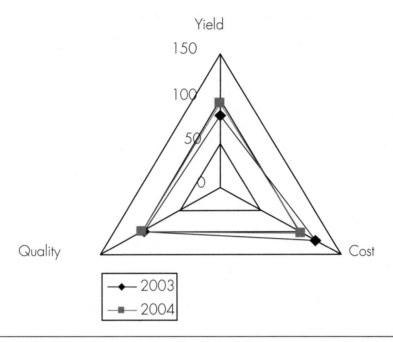

FIGURE 4.10 Illustration of a radar diagram for benchmarking factor comparison

Note: Data plotted using Excel Chart Wizard for radar plot.

claims about 100 percent increases in performance gains or 50 percent less in cost. However, these percentages are meaningless if they are not accompanied by the data that allow the customer of the data to understand the base of comparisons from which the claim of a gain was made. For instance, if one makes a 50 percent reduction followed by a 50 percent gain, is the net result back to the same level? No, of course not—the net result is still less than the original position because the base of comparison has changed. However, such numerical shell games are often played when dealing with percentages. So what can be said? It is always best to reference any percentage-based comparison back to the original units and to maintain the same base for performance assessment instead of changing it as time passes. This is why economists will reference the value of money to a given year so that the effect of inflation may be understood.

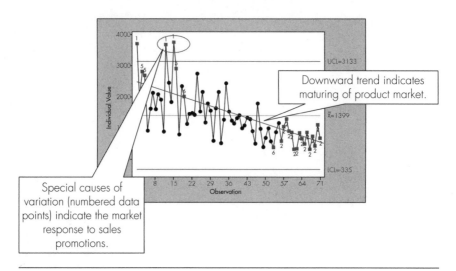

FIGURE 4.11 Illustration of graphical communication clarity

WHAT CAN GO WRONG IN A STATISTICAL COMPARISON?

There are many other ways to misinterpret a statistical analysis—and perhaps more will be invented in the future! A delightful classic on this subject is Darrel Huff's book *How to Lie with Statistics!* This book is not a primer on how to do it, but rather it illustrates some of the major problems that come about from what he calls *statisticulation*—the abuse of statistics or statistical manipulation.[4]

Gaining clarity in drawing statistical conclusions requires good planning from the start as the questions to be answered are formulated and all the way through the specification and assessment of the measures to be used, collection of data, choice, execution and analysis of statistical methods, and the interpretation and presentation of results. It is for these reasons that the recommended approach for benchmarking is to assign a specialist to each benchmarking project to assure that the data management approaches the rigor expected of scientific research. When the

---

4. Darrell Huff, *How to Lie with Statistics* (New York: W.W. Norton, 1954).

benchmarking specialist has received training to the level of performance of a Six Sigma Black Belt, then he or she should have mastery of all of the topics that have been presented in this chapter.

SUMMARY OF COMPARATIVE ANALYSIS

This chapter has highlighted statistical methods that can more effectively support process benchmarking studies. This chapter is not considered a complete treatment of this topic as the statistical foundations that are taught in a Six Sigma Black Belt training program are required to understand this fully. However, a few summary lists of the main points will help to review the learning in this complex topic that are important for managers.

The following set of questions serve as a checklist to summarize the approach to gathering good data for a comparative analysis:

- What do we need to know?
- What questions do we need to answer?
- How will we recognize and clearly describe this answer?
- What types of data analysis tools should we use to have the best communication of outcomes (graphical display)?
- What type of data is needed to construct this tool and answer the question, and how much data is needed?
- Where in our process is the best data measurement point?
- Who in the process is in the best position to give us this data?
- How can we collect this data from this person with minimum effort and chance for introducing measurement errors?
- What additional information is needed for future reference (to uniquely identify this data set), analysis, or for traceability?

The process for applying statistical analysis can also be summarized in the following bullet points:

- Describe the physical process to be measured.
- Choose the right variable to measure.

- Assure that the measurement system is good.
- Sample data randomly and independently.
- Collect enough data to assure analytical confidence.
- Analyze the central tendency.
- Compare the actual to desired or target performance.
- Evaluate the contributors to variation.
- Determine which sources of variation are the drivers.
- Link the statistical measures to the physical process.
- Draw conclusions on how to manage the work better.

When comparing data from two different organizations, the complexity of data collection and analysis increases as an exponential function as the number of organizations that are involved in the study increases. In addition to the selection and operational definition of a common measurement and need to assure the validity of measurement systems, there are four critical statistical factors that must be agreed upon when conducting a cross-company comparison of performance data:

- Definition of the measurements used for the comparison
- Sampling method and size to be used for data collection
- Analysis method for processing the data
- Graphical presentation of the data for comparison

When there is no common agreement between the benchmarking partners on these items, then the study is susceptible to analytic error, and caution must be used in interpreting the results that are presented.

Now we are able to turn to the next issue: How can we use benchmarking studies to help stimulate business improvement? This is a topic for the following chapter!

Applying Benchmarking Results for Maximum Utility

Strategy is the deliberate search for a plan of action that will develop a business's competitive advantage and compound it. For any company the search is an iterative process that begins with the recognition of where you are and what you have now. The differences between you and your competitors are the basis of your advantage.

—BRUCE D. HENDERSON

BENCHMARKING FOR COMPETITIVE ADVANTAGE

Strategy is a word that can be used as either a verb or a noun. When it is used as a verb, then the quotation from Bruce Henderson is correct—strategizing is the deliberate search for a plan of action that will create and sustain competitive advantage. When strategy is used as a noun, then it is a state of organizational performance—the objective that the organization must achieve in order to gain its stated purpose. "Strategy is the persistence of a vision—the ability to see where one wants to go and do those things necessary to stay on track and get there."[1] But how does one achieve purpose in a business? This is done by clearly defining the end-state or vision they wish to achieve and aligning the resources that have

1. Watson, *Strategic Benchmarking*, 26.

been structured into a business to focus on moving in this desired direction. Success means achieving a better position in the competitive market than companies that offer alternative choices—to do this the commercial offer of an organization must be clearly differentiated in the mind of the consumer, and an advantage must be perceived at the price point at which it is offered. This description summarizes Business Basics 101. So how does benchmarking contribute to achieving success?

The application of benchmarking in the domain where business strategy is created is the subject of this chapter. This chapter develops the organizational theory and principles that establish strategic benchmarking as an essential management practice and place it alongside other business practices that facilitate business differentiation: market research, competitive analysis, technology assessment, and customer analysis. To initiate a journey of inquiry into this subject will begin with defining this domain of strategy and the core concepts that it entails. Focus will be placed on how competitive differentiation is achieved and the role of strategic benchmarking as a source of innovative inspiration in identifying and shaping the business direction of an organization.

PLACING STRATEGY INTO A BUSINESS PROCESS MODEL

The starting point for this discussion will be to identify how strategy development fits into an organizational structure. All organizations tend to operate using three levels of management structure—one level that is focused on the enterprise as a whole, a second level that is focused on the business of the organization, and a third level that delivers the operational performance of the organization—its output. Each of these three levels has its own unique customer focus, strategic work, and performance measures. The structure of this performance management system is illustrated in Figure 5.1 and is also summarized in the following bullet points:

- *Enterprise Level:* The customer of the enterprise is the business owner or shareholder of the organization. The strategic work that occurs at this level of an organization is its governance. Performance mea-

Organizational Level	Primary Customer	Chief Objective	Main Metrics
Enterprise	Shareholder	Maximize the value propositions of both shareholders and target customers	• Shareholder Value • Brand Value
Business	External Customer	Establish a demand-driven pull for products and services	• Profitable Growth • Customer Loyalty • Deliver to Promise
Operations	Internal Customer or Next Process	Deliver to promise and establish a truly reliable organization	• Productivity • Cycle Time • Quality Level • Cost of Operations • Job Satisfaction

FIGURE 5.1 Measuring performance management

sures that must be optimized at this level to deliver excellent results
are shareholder value and brand value.

- *Business Level:* The customer of the business level is the consumer in
  the marketplace. The strategic work that occurs at this level of an
  organization is commercial relationship development and the service of customers in targeted markets. The measures of performance that must be optimized at this level of the organization are
  profitable growth, customer loyalty, and delivery to promise.
- *Operations Level:* The customer of the operations level is the user of
  the product or service and the internal partners who collaborate in
  its production. The strategic work that occurs at this level of an organization is the production, delivery, and support of the goods and
  services of the organization. The measures of performance that
  must be optimized at this level of an organization are productivity,
  cycle time, quality, cost of operations, and job satisfaction.

How do these three levels of management abstraction relate to the core
business processes of an organization? The answer is that core business

processes are cascaded into an organization from the business level. There are three core processes in any organization: the product creation process, the product realization process, and the management process. The relationship of these two models is illustrated in Figure 5.2, and each of these processes is defined in the following bullets:

- *Product Creation Process:* Product creation generates a design for an organization's products and services and also creates the commercial business case for investment in developing future offerings for its market.
- *Product Realization Process:* Product realization translates the designed products or services into delivered outcomes of the organization by producing the deliverables and supporting their application in a customer's environment. Service organizations would define this as a service delivery process, while organizations producing durable goods would consider this to be the product delivery process that encompasses both manufacturing and global logistics.
- *Management Process:* The management process facilitates the development and allocation of resources (financial capital, human capability, and operational capacity) to achieve the desired results of the overall performance management system.

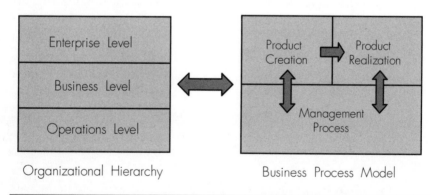

FIGURE 5.2 The architecture of organizational structure and business processes

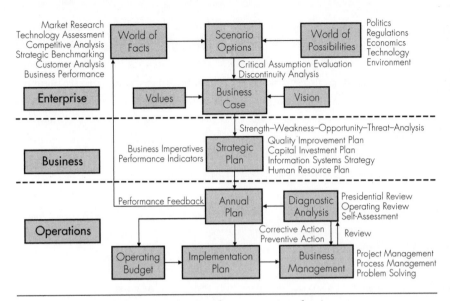

FIGURE 5.3 Translating organizational structure into business processes

The three levels of management abstraction and the core business processes are merged into the business operations model that is addressed by the structure and mechanisms that define the organization as a system. This merged model is illustrated in Figure 5.3.

The level of abstraction in the detail to which work is performed across the three levels of an organization's structure becomes increasingly controlled, and the horizon for executing this work performance becomes more real time as work cascades down the hierarchy. At the top level of the organization, the planning is directional, and the planning horizon is measured in long-term (sometimes over 10 years). At the middle organizational level, the plans are made for a medium term (typically no longer than three–five years), while at grassroots, decisions are within a one-year planning horizon, and most frequently are focused within a monthly or quarterly planning window — the work we must get done to achieve the most pressing performance objectives. Some of the key characteristics of the detailed work that is performed at each level of this hierarchy include the following:

- *Enterprise Level:* The key work of this level is defining critical governance policy or decisions to establish the operating boundaries of the organization. Areas of focus for this work include setting a long-term vision or purpose of the organization; defining the strategic intent of the organization; assessing business implications of commercial markets, competitors, and technologies; choosing business areas to develop; allocating resources to achieve business goals; evaluating the effectiveness of the strategic plan; and developing the business case for key strategies and monitoring overall effectiveness of the execution of the organization's plans. The role of strategic benchmarking at this level of the organization is to serve as a catalyst or stimulus for defining future direction or establishing the context for the detailed work of the organization.

- *Business Level:* The key work of this level is defining the specific strategies that will be implemented to achieve the organization's strategic intent in its chosen markets by its specific product or service lines. Areas of focus for this work include developing product marketing plans; designing and developing products and services; setting the objectives for organizational performance; allocating resources of the organization to achieve its specific commercial objectives; aligning organizational support systems to coordinate efforts in addressing business plans; and continuously monitoring the work through self-assessment to adjust plans based on observed shifts in the business environment, competitive domain, or critical technology areas. The role of strategic benchmarking at this level of the organization is to specify requirements for an ongoing environmental scan or business monitor system that will detect changes in the critical business assumptions and point business leaders toward developments that require their attention.

- *Operations Level:* The key work of this level is planning and executing the routine work of the organization in alignment with implementation of its strategic plans. Areas of focus for this work include developing implementation plans for change projects; developing and managing operating budgets; managing work processes; change

136

management and problem solving; reviewing results and adjusting performance to meet objectives; and reporting on progress to senior management. The role of strategic benchmarking at this level is to focus upon the identified areas of best practice and perform follow-up operational studies of business process enablers that could create a chain reaction causing improvement in critical areas that require development and were recognized as opportunities for improvement during the organization's business self-assessment.

Thus, the top tier of the organization structures its focus, the middle tier identifies metrics for monitoring to assure ongoing competitiveness, while the frontline of the organization identifies the practices that must be executed to assure continuing leadership.

Because the customers change across these levels of work abstraction, how is quality assured in such a business model? How is the focus on delivering the best performance to customers actually achieved?

DEFINING QUALITY AS THE KEY BUSINESS OUTCOME

Over the past century, many definitions have been offered for the term *quality*—indeed, it almost seems like a subjective term that has no fixed meaning! However, in order to fix the meaning of this term, let us examine how quality is developed. The first important observation to make is that quality must be defined from the perspective of a perceiver and, most important, from the individual who is the target of the object of that quality. Thus, the customer is final determinant of what is and is not quality. Measurement of quality thus compares what a customer wants (expectation) to their perception of what was received (deliverable). Thus, the development of quality performance follows a process as illustrated in Figure 5.4.[2] The process includes three steps: creating an understanding of

2. This model is further described in Gregory H. Watson, "Customer, Competitors and Consistent Quality," which appeared in Tito Conti, Yoshio Kondo, and Gregory H. Watson (editors), *Quality into the 21st Century: Perspectives on Quality and Competitiveness for Sustained Performance* (Milwaukee: ASQ Quality Press, 2001), 42.

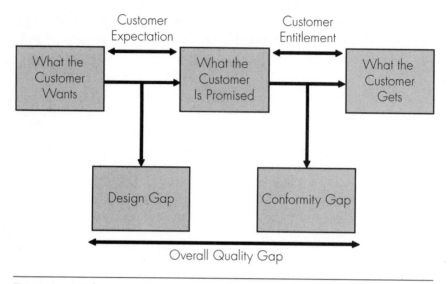

FIGURE 5.4 Relating quality to an organization's business process model

what the customer wants (needs); defining a promise in terms of what the customer will be offered (service guarantee [e.g., service-level agreement] or product specification); and evaluating the follow-through on the delivery of that promise to what the customer actually gets.

By drawing this model, it is evident that there are three failure modes possible by which quality is not delivered to the customer. In the first failure mode the expectation-setting process (defining the promise or commercial offer to the customer) does not meet the true need of the customer—thereby creating a design quality gap. In a second case, customers do not receive performance that fulfills the promise or offer to which they were entitled (if the company is operating as a first-class citizen and seeking to deliver on its promises). In the third case, both conditions can fail—the promise does not reflect the customer's true needs, and the customer does not have even a partial promise fulfilled! This third case is a sure way to destroy shareholder value—who wants products that don't do what we need them to and perform poorly to their own design?

This model establishes a framework for delivering quality, but this model does not specify the deliverable that will meet these expectations or how well these deliverables will influence the commercial decisions of customers—two key ingredients in any quality definition! In order to address these issues, another model must be introduced to increase understanding of the customer dimension—the Kano model for attractive quality.

Dr. Noriaki Kano, professor emeritus from Tokyo Science University, developed a sound thinking model to explain how customers are satisfied by the design and delivery of the quality practices of an organization. Kano's model identified two axes in which to learn about customer behaviors: customer satisfaction and degree of fulfillment of the promise to the customer (labeled "execution excellence" in Figure 5.5). Kano observed that there are three functions that describe the fulfillment of quality from the customer's perspective and that these are based on the ability of the customer to articulate his or her needs as well as the ability of an organization to understand these needs.

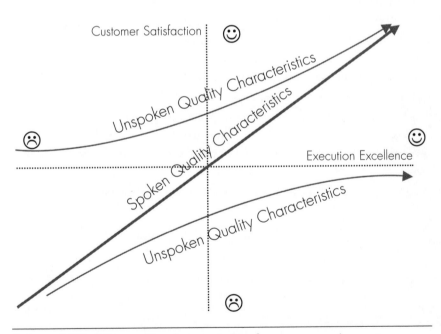

FIGURE 5.5 Defining quality characteristics of customer requirements

Having worked with the original Kano model for a number of years, I found a need to adapt its interpretation in order to provide a clearer understanding of customer behavior in a competitive market.[3]

The three functions of the Kano model describe different responses to customers in defining quality that is suitable for their needs. The central function is described as a spoken quality characteristic because this basic definition of quality serves a competitive environment. This function increases quality with the strength of the value proposition in an offer relative to the spoken request of the customer (e.g., function, performance, and cost requirements contained in a request for proposal or competitive bid). The winning competitor for fulfillment of quality through this functional behavior will deliver the best feature performance for customer-desired features at the best price point—or the best performance for value. However, customers do not or cannot always explain what it is that they want; thus, there are two functions that Kano further described as the "unspoken quality" fulfillment needs of customers. These two functions have very different ways of influencing customer satisfaction. Applying the basic quality function, we note that the customers are never satisfied. This occurs because the performance expectation is so high that quality is a given—it doesn't delight; it only can dissatisfy the customer. For instance, we are not exceptionally happy that the octane in our gasoline is correct—indeed, we are only upset if the octane is low, and it affects the performance of our car. Thus, this basic quality function never satisfies—it only dissatisfies customers, and the type of reaction customers tend to have to performance issues is not the rational choice that is made in a competitive purchasing decision. It is the emotive response of betrayal that an expected quality characteristic has not been delivered. Kano called this level of performance "must be" quality—it is not op-

---

3. The Kano model for attractive quality was first described in Noriaki Kano et al., "Attractive Quality and Must-Be Quality," trans. Glenn Mazur, *Quality Journal* 14 no. 2 (1984): 147–156. I developed this more distinctly competition-focused version of this model in "Customers, Competitors and Consistent Quality," 23–43.

tional. At the opposite extreme of customer response is the upper curve on the diagram, which Kano called "attractive quality" and for which his model is named. Note that here even poor design warrants satisfaction from customers. Why? Simply because the designer has anticipated a need before the customer recognizes it—the customer is then delighted that their life has been made better in this way or that his or her job has become easier! Kano noted that the status of any particular quality feature can be very dynamic in this model. What begins as an exciting level of quality that is delivered to customers may quickly become competitive as the feature is emulated in the market. When customers get to the point of near-total acceptance of the feature, then that capability simply must be included in the product as it has become a commodity. For instance, when the automobile was first introduced, people were excited that they could go from one place to another in it. Now transportation is so basic that the car's movement is assumed—and when a car doesn't move, then there is a highly emotional reaction!

COMPETITIVE ADVANTAGE THROUGH CUSTOMER ALIGNMENT

One of the factors implicit in Kano's model is the concept of customer choice. It is this concept that allows us to use the Kano model as a basis for choice among alternative value propositions offered for features—competitiveness. How should we characterize the dimensions that drive competitiveness in an organization? This question has been authoritatively addressed by Harvard Business School professor Dr. Michael Porter in his books *Competitive Strategy* and *Competitive Advantage.*[4] Porter identified five forces that characterize the ability of rivals to displace an organization in a competitive market. Porter uses his model of forces to describe the relative attractiveness of a market. The following are five forces that act on a market:

4. Michael Porter, *Competitive Strategy* (New York: Free Press, 1983) and *Competitive Advantage* (New York: Free Press, 1989).

141

- *Supplier Power (Supply Chain):* The power of suppliers in an industry can affect the freedom of choice of a firm for its product development and market penetration. The factors that affect the relative strength of industry suppliers are concentration of the commodity in the market (uniqueness of the technology, number of suppliers, availability of the product, etc.); factors related to the individual supplier (significance of product volume, proprietary nature of the product, flexibility of production capability, etc.); and relationship factors (relative ease of changing suppliers, degree of differentiation in alternative sources, transition time for changing suppliers, etc.). Examples of power suppliers are both Microsoft and Intel.
- *Buyer Power (Supply Chain):* The relative power of a buyer in the industry can also lock up the entire supply chain and make it difficult to enter a market. The factors that determine the strength of a buying organization include the relative dominance of the buyer (brand identity, buyer market share in industry, volume purchased, price sensitivity, incentives for purchase, etc.) and product line dynamics (product differentiation, ease of substitution of parts into the product, available substitutes, etc.). The entire automotive industry illustrates the impact of a dominant buyer on a relatively small-to-medium-sized business supply chain.
- *Barriers to Entry (Asset Uniqueness):* This is the relative strength of the assets that have been developed and deployed by an organization — the uniqueness of its assets can also establish a significant competitive advantage. Barriers to entry in an industry may be established through government regulation, strength of competitor branding, proprietary processes or knowledge, intellectual property ownership, access to the distribution channel, and so on. The semiconductor, steel, petroleum, chemical, and pharmacological industries illustrate the impact of uniqueness as a barrier to entry in their industry.
- *Threat of Substitutes (Technology):* The availability of alternative choices is another of the key competitiveness dimensions. What does it take to change to an alternative option? Is the cost equivalent? Is there additional risk? Is performance truly equal? Is there

142

any trade-off involved? How inclined is the consumer to making a change? In some industries, people change based on price alone (gasoline purchasers will change loyalty for tenths of a penny!), while in other industries consumer habits die hard (brand association in food products is a good example).

- *Rivalry:* The degree of intensity in the rivalry among the firms in a market is the outcome of the prior four forces and their impact on the dynamics of the market. This force considers the situation within the industry (its concentration, rate of growth, capacity, influence of technology, etc.) as well as the nature of the competitors (cost structure, commercial diversity, corporate investment stake, brand identity, etc.) and product comparison for the relative merit of the consumer choice (product feature and performance, cost, etc.).

The capabilities that distinguish an organization's uniqueness in its market also reflect the set of critical assumptions regarding the business model as well as areas in which it is imperative that the organization monitor for changes or discontinuities that could cause an inflection point in its market growth trajectory. Furthermore, the competitive analysis using the five forces also addresses Kano's *spoken quality* or the differentiation characteristics that are publicly known and shared—this is explicit market knowledge. However, Porter's analysis does not include the tacit market knowledge embedded in the two forms of unspoken quality in Kano's model. By taking a different approach to understanding the strategic choices about delivery of value, a new perspective on competitiveness emerges.

To create a unique competitive position (differentiated from the rivals), an organization must choose strategies that will define its uniqueness, and these choices can be made at three levels: enterprise, business, and operational levels! Porter's interpretation of these leverage points for changing strategy align with the model of business that I first proposed in my earlier book *Business Systems Engineering*.[5] This provides the point of depar-

5. Gregory H. Watson, *Business Systems Engineering* (New York: Wiley, 1994).

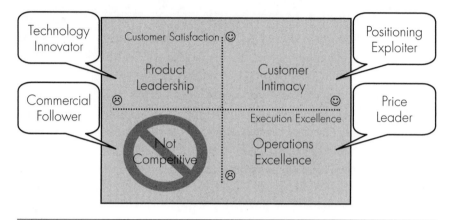

FIGURE 5.6 Mapping value disciplines to customer-focused strategies

ture for extending Porter's model to address the tacit knowledge of the organization. The focus of change that can influence the value proposition of a company relative to its customers was defined as a three-dimensional choice by Michael Treacy and Fred Wiersema in their book *The Discipline of Market Leaders*. This model is illustrated in Figure 5.6, where these three competitive choices are superimposed on the Kano Model.[6]

Treacy and Wiersema propose that the value disciplines of an organization (the ways that it delivers value to customers) are threefold:

- *Product Leadership:* In the value discipline of product leadership, technology is the king. The objective in this approach is to deliver the best product to the market by being the time-to-market leader with breakthrough technology that creates attractive quality for the targeted customers. Thus, management focus is on attractiveness of the product offering, and it is willing to cannibalize its current products and sales in order to remain at the leading edge of its technology (companies applying this type of strategy include Microsoft,

6. Michael Treacy and Fred Wiersema, *The Discipline of Market Leaders* (New York: Basic Books, 1995).

Intel, and Nokia). Thus, management focus is placed upon invention, commercialization, and market exploitation by delivering advanced product technology and using applied research focused to develop insights into innovative opportunities to delight customers. The major challenges for this strategy occur with a transition to new technologies or the emergence of a disruptive technology.

- *Customer Intimacy:* In the value discipline of customer intimacy, both customized solutions and customer relationships share the throne. The objective in this approach is to achieve the best total solution to allow customers to get their job done more effectively, efficiently, and economically, so the golden rule for management is to "solve the client's broader problem" (companies applying this type of strategy include Ritz-Carlton Hotels, Nordstrom, and eBay). Thus, management focus is placed on client acquisition, development of an intimate level of knowledge about the client's job, and development of solutions that facilitate his or her job. A winning strategy for an organization to compete using this discipline is to develop expertise in the client's business area and to customize their products or services to help the client in both its sustaining technology and create appropriate market disruptions so it can remain in a leadership position. The major challenges for this strategy occur with a change in the solution paradigm (i.e., the emergence of the Internet as a commercial channel).

- *Operations Excellence:* In the value discipline of operations excellence, cost is the king. The objective in this operating approach is to achieve best total cost and the golden rule for management is that "variety kills efficiency" (companies applying this type of strategy include Wal-Mart, Southwest Airlines, and Federal Express). Thus, management focus is placed on the end-to-end product delivery and customer service cycles, and the leverage areas for improvement are on process redesign to achieve continuous improvement of the use of the asset base through cost-effective process technology. The major challenge for this strategy is the requirement to shift to a new asset base or process technology as the current capability becomes obsolete.

Given that these value disciplines represent choices that are driven by considerations about the strategic direction of an organization and that this direction is set by choices that are made at the enterprise, business, and operational levels of an organization, how does an organization learn what it needs to know to make the right choices? This final element of the context of benchmarking was addressed in *Strategic Benchmarking,* and it is defined through the process of setting and executing strategy — or the strategic planning process.

GENERATING STRATEGIC LEARNING EXPERIENCES

As Porter correctly identified, it is in establishing strategy that an organization creates the distinctions that drive its competitiveness. The process for strategic planning engages an entire organization at all three levels of its functionality; however, what is unique in this planning process is the set of questions asked and the performance areas that are assessed at each level of the organization. Thus, the benchmarking process will engage strategic planning in different ways at different levels:

- *Enterprise Level:* At the highest level of the organization, the process of strategic benchmarking seeks to learn about factors that could influence the trajectory of its profitable growth. This level of investigation seeks to discover disturbances in the environment (such as disruptive technology, political unrest, economic uncertainty, commercial unrest, etc.) that represent a risk of continuity to the sustained performance of the organization (e.g., changes in its critical business assumptions). Such changes could mark an inflection point in the function for diffusion of its products into the commercial market. Anticipation of such change permits greater responsiveness to the market changes.
- *Business Level:* At the business level of the organization, management must be aware of the threats and opportunities that are offered by shifts in the competitive markets, and the strategic benchmarking process must provide imaginative studies that support the continu-

ing viability of the organization's product line strategies. At this level of investigation, the focus is on discovering disturbances in the appropriate competitive dimensions, as defined using Porter's competition model. Distinctions observed in a study at this level must be addressed by examining how reallocation of the resources and efforts of the organization should be prioritized.

- *Operations Level:* At the grassroots of the organization, the strategic choice is focused on choosing the best implementation strategy for realizing the changes that have been identified at the upper levels of the organization. Here concreteness in specification of the change is essential, and the strategic benchmarking studies at the higher level will give way to the operational benchmarking studies that are essential for gaining the detailed knowledge of best practice that is required for designing appropriate process improvements.

How does this operate in the context of an overall strategic planning process? Consider the model that was presented in *Strategic Benchmarking* and is illustrated in Figure 5.7.

This model for strategic planning begins by understanding the environment — the activity the enterprise level performs to define the business case and the organization's purpose. The head-to-head competitor analysis depicted in this flow chart describes the analysis that occurs at the business level of the organization. At this level, it is essential to make detailed observations of the developments of your competitors, related technology fields, and the expectations of your targeted markets in order to determine how to deliver on the expectations of your investors. At the operations level of benchmarking, focus is on developing a creative understanding of how business process change could be implemented in a way that yields an advantage over the way competitors work. Gaining such an incremental advantage at each level of the organization can result in optimizing processes in a way that can be described using a strategy called the *Boyd Cycle.*[7]

---

7. Boyd taught tactical engagement to USAF pilots and developed his cycle into a general theory of war that can be applied to competition. He applied his ideas in the design of the USAF F-16 fighter. This process is discussed more fully in *Design for Six Sigma* (GOAL/QPC, 2005).

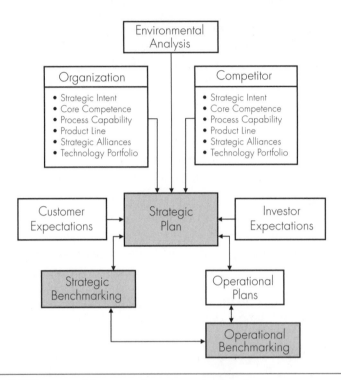

FIGURE 5.7 The essential approach to strategic planning

LEARNING QUICKER — DECIDING FASTER — ACTING CONFIDENTLY

The Boyd Cycle focuses on achieving efficiency over an adversary's decision-making process by observing, analyzing, making, and executing choices faster than competitors are able to do so. This is important because the competitor who acts fastest most often wins! How does this work? Business competition takes place under conditions of a real-time competitive rivalry. Thus, success depends on an ability to introduce a series of innovations at a faster rate than your opponent. Faster learning and action means more time for analysis, discovery, and adaptation of this learning. Moving slow means less time, and you become reactive, falling behind the competition. Developing a culture that rapidly orients itself to external conditions, observes the effect of actions, decides on the alternative that has the best advantage, and acts fast will allow a competitor to better understand cause-and-effect relationships by reducing the time between observations of the causal events and their outcome. This performance feedback can be processed and used to recalibrate actions for the next round of market changes such as new technology adaptation or design of product features.

The Boyd Cycle encourages accelerated competitive activities and management of their impact through a series of systematic, repeatable processes that moves strategic planning from a once-a-year event into part of an organization's continuous innovation process. If a rival in a head-to-head competition can consistently operate its strategy cycle faster than others, then it will gain the competitive advantage. This means that it is operating inside the opponent's decision loop—acting quickly to out-think and outmaneuver the competition. By the time a slower adversary reacts, the faster one is doing something different, and its adversary's action becomes ineffective as it addresses what was happening in the past rather than anticipating the future. With each cycle of progress, the slower party's action becomes more ineffective by a larger margin. This rapid action appears ambiguous to an opponent and generates confusion and disorder in its thinking. The aggregate effect of this rapid, incremental improvement is to disorient the planning capability of opponents.

Because strategy is intended to improve our ability to shape and adapt to unfolding events, it is essential that the process for learning from the outside (orientation to the external world) be conducted using efficient observation processes for critical or differentiating events. The secret of moving faster than your opponent lies in the continuous reduction of friction (things that hold back an organization) through simple, reliable administrative structures and the use of flexible tools that can be adapted rapidly in response to changing tactics. Thus, assuring that the principles of a lean organization are applied to the strategic planning process will provide an advantage in terms of decisions implemented. When this happens, your opponent will not understand what you are doing because they will always be working on a technology generation or product concept that is lagging. The ability to apply the concept of the Boyd Cycle depends on good information about the business—beginning with a sound process for strategic benchmarking converted into operational action through a flexible, real-time planning process.

The foundation for this entire management system is measurement, which was also the begging point of this chapter (review Figure 5.1 to understand the implications it has for business process measurement).

MEASURING AND MANAGING ORGANIZATIONAL PERFORMANCE

However, as the old saying emphasizes, "What gets measured gets managed." It is essential to develop a Six Sigma customer dashboard to support the Recognize phase of DMAIC embedded in the strategic planning process. A customer dashboard streamlines the way a Balanced Scorecard is implemented.[8] It is essential that a sound measurement system be developed that contains both balance and alignment—the two essential ingredients of performance management. In order for this system to be broadly useful, it must also have predictive and diagnostic capabilities and permit traceability of actions and activities from initialization to outcome so that causal linkage can be established. What do these measurement requirements really imply? Let's consider how these five characteristics of a performance management system should be developed and what this implies for a benchmarking program in terms of the design, application, and control of the supporting measurement system.

- *Design Rules:* There are two rules for designing a measurement system. Rule one is that the performance measurement system must be *balanced* in terms of perspective. This balance must be achieved so the measurement indicates both financial and operational perfor-

---

8. These ideas are a further development of two articles that I wrote several years ago: "Peter F. Drucker: Delivering Value to Customer," *Quality Progress Magazine* May (2002): 55–61 and "Selling Six Sigma to Upper Management," *Six Sigma Forum Magazine* 2 no. 3 (2002): 26–37.

mances, both customer and shareholder perspectives, and compares both internal with external performance. Rule two is that performance measurements must be *aligned* and illustrate collaboration required for success in many dimensions: cross-organizational, cross-functional, cross-market, and cross-disciplinary.

- *Application Rules:* Performance observations should be both *predictive,* indicative of future performance, and *diagnostic,* able to break down the components of current or current performance in order to determine the drivers of performance, which are the root cause reasons for change.
- *Control Rules:* These rules are aimed at designing measurement systems that can be applied to support the business control function. Three rules apply: Performance must be *traceable* across the organization's hierarchical layers; the *strength of association* between process variables and results variables must be established; and *comparative assessments* must be made against targets or requirements, benchmarks or best level of performance observed, and process design capability.

When a business measurement system follows these rules, then it will be able to support the scientific management of the business operations and will properly portray how the operating space of the organization performs.

EVALUATING YOUR BUSINESS MEASUREMENT CAPABILITY

An organization's senior management team is responsible for the outcomes of work in the Recognize step of deploying Six Sigma. The key aspect of management's work is to begin by conducting a self-assessment of their organization's measurement system. If the old observation is true, "You don't manage what you don't measure," then it is really important to know what and why you take measurements and how good those measurements are for supporting management decision making.

Why is measurement so important? Measuring work processes provides understanding by characterizing process performance. Measurement takes time and costs money—so measurements must be taken with rigor and follow a deliberate step-by-step process to reveal the deepest insights into process performance. Organizations should not just capture convenient numbers that are easy to measure or develop a massive collection of data stored in computers to provide a history of everything that is done. Good measurement helps to resolve problems quickly and to illuminate the inner operations of work processes. But the benefits of process measurement must outweigh the costs of merely collecting and storing data. The measurements must indeed illustrate critical business performance that management must understand, and the measurement system must be sensitive enough to identify changes that are significant for indicating progress toward achieving the business objectives of the measurement. Measures must be timely, and decision delays resulting from data collection and measurement analysis procedures must be minimized in the design of the work process. How will you know if you are following these best measurement practices in your organization?

By asking a few tough questions, management can evaluate the design effectiveness of their current business measurement system. Ask the following critical questions as means to assess your measurement system performance:

- What do we need to know? By what means will we learn?
- What measure provides this knowledge?
- What does this measure enable us to do?
- How can this information be presented for a clear decision?
- What analysis method will deliver this type of information?
- What type of data is required to use this analysis method?
- Where is this type of data available?

If you do not have clear answers to these questions, then you should stop and reconsider the measurements that you are using and determine how to improve your approach for gaining understanding about your business processes. How should a sound measurement system be constructed?

ELEMENTS OF A BUSINESS MEASUREMENT SYSTEM

A measurement system must be aligned to the flow of work processes if it is going to be capable of detecting changes in the activities that produce the outcome of the business system. One way to align the business system is to design measures at its critical control points. But what is a control point?

It is essential to know where the measurement should be taken in order to achieve the greatest opportunity for decision making that supports process adjustment and business control. The points where critical measurement observations are taken may be called *control points* if they meet two conditions—an ability to take a real-time measurement of process performance, which affects the outcome *and* the ability to adjust or control the process flow to influence the outcome. A control point is a point in a business or work process where not only may a red flag be raised when the process is in trouble (as indicated by the observed measure), but also where the operators can perform an adjustment of a controllable business process factor to bring the work process back into a controlled operating state to self-regulate the quality of their work outcome. The following control point observations may be made:

- Control point location can be used to manage process throughput.
- Observations about process performance available at the control point monitor rate of process flow, which may be used to increment the initial process observation to establish a performance level.
- Feedback, adjustment, or regulation of the flow is possible at the control point to modify throughput rate to achieve performance objectives.

Characterizing measurement control points is one of the most important tasks in building a measurement system. Without knowledge of the mechanism by which control can be exercised and determining the degree of effectiveness that can be achieved at that point, it is impossible to design a useful feedback mechanism at the measurement observation point. This is one problem that must be avoided during a measurement system design. Two other considerations are also exceptionally important:

- *Measures may not relate to strategy:* The strategic direction chosen by a company's management team may be a departure from its past. It may represent a significant modification of the past direction. When this happens, the measures of process performance that were used to develop a steady-state condition may not be very satisfactory to capture all the nuances in the change process. In addition, the old set of performance measures may not provide good indication of the progress that is being made toward achieving the new objectives. Progress toward accomplishment of strategic changes must be measured as both an in-process measure as well as a measure for achievement of the desired result.

- *Operational performance may not deliver measures:* The routine way of working in an organization may result in lack of connectivity to a strategy-based measurement system. For instance, if the work processes do not capture the components of the measurement, then it will not be possible to accurately portray overall performance for the process. If an organization wants to make time to market a critical measure of performance, then the organization's work processes should measure all actionable subcomponents of the time equation. However, some work processes may measure cycle time, while others do not; some work processes may distinguish between the various components of cycle time (waiting time, movement time, set-up time, and value added working time), while others don't. For a measurement system to deliver Six Sigma results, it must have connectivity from top to bottom *and* from bottom to top!

CRITERIA FOR SOUND PROCESS PERFORMANCE MEASURES

What does it take to have a good process performance measure? The criteria for a sound performance measure were identified in Chapter 4. When a measurement system meets all of these design criteria, it has achieved best-practice status as a daily management control system. Such a measurement system is capable of tracking performance from the Business Y (top-tier metrics of strategic performance) to the Process X

(frontline measures of process performance), as well as tracking performance contributions from frontline measures of process performance to the top-level metrics of business success. From a starting point definition of success for the organization — the global metrics of success — it is necessary to determine how the frontline work processes will actually deliver desired levels of performance. To achieve this type of connectivity, it is essential that an organization develop their *line of sight* — a linked and aligned performance relationship structure. Line of sight allows business leaders to look into the organization and see how the frontline workers are delivering on the strategy that was planned, and it also permits frontline workers to understand how their activities will deliver the company strategy. Both directions are essential for continued success. To achieve this connectivity, performance measures must be linked by a cascade of action objectives that deliver predictable outcomes through integration of the organization's actions (see Chapter 9 for an in-depth discussion of how to achieve this alignment). Then, the work-process teams can manage a coherent set of coordinated actions that deliver the customer's needs on a profitable and sustainable basis.

Process measures, cost measures, and customer measures must all be integrated at the frontline level using a work-process performance scorecard to exploit this profound knowledge of work-process operations. How is line-of-sight knowledge and management accountability achieved? The first step to achieving scientific business control is to create a capable business measurement system.

CREATING A CAPABLE BUSINESS MEASUREMENT SYSTEM

There are four steps in developing a sound performance measurement system. The first step defines which factors are critical to observe and the purpose of monitoring this data. Second, the organization must map its cross-functional processes that deliver results so it knows where it may control these success indicators. Third, the organization must identify those critical tasks and capabilities required to keep the process operating in the performance envelope that is required by its customers.

Finally, the organization must define the measures that track these tasks and capabilities.

Professors Robert S. Kaplan and David P. Norton of Harvard Graduate School of Business created the idea of a balanced scorecard to give managers a comprehensive insight into business performance at a glance.[9] The balanced scorecard supplements the financial measures of an organization's performance with operational measures that illuminate performance, according to the perspectives of all business stakeholders (customers, employees, managers, and shareholders). Typically, a scorecard is developed to let senior managers see all of their key performance indicators together in one place. However, these scorecards can appear more like a smorgasbord of measurements. The connectivity of one measure to another is not required, and neither is the linkage nor cascade from one tier of management to the next. Without rigor in the development of such a system, many organizations have just adapted a set of measures that seem right but do not have a causal impact for improving business results.

Other concerns exist with the scorecard approach to measurement systems. For example, scorecards follow the analogy of baseball—they provide a detailed report that is useful for after-the-fact analysis of events. However, this analogy does not provide a good role model for supporting the routine daily business operations and decisions—scorecards fail to provide the action orientation needed for daily management. What characterizes this baseball scorecard analogy?

- A scorecard provides a completely detailed log of performance.
- Scorecards are kept by workers who have been dedicated to just recording data—they do not actively engage by participating in the action.
- The record-keepers sit above the crowd and observe, having no interaction with the players.

---

9. H. Thomas Johnson and Robert S. Kaplan, *Relevance Lost: The Rise and Fall of Management Accounting* (Boston: Harvard Business School Press, 1987).

- Neither the record-keeper nor scorecard is consulted for advice during the action.
- Scorecards are provided to coaches after the game to evaluate player improvement opportunities for the next round of play.

What is a better approach? Consider the approach developed by General Electric, which is called a *customer dashboard*. The Six Sigma measurement approach works on the analogy of the pilot's cockpit. First, consider the kind of measurement architecture that exists in the cockpit of an airplane. In front of the pilot is a heads-up display that has the most important indicators to assure safety of flight. These measurements are "in the pilot's face" in a way that the pilot is not able to ignore the facts and is therefore most likely to take appropriate action. When the display illustrates that something is wrong with a key mission indicator, then the pilot turns to a secondary set of much more numerous measurement systems on the overhead panel to diagnose the problem in order to determine the appropriate action to take. For all those factors that are not mission-critical or safety-of-flight factors (Xs that contribute to this Y), there is a third location — behind the pilot's back on a panel of circuit breakers we find the attribute data (go/no-go), such as the entertainment system, the overhead lights, and the systems that provide power to the seats in business class. This arrangement inhibits pilots from gaining bad habits about monitoring measurements — the only ones that they see are the most important ones, and the aircraft system designers have engineered the entire platform to keep pilots from making fatal mistakes like flying by a decision rule to just use "my favorite instrument," as an indicator of safety of flight. A Six Sigma customer dashboard measurement system takes exactly the same approach as the designers of the aircraft system.

What are the artifacts of a Six Sigma customer dashboard measurement system? How would you know that one has been implemented? Several design features distinguish a Six Sigma performance measurement system from a balanced scorecard system:

- A Six Sigma approach to measurement applies the function $Y = f(X)$ to decompose the work-process activities and assure statistical connectivity of measures with business activities at the control points of the process.

- Measurement is always linked from the customer (illustrating how market issues that are critical to satisfaction issues [CTS] are embedded in the work processes as critical to quality [CTQ] factors).
- The customer requirement for performance is embedded in standards for expectation of results and becomes the reference for measuring achievements.
- Causality is determined using statistical inference to characterize what quantitative relationships exist among the in-process results measures.
- Response to performance concerns is based on variation analysis that is aimed at the reduction of variation in both special-cause and common-cause variation (where the special-cause variation is due to fine-tuning of the process features, while common-cause variation is due to management assumptions or design of the process).

These distinctions seem to cut a fine line between scorecards and dashboards. How can the two approaches be more clearly differentiated? There are four distinctions that exist between these two methods that are found in the customer dashboard system but do not necessarily exist in a balanced scorecard:

- Variation is the basis for evaluation of the measurement process. Good processes will have less variation for critical measurement parameters than poor processes. If management wants to improve a process, then management must reduce the variation in the process that is due to common cause — the natural variation that is designed into the core process activities.
- Connectivity among performance indicators is based on statistical analysis that demonstrates causality, not just on groupings of measures that appear to have some affinity for influence.
- Ownership is established for implementing the process measurement system and for monitoring the measures to achieve desired results.

- Accountability for performance is a requirement of process owner-ship. There is no option for executive excuses for performance short-falls (or overachievements, for that matter). If the performance is unexpected (whether good or bad), then it must be understood and explained.

How does an organization's leadership team begin to develop such a cus-tomer dashboard? The following sequence of activities provides a step-by-step high-level work process for creating a customer dashboard:

- *Setting the direction:* Determine the value proposition for the main-stream business.
- *Determining the context:* Establish a competitive market proposition for the entire business
- *Mapping the enterprise:* Analyze how necessary business and work-process actions are integrated with the measurement system.
- *Identifying critical business control points:* Determine where all critical measurement drivers of the business results have control points.
- *Delegating responsibility for processes and measures:* Delegate authority for control of these key measurement control point decisions to pro-cess owners.
- *Calculating the measurement baseline:* Determine current performance level and discover benchmarks in external organizations that chal-lenge business leaders to improve beyond benchmark level of busi-ness excellence in your critical performance areas.

USING A CUSTOMER DASHBOARD FOR DAILY MANAGEMENT

Another consideration regarding customer dashboards is how to use this measurement system to manage the daily work and routine operations of a business. When it comes to execution of its business plans, management has two distinct activities: evaluating the quality of their work and stew-arding their resources to achieve their performance targets.

Managers are to make a clear distinction between self-assessment objectives that define the organization's approach to business improvement and evaluate the completeness of its deployment (process measures — the Xs in a Six Sigma measurement system) and those objectives for evaluation of achievement using the measures of business results for ensuring stewardship and recognizing accountability (results measures — the Y measures in a Six Sigma measurement system). Self-assessment methods should be divided into two categories for review. The first focuses on the approach taken or plan for improvement and the deployment of that plan. This review focuses on changes in the process Xs. The second review focuses on the operational results that are delivered by the changes in the Xs on the business results in time of the Y measures.

Process monitoring is a stewardship activity that continuously samples work-process performance to determine how well a process is operating over time. As long as a process is operating within its desirable performance envelope, the process is considered to be in a state of control (either statistical control or business control depending on the operating limits used for this comparison). When a process exceeds these boundary conditions for good control, it may be considered a rogue process that requires process improvement (through variation management). The purpose of process monitoring is not to say how good it is performing, but to capture early indicators of performance shifts that will lead to poorer performance than desired. Early estimation or inferences of change are one of the most important benefits from implementing a Six Sigma customer dashboard measurement system — like the pilot, a business leader must learn how to detect and stay ahead of emerging problems that the dashboard indicates are developing.

Customer dashboards provide a balanced, real-time, customer-focused, action-oriented approach for the objective management of business and work processes. Their drawback is at the point of implementation because putting these measurement systems into place requires "sweating for quality" — it is not easy work and involves the cross-functional efforts of the entire management team. Even more important, daily use and operation of such systems must become the core of a business's way of working. It is the execution of management using the customer dashboard that requires both disciplined application and thorough follow-up using the variation investigation methods of Six Sigma tools and analysis methods to determine and eliminate the root cause of critical business problems.

If management does not learn to focus on diagnosing common cause of systemic performance issues, then they will abrogate their responsibility as effective business leaders. When senior managers continue to lead the investigation of special-cause variation (and assigning the cause — or blame — for the problem), they undermine the organizational structure by not holding the process owners accountable for their performance results. Not only is this micromanagement, but it also confounds the decision rights of an organization and muddies the empowerment process by failing to match responsibility and accountability to the activities required to successfully manage and monitor work processes. Use of a customer dashboard assures business leaders that management's objective for process information is satisfied, but not at the expense of a broken business process (loss of stewardship for resources), which is fundamental to the work of process owners. Dashboards are intended for all the players to use, and self-management continues to be the best principle for process operations.

BEGIN BY BENCHMARKING ORGANIZATIONAL PURPOSE

Measurement is necessary to properly define the *operating space* of an organization — the part of the commercial domain that it carves out as its own unique area for business. The first five chapters of this book have described an approach for defining where an organization can achieve a competitive advantage through benchmarking critical aspects of its business strategy — using strategic benchmarking. The remainder of this book will focus on the ways to make this method practical and to link it into operational activity — the work the organization accomplishes in order to satisfy its customers. It is only when strategic benchmarking completes a loop of learning — from discovery of trigger points and leverage opportunities to execution of actions required to successfully implement differentiating activity—that benchmarking is able to truly make a difference.

In order to discover how strategic benchmarking makes a difference in companies, case studies will be presented that depict the transition from strategic illumination to creative imitation and faultless execution—the discovery journey of successful benchmarking.

DEVELOP A BENCHMARKING BUSINESS PRACTICE

Part 3 of this book contains three chapters that present case studies. In Chapter 6, the set of case studies that were included in *Strategic Benchmarking* are updated, and lessons learned based on hindsight are presented. Chapter 7 presents a case study that describes how to gain strategic illumination of trigger points and improvement leverage opportunities. Chapter 8 follows through with a case study that defines the creative imitation process of operational benchmarking, which is necessary in order to achieve the end result of faultless execution of appropriate business practices.

The purpose of the case studies is to provide a convincing argument that benchmarking at the enterprise level of policy definition and strategy formulation is a viable practice that can lead to competitive advantage.

INTEGRATE BENCHMARKING INTO YOUR BUSINESS STRATEGY

Enduring competitive advantage, however, is only achieved if benchmarking becomes mainstreamed into the strategic planning process and applied on a regular basis to detect changes in critical business assumptions, technology applications, or other emerging differentiators. In this chapter, we have defined the relationship between these methods, while in Chapter 9 an approach for merging these concepts is presented in the context of a policy deployment management system (which is defined as a *hoshin kanri* system in Japanese management methods). Thus, benchmarking finds an organizational *home* in the management process alongside strategic planning and business development.

CREATE BENCHMARKING OPERATIONAL PROCEDURES

Implementation of benchmarking requires a development of a detailed program that is aligned with accepted industry practice and that defines the procedures used for conducting a study. Support for these implementation decisions is found in Appendix A, which presents the generally accepted Benchmarking Code of Conduct as promulgated by the American Productivity & Quality Center's (APQC) International Benchmarking Clearinghouse (IBC). In addition, Appendix B presents a detailed Standard Operating Procedure (SOP) for benchmarking. Together, these documents define a detailed way to implement benchmarking and support its deployment in organizations. The subject of the implementation of benchmarking programs is contained in much of the literature on this subject (see Appendix E for a comprehensive bibliography of benchmarking books that have been written since 1989), so this information will not be duplicated in this book.

PLAN YOUR BENCHMARKING PROGRAM

If benchmarking is to become part of the institutional management program, then it must become a sustainable capability of the organization. This topic is discussed in the final chapter of this book. In addition, Appendix C identifies web-based benchmarking resources that can aid in the development of your benchmarking capability.

PART 3
Case Studies in Benchmarking

Reviewing Lessons Learned from Old Case Studies

What learning is the most necessary? Not to unlearn what you have already learned.

— DIOGENES LAERTIUS

THEORY IS ESSENTIAL AS A BASE FOR PRACTICE, BUT DOES IT WORK IN PRACTICE?

At a 1993 meeting of business school professors and quality executives from some of the Fortune 50, one of the senior professors quipped: "That's nice — quality works in practice, but does it work in theory?" This illustrated to me the gap between the pragmatic, get-it-done attitude of an operations manager and the lack of urgency and theoretical basis of an academic. Now, I have feet in both camps and can see value in both viewpoints. But if I am to err on either side of this equation, color me a pragmatist. Thus, we need to see how the theory works in practice.

The next three chapters describe how these different approaches to doing a benchmarking study operate and illustrate these methods with case studies. This chapter will compare and contrast the different types of data collection strategies used in the initial taxonomy of benchmarking studies and identify lessons learned from the cases that were previously described in benchmarking literature. The next chapter will focus on how to do a strategic benchmarking study and will illustrate this approach with a case study. The final chapter in this section will focus on the methodology and techniques used in doing an operational benchmarking study.

However, to introduce case studies from *Strategic Benchmarking,* we must consider management's motivation for conducting a benchmarking study. In the following section, three examples of studies are identified, and the motivating forces behind each are discussed.

WHAT IS THE BUSINESS MOTIVATION FOR DOING A BENCHMARKING STUDY?

Why do organizations conduct benchmarking studies? Consider three of the "classical" examples of benchmarking studies and the factors that caused their management to initiate each study.

EXAMPLE: XEROX AND L.L. BEAN — TRIGGER: BUSINESS CRISIS

In the late 1970s, Xerox Corporation was faced with a severe business crisis. The market that Xerox had created for business copiers was under attack by Japanese competitors, and Xerox was steadily losing market share and saw its shareholder value steadily declining as return on assets dropped from over 22 percent in 1974 to just 4 percent in 1984. What action should be taken in this business crisis?

The answer to this crisis for Xerox was the development of a process for benchmarking. Xerox used its strategic opportunity of a subsidiary operating in the Japanese market (Fuji Xerox) to triangulate on learning about its competition as described in the Preface to the book and subsequently in this chapter. Xerox was able to directly observe their internal costs and processes as well as the internal costs and methods of Fuji Xerox. By using the known market prices to establish a comparative baseline, Xerox was able to estimate the cost of operations by their competition and to identify areas in their financial performance that pointed at achievement of improved effectiveness or efficiency. By studying what other businesses were doing in these areas (most famously the logistics comparison Xerox made against mail order company L.L. Bean) and comparing to Xerox practices, it was possible to identify improvement opportunities that would close the performance gaps. Xerox took the natural act of making comparisons and turned it into an operational science.

An important observation of this study is the motivation that initiated the benchmarking study. Just as Deming observed, quality often comes "out of a crisis" that focuses management and stimulates a need for change. Business crisis was the dominant factor that drove management to benchmark.

EXAMPLE: FORD AND MAZDA—TRIGGER: PARADIGM SHIFT

In 1981 when Dr. Deming's white paper "If Japan Can, Why Can't We?" was broadcast on NBC, Ford CEO Don Peterson called Deming and asked for support in helping to improve the level of competitiveness of Ford against encroaching Japanese automakers. As part of Ford's strategy to improve, they acquired a 25 percent share in Mazda and began directly studying how this Japanese auto manufacturer did business differently. One discovery that amazed the financial managers of Ford was that the work of the Mazda accounts payable staff was accomplished by 5 individuals, while the work at Ford's organization required some 500 people. The observation that Ford made was that the Mazda people had changed their entire approach for this task from a functional perspective that only optimized accounts payable, to a process perspective that optimized the entire procurement process resulting in less cost and process for managing corrective action at the end of the process (accounts payable).

The approach that Ford took to this revelation was the detailed study of the Mazda methods for managing the entire procurement process in relationship to its suppliers, not merely a traditional study of accounts payable staffing policies or dictating a "do more with less" encouragement to workers. Ford had learned from Deming that the problem was not with the workers, but with the common-cause management system that it had defined. Therefore, process change had to be made by management in order to achieve improved productivity at the worker level.

169

This study (described more fully by Michael Hammer) is credited with providing the stimulus necessary for streamlining Ford procurement processes in the mid-1980s. The motivation that initiated the detailed study of Mazda by Ford was the observation that better work performance was being achieved at an order of magnitude in labor productivity as a result of a change in the paradigm of work performance.[1]

EXAMPLE: COMPAQ AND FEDERAL EXPRESS — TRIGGER: INNOVATION STIMULUS

In the decade of the 1980s, Compaq Computer Corporation was the darling of the high technology industry. It had sustained annual growth rates exceeding 20 percent since it was founded and established numerous records for business performance. This did not make Compaq invulnerable to change or external attack. In 1990, Compaq suffered an unprecedented collapse of its network of independent dealers as consolidations shifted its distribution from 10 dealer chains to 6 under the pressure of the Dell direct sales model and a move toward superstores in the retail channels. Consolidation of the dealer channel took less than a month and caught Compaq, along with all other producers, by surprise. The impact on the Compaq business was the strongest as Compaq relied solely on this dealer channel for its distribution. The consolidation left an excess inventory of some $400 million in the distribution channels and forced Compaq to issue it's first-ever profit warning — causing the price of its stock to tumble from $85 to $55 per share overnight.

What was the problem? The top management of Compaq discovered that their business model needed to be changed rapidly. They needed more flexibility and had to create an approach to the market that was more aligned with direct sales, rather than relying so heavily on a single distribution channel to access the consumer market. As a result, management realized that they needed to have a capability for direct communication with customers — both to provide technical support and to per-

1. Michael Hammer and James Champy, *Reengineering the Corporation* (New York: Harper, 1993).

mit direct sales. This required an entirely new business process—a call center—and Compaq turned to benchmarking the best call centers, such as the one operated by Federal Express, in order to determine how to rapidly design and implement this new capability.

This study (documented in *Strategic Benchmarking* [1993]) is credited with providing the necessary stimulus to regain the Compaq market leadership position in the personal computer industry in the early 1990s.

The motivation that initiated this study was the need to create a business process that did not exist in the past and to do it with a sense of urgency so that business results would not suffer from the setback for any sustained period of time. By 1994, Compaq had executed the turnaround strategy and once again doubled its revenue from the pre-1991 level.

CASE STUDIES REVISITED

Observing that businesses are faced with a variety of motivational factors that drive them to initiate a benchmarking study, how do they actually perform these studies? The way these benchmarking studies were conducted was illustrated in *Strategic Benchmarking* through four chapter-long case studies. These studies are reviewed and updated in the rest of this chapter.

INTERNAL BENCHMARKING AT HEWLETT-PACKARD

Hewlett-Packard (HP) was reported to have conducted internal studies of its R&D process at its different business units to determine how to develop new products in the shortest time to market.[2] This study also illustrates how many studies will cross the lines distinguishing between strategic and operational studies. The initial emphasis of this study was on the development of a performance measure that would permit cross-business unit comparison of performance on time to market. This measure—break-even time (BET)—was then the indicator used to determine which proj-

2. Watson, *Strategic Benchmarking*, 93–107.

ect teams were implementing practices leading to a faster payback period based on the relative investment of resources. The motivation for this study was the observation that Japanese competitors were developing products in less time than were Hewlett-Packard divisions and that the quality levels of the products were equal. Management made a strategic decision to change its R&D process in order to stay competitive and deliver market-oriented innovative products to continue to delight their customers. There were two outcomes of the operational aspect of this study that changed the way HP designed its products — the implementation of the BET metric to objectively define the progress of projects in a uniform manner and the implementation of quality function deployment (QFD) to keep projects focused on delivering real market needs.[3]

Indeed, when one reviews the lessons learned from this HP study, it is evident that they contain the seeds of Six Sigma. The approach taken by HP was to follow the sequence of "document the process, measure the process, reduce the variability within the process and think of ways to continually improve the process."[4] Note that this sequence of activities follows the same logic as the DMAIC process used in today's Six Sigma projects!

Note as footnotes to this study that Hewlett-Packard is still a dynamic competitor in its industry, having taken over many of its previous competitors through mergers and acquisitions (Apollo, Tandem, Digital, and Compaq were all implanted into HP) and the company continues to flexibly redefine its approach to the market as it has survived a major organizational transition in the mid-1990s, including the transfer of management oversight to the first noninternal CEO — Carly Fiorina. This transition of Hewlett-Packard will be described further in the second article in this

3. At the same time Hewlett-Packard implemented BET, it also implemented QFD as a change mechanism in order to align the desires, needs, requirements, and expectations of its customers with the functional requirements that it designed into its products and assure that quality is built into the product design as it moves from a conceptual stage of development to the level of detailed engineering drawings.

4. Watson, *Strategic Benchmarking*, 107.

series to illustrate how strategic benchmarking can help refine an organizations understanding of its purpose or strategic intent and refine that intent as it understands the opportunities it has for changing direction as it defines and embraces its own future.

COMPETITIVE BENCHMARKING AT FORD

Ford was reported to have conducted competitive studies in the process of designing the initial model of the Taurus.[5] Like the retrospective view of HP's internal benchmarking study, the Ford "Team Taurus" approach laid the foundation for many of the lessons of the Six Sigma Define-Measure-Analyze-Design-Verify (DMADV) or Design for Six Sigma (DFSS) efforts of the coming decade. While Ford was not the market leader in innovation of many automotive design features and functions, it did recognize the need to develop a product offering that could excite its customers and provide them with capabilities that equaled or exceeded the capabilities available in competing car choices. This desire was at the heart of the competitive study conducted to support the Taurus product development. The motivation for the study was to regain market share and its reputation for an innovative automobile product line by the analysis of attractive features of competing automobiles and determining which features represented best-in-class designs—then these were the designs that had to be equaled or exceeded in the Taurus. The competitive product analysis of some 400 features found in 50 automobiles provided the core of the learning process for Team Taurus engineers. One important aspect of this study was the fact that Ford did not isolate its investigation to the best of the best but rather surveyed the entire industry

5. Ibid., 109–128. Ford is also reported to have conducted a competitive study with Mazda regarding the function of managing accounting (Michael Hammer and James Champy, *Reengineering the Corporation* [New York: Harper, 1993]). It is interesting to note that this study began as an operational benchmarking study and migrated into a strategic study as Ford learned that its organizational structure must change as a result of the technological capability of the new software applications for "paperless" management.

from BMW to the Opel Senator, which turned out to contribute best-in-class features in the final 400, even though this car would not typically be considered a real rival of the Ford Taurus. The results of this effort were to introduce an automobile that was not only a "Car of the Year" winner, but also a market leader!

However, a retrospective on the study provides some interesting insights into the need for constancy of purpose in the management process. While the Taurus was an initial market success, problems in the execution of its transmission design lead to its reputation as a lemon in following years, which led to a series of redesigns—each one slowly chipping away at the original design concept. The initial concept of competitive features led to an unusual situation by the late 1990s, where the car had over 250,000 *buildable combinations* or variants of options and features that could be ordered, but sales of the car dropped from a 1992 high of 400,000 units to less than 60,000 by the end of the decade, and it was last produced in August 2006. In hindsight, a key lesson of this Ford project is that competitive benchmarking should not be a single-point event—looking at the market at an instance in time then preserving that viewpoint for posterity. As originally observed in *Strategic Benchmarking:*

> A "single point" observation of competing product can reveal the features, technologies, design rules, and safety standards incorporated into that one product. It fails, however, to the trend of improvement, the mix of new versus old features, the speed with which a competitor is capable of implementing new technologies or adapting to environmental change, or clues as to the underlying process technologies. Doing analysis *over time,* on the other hand, provides insight into these issues. A robust approach to competitive analysis looks beyond today's product features and production methods to development of a broad profile on the competitor—its core capabilities [as well as its core rigidities!], its technological velocity and trajectory, its strategic investments. These charac-

teristics cannot be learned from a single-point product analysis. (Watson 120)

In order for a competitive benchmarking study to have an enduring effect, it must be kept evergreen—it must be updated regularly and refreshed with new competitive information that is gleaned from changes and strategic shifts that occur based on management-level decisions that occur *between* the car models, as well as the design changes reflected *within* the car models! This observation illustrates the Six Sigma way of thinking as the sources of variation are examined and the lessons learned are exploited to create not only a short-term snapshot of competitive performance but to develop a long-term documentary film of the history of competition. The choice that management is able to make about the product is based upon all of the effects of variation in competitive product decisions, not just the short-term impact of model changes. This lesson illustrates what is required for enduring success—continuing innovation must be based upon a continuous discovery process and sound data analysis that captures all lessons that may be learned from the investigations. This lesson illustrates the merging of Six Sigma program features with strategic benchmarking to create an enduring competitive position for an organization.

FUNCTIONAL BENCHMARKING AT GENERAL MOTORS

General Motors conducted a two-year benchmarking study of alternative ways to manage the quality and reliability functions, which was completed in 1984.[6] This study was conducted at a time when quality dominated the attention of most thoughtful managers resulting from a 1981 broadcast challenge by Dr. W. Edwards Deming. This TV program demonstrated that quality is a competitive differentiator—and Deming's logic was further endorsed by the academic results of the Profit Impact of Market Strategy (PIMS) study that was funded by General Electric

---

6. Watson, *Strategic Benchmarking*, 129–148.

and conducted by the Wharton Graduate School of business. This study reported "quality is king" — quality perception of product customers is an accurate predictor of commercial profitability.[7]

While by today's standards of knowledge the insights of the GM study represent basic knowledge of quality, these ideas were fresh insights at the time, and they helped to focus the attention of many of the participating companies (e.g., Hewlett-Packard, 3M, John Deere and Company, etc.) on ideas that could enhance long-term quality performance. In the design of this study, GM began with ten *null hypotheses* or *Theory O* statements about strongly held beliefs that were to be tested for validity using the benchmarking partner companies.[8] In applying this hypothesis testing logic, GM also anticipated the use of the scientific method in the analyze phase of Six Sigma DMAIC projects to test the Theory O of management opinion against the facts of the workplace and determine the factors that drive performance in order to put them into a state of business control. The most enduring result of the GM study was the way it made an objective assessment of the entire quality management system, which facilitated understanding of the way that quality contributes to business performance among the participating organizations. Discovery of this linkage predated the introduction of the two major quality systems innovations of the 1980s — the criteria of the Malcolm Baldrige National Quality Award and the set of ISO9000-related standards for quality management systems. While the study's results, in hindsight, were unremarkable, it is important to note the timing of the discovery that was made by GM and its partners. The report was produced and available to the partners in September of 1984. However, the similar conclusions doc-

---

7. Robert D. Buzzell and Bradley T. Gale, *The PIMS Principles: Linking Strategy to Performance* (New York: Free Press, 1987).

8. Indeed, at this period of time, many of these companies participated in a number of learning events as a cohort of organizations that helped them to develop a common perspective of the approaches to quality that could be effectively deployed to create business results. Many participated in the early work of the GOAL/QPC Research Committee as well as the development of the Malcolm Baldrige Quality Award Criteria (which may be interpreted as a self-administered benchmarking survey to compare the internal quality management practices of an organization against those features found in recognized leaders).

umented in both the Baldrige Award criteria and ISO9000 were not documented for public consumption until late in 1998. This three-year lead time in knowledge acquisition allowed the participants in the GM study an advantage over their competitors. They could define their system for quality management in a way that allowed them an opportunity to create an advantage in the perceived-quality level, which the PIMS study demonstrated was important to create an enduring profitability for the organization. Thus, while the GM study may not have provided the once-and-for-all long-term solution, it did a good job in meeting the more immediate need of defining the characteristics of a quality system that would force the organization to change now, while recognizing that this process is evolutionary and that a further round of study would be required in order to define the next level of process change and performance improvement that must be attained. Unfortunately, there is no evidence that GM had the management willpower to conduct a second round of the quality and reliability study, as they turned their focus first to a common industry standard (QS9000 or the automotive industry version of ISO9000 for its suppliers), and then to the pursuit of the Malcolm Baldrige National Quality Award (won by the Cadillac motor car organization in 1990), and ultimately to Six Sigma at the turn of the century. Again, a big weakness is observed in the application of benchmarking in terms of a lack in constancy of purpose, to continue analyzing the critical business assumptions of the organization and its core processes as a means to challenging the organization to improve itself.

GENERIC BENCHMARKING STUDY AT XEROX

The Xerox generic study of logistics performance is perhaps the most widely documented benchmarking case study.[9] The trigger for conducting this benchmarking study was a crisis. In the late 1970s, Xerox was

9. This study is documented in Camp (1989) and Watson (1993) as well as in Gregory H. Watson and Richard C. Palermo, eds. *A World of Quality: The Timeless Passport* (Milwaukee, WI: ASQ Quality Press, 1994).

177

faced with a severe business problem. The market that Xerox had created for business copiers was under attack by Japanese competitors, and Xerox was steadily losing market share and saw its shareholder value steadily declining as return on assets dropped from over 22 percent in 1974 to just 4 percent in 1984. What action should be taken in this business crisis? In response to this crisis, Xerox developed the process of benchmarking in order to learn how it could manage its business in a more competitive way. Xerox used its strategic opportunity of a subsidiary operating in the Japanese market (Fuji Xerox) to triangulate on learning about its competition. They were able to directly observe their internal costs and processes as well as the internal costs and methods of Fuji Xerox. By using the known market prices to establish a comparative baseline, Xerox was able to estimate the cost of operations by their competition and to identify areas in their financial performance that pointed at achievement of improved effectiveness or efficiency. This study of the competitors helped Xerox to learn the size of their performance gap; however, it didn't provide lessons learned about what to do to close the gap. In order to determine how to close the gap and gain an edge over competitors, Xerox chose to complete their study by looking at what leading businesses were doing in the areas where they had shortfalls and comparing the practices of these companies to Xerox practices. Using this approach, it was possible to identify improvement opportunities in a wide variety of operational processes that allowed Xerox to close the performance gap by 1987.

One such area identified was in the amount of inventory carried at all levels of supply (e.g., raw material, work in process, and finished goods) by competitors. One of the major lessons that Xerox learned to improve its logistics management processes came through a study of the warehouse management processes at retailer L.L. Bean. This study is credited with providing the needed stimulus to make significant improvement at Xerox. An important observation of this study is the motivation that initiated the benchmarking study. Just as Deming observed, quality often comes out of a crisis that focuses management and stimulates a need for change. Business crisis was the dominant factor that drove management to benchmark.

There are a couple of footnotes that should be added to this study. First, the study began as a strategic benchmarking study—dealing with the core ability of Xerox to compete in its global markets. However, midway through the study it transitioned into an operational study, as Xerox focused on process improvement changes that would permit it to increase its own performance beyond the capability of its competitors. But in hindsight, it is clear that the Xerox benchmarking effort was not a magic bullet that helped it to avoid basic business problems for decades to come. In the early 1990s, Xerox was faced with another major business challenge—the transition of its technology from analog to digital, while at the same time changing the organizational structure from a massive functional organization to a streamlined, divisional structure that was divided into discrete lines of business and managed as a portfolio of individual businesses. Indeed, as Xerox migrated through all of these changes, it lost its business process focus and de-emphasized its efforts in both leadership through quality and benchmarking. An external CEO from IBM completed the transition and shifted the emphasis more toward pure financial management of the portfolio of divisions. Xerox ultimately recognized these problems and brought back its former CEO, Paul Allaire, and then transitioned back to a core team of senior managers who have been attempting to resurrect the culture of the organization that was lost. The lesson in this effort is that benchmarking is only a tool—it is not a panacea that alleviates all business issues by "copying from the best" those practices to differentiate performance of the organization from its competitors. Benchmarking must be a significant part of the ongoing process of management, and lessons must be refreshed on a regular basis in order to optimize the value of this methodology.

UNDERSTANDING BENCHMARKING STUDIES

Upon reflection on these examples of studies from the history of benchmarking, it is clear that there are several indicators that can be used to define what type of study is being conducted. First, the business objective can be defined as either strategic or operational. Second, the benchmarking partner can be identified as either competitive or collaborative. Third, the source of data may be internal or external. The type of data collected may be either attribute or variable data whose source is an Internet database, a dedicated survey or questionnaire, specific measurement of agreed factors, or it may be anecdotal and based on subjective opinion. Finally, the trigger that exposed the need to do the benchmarking study may be an external influence from the environment (e.g., a shift in technology, a move by a competitor, a change in regulations or laws, an economic change, etc.) or it may be internal (e.g., perceived need to improve performance, observed weakness in an organizational strategy, core competence, or key performance area, etc.).

While these distinctions are helpful for development of a clearer understanding of *how* to benchmark, they really do not help determine *what* to benchmark. Indeed, they also are not helpful in understanding the question, *should* we benchmark? Many of benchmarking case studies illustrate the results obtained by large organizations and apply to massive core business processes (as is the case in the Xerox example where they are looking to improve their global logistics process or in the case of Hewlett-Packard where they want to improve their time to market for new product development). This raises the natural question: Does benchmarking apply to all organizations? Yes, it does, in particular when considering a small to medium enterprise; however, the explanation of the applicability of benchmarking takes more than just this quick answer — yes, it applies!

There are a number of barriers to benchmarking that concern smaller organizations.

- *No Small Companies Seem to Do It!* First, benchmarking literature favors examples or case studies from larger organizations. This is because it is typical that only the larger organizations have enough resources to document their case studies. They tend to have specialists who support the practice on either a full-time or part-time basis, and these people demonstrate their professionalism in the field of benchmarking by publishing their results. In smaller organizations, people attempt to master many trades while becoming expert in none! This creates a bias in published literature toward sources from larger organizations for any quality improvement topic such as benchmarking. It is more likely that the articles and books written on these subjects will come from a large organization or a consultant who provides services to smaller organizations and uses the case study as promotional material.

- *Size Does Matter!* Second, even in a large, multinational company, the business unit or division is typically equivalent in size to a small- to medium-sized enterprise, and the lessons learned at that level should be transferable to a small company. This means that the lessons learned from a benchmarking study are transferable or scalable to smaller organizations by using appropriate analogies to assure goodness of fit.

- *Search for the Best of the Best:* Finally, many of the smaller organizations are concerned about the effort that it will take to discover the world-class level of performance and are justly concerned that the large companies where this may tend to occur will not be willing to share with them. This concern should not be a driving issue that determines whether an organization benchmarks. It is not necessary to find the one best or world-class organization to improve—it is only necessary to find someone who does it better! Additionally, there are other strategies, such as joining a benchmarking club or consortium where your resources are multiplied by the support of partner organizations and access to large companies is more readily available than is typically achievable by a single, smaller organization.

After reviewing these cases, it is hopefully clear that benchmarking can provide insights leading to significant opportunities for business improvement. The next two chapters will describe how strategic and operational benchmarking is done and will illustrate their use with case study information.

CHAPTER 7

Conducting a Strategic Benchmarking Study

The principle of strategy is having one thing, to know ten thousand things.

—MIYAMOTO MUSASHI

INTRODUCTION

What is strategic benchmarking? It is a management practice that integrates the process of benchmarking with strategic planning methodology to uncover unique opportunities to gain business advantage over competitors. The data sources may come from any of the four types that were described in Chapter 1. However, the issue that is most important is how management interprets the information and applies it to define the options it has for choices of its strategic intent, as well as the plans it makes to execute that intent. In the process for strategic benchmarking, management is not seeking to gain knowledge of a process—that is the objective of operational benchmarking—rather, it is seeking to discover either trigger points that will induce change in its business model or management practices that it may leverage to facilitate strategic change. Strategic benchmarking studies current competitors, latent competitors, and organizations' lead in business practices that are of strategic interest to the top management team.

Strategic benchmarking can change an organization's strategic direction by studying how its competitors or frontrunner organizations have made their choices about strategy and resource allocation; alternative structures for governance of the business; decision options that support business mergers, acquisition, or investments in R&D projects; decisions affecting management choices about either business or product line positioning; or opportunities for implementing change management strategies (e.g., pursuit of a specific strategy such as implementation of an enterprise software product or management's choice of an improvement methodology [for example, ISO9000, Total Quality Management (TQM), or Six Sigma] as a way to induce change in the organization).

Thus, strategic benchmarking begins with business strategy and ends with allocation of the organization's resources. In between is the study of opportunities to differentiate the approach you take to the market, the way your organization operates, or the products that you develop. This chapter will describe how this is done through the description of the case study of Nokia Mobile Phones that occurred in 1995 to 1998. However, before the case study is described, two preliminary discussions are necessary: (1) How did the strategic planning process operate? and (2) How were resources allocated to achieve the desired market advantage?

BACKGROUND INFORMATION

I became involved with Nokia Mobile Phones (NMP) shortly after the publication of *Strategic Benchmarking*. The first engagement was requested by Pekka Ala-Pietilä, then the relatively recent CEO of NMP, who requested that I join Professor Gary Hamel as a speaker to the NMP senior management team at their annual business kick-off meeting, which was held in December 1993. I was invited to speak about how to use strategic benchmarking to stimulate organizational change, while Hamel spoke to them about the core competence of organizations and how to create competitive advantage through the creation of a unique set of competences. These speeches planted the seed that grew into my future work with Nokia.

After leaving Xerox in May 1994, I received a request to support Lew

Platt, the new CEO of Hewlett-Packard, by managing a strategic bench-marking study to define the direction that HP should take its quality efforts over the coming 25 years. Hewlett-Packard enjoyed taking the long view of the world and used such stretch horizons for studies to assure creative thinking in the application of study findings. Dick LeVitt, a newly appointed corporate quality director, was the sponsor of the study. This study was designed to evaluate the concept of *competing through quality* and finding a differentiation among the leaders that would suggest what directions HP should pursue in its strategy.

THE HP STRATEGIC BENCHMARKING STUDY

The study that HP conducted recognized that the seeds of future performance in its industry would most likely be found among today's leaders in that industry. So the senior management team decided to make some simplifying assumptions in setting a direction for this study. First, they wanted to evaluate companies who had achieved a degree of hyper-growth (annual growth rate of 25 percent or more) as one indicator of their success in creating innovative products that were sensitive to market needs. Second, a focus of the study would be the electronics and telecommunications industry as this sector was growing at the fastest rate at that time. Third, the company wanted a global perspective in its results and decided that companies should be chosen for comparison from three regions: United States, Europe, and Japan. Fourth, the company had to have been externally recognized for excellence in its approach to quality management. And finally, the business leaders at HP limited the scope of the study to five companies in each region whose management system they respected.

In order to assure objectivity in the study, a questionnaire was developed, and the study leader requested that each of the participating companies complete the questionnaire during a site visit that was performed by two HP executives supported by a consultant. The job of the HP executives was to interview key business leaders from each company using the questionnaire, while the task of the consultant was to collect the data, develop trip reports for each company, and facilitate an HP-only meeting following each site visit to record lessons learned and develop a presentation about the implications of their findings. Each participant in the study received a copy of the trip report that was tailored to them, described the observations of the HP executives, and also provided a critique of their quality management system by the consultant.

This study was significant to Hewlett-Packard because of its finding that there were two different quality approaches that applied in its future direction—one that supported the need to design quality into the product function and features through innovative practices as the dominant business emphasis and another that supported building quality into the product through the production process to support the mass production requirements of an ever-expanding electronics consumer market. These two findings implied that HP may require separate business models, based on the quality system requirements, to support the more highly customized, low-volume business of electronic instruments and systems, as compared to the standardized, high-volume business of consumer electronics and computer systems. It is interesting that Platt eventually divided the business along these lines; however, I cannot claim that this study was the only stimulus for his thinking. What did this study mean for the people at Nokia Mobile Phones?

BUSINESS REASON FOR A NOKIA STUDY

To answer the question from the NMP perspective, it is necessary to understand the type of organization that Ala-Pietilä received when he took over the reins. This perspective is best achieved by considering the market impact that the organization had on the mobile phone industry at the time. Nokia was a distant third in market share behind the stronger brands of Motorola and Ericsson. Indeed, following Nokia were the also-rans in this business. The cellular phone industry up to this point in time had achieved modest growth, but it had not passed the initial inflection point in its S-curve of growth that signals the entry into the early adapter market. It was mostly the technophiles who were buying the products.

Nokia conducted a survey of the market to consider the strength of its brand and found that it had no brand value—indeed, people were confused about the company, and over three quarters of those surveyed believed that the company was based in Japan, rather than Finland. Of course, NMP was guilty of creating this confusion as it marketed its product line under a number of different brands: Mobira, Technophone, and Cityphone were three that ultimately were merged into a single brand—called by the company's name—*Nokia* (the company had been named after the Finnish city where it was first established in the mid-1800s as a pulp and wood products company). At this time in its history, the cellular phone business contributed 20 percent of the total revenue for the entire corporation, which also sold cables, consumer electronics, rubber boots and tires, as well as a variety of other products. Clearly, its mobile phone technology and wireless communication business was significant but not "top of mind" to the business before 1992.

In 1992 Jorma Ollila, the former president of NMP and newly appointed CEO of Nokia Corporation, decided to divest these other product lines in order to focus on wireless communications, and at the same time the NMP team decided to create a brand strategy to develop value that would allow it to have more enduring competition edge in its market and become a global leader in wireless telecommunications.

Under Anssi Vanjoki, the head of marketing and sales, NMP developed a 25-year strategy to make the Nokia brand the dominant brand in the European cellular phone industry. The NMP management team called this journey's purpose to become the *dynamic champion* in the wireless industry. The meaning of this term was twofold. First, *dynamic* implied that the underlying technology for this industry was not really assured, as there were five different competing technologies at this time, and no crystal ball could clearly see which would win (note that the older technology AMPS, was being attacked by GSM, TDMA, CDMA, and a proprietary Japanese technology—each with their own godfathers in terms of a major industry corporate sponsor and a national telecommunications provider as their backers). The choice of the word *dynamic* meant that NMP would not select a single technology, but would pursue a broad development of technology that allowed it flexibility to choose among all five and compete on a global basis until the industry sorted itself out and a common technology emerged. The second meaning came from the word *champion,* which implied that NMP would achieve at least a 25 percent market share in all of its regional markets. This was an audacious goal when compared with the company's initial positioning with less than 10 percent of the global market share and no real market visibility for its brand.

Nokia was also sensitive to the fact that competing on quality was a major issue in the cellular phone industry — both Motorola and Ericsson had received major awards for their quality management systems (Motorola received the Malcolm Baldrige National Quality Award [MBNAQ] in 1988 and Ericsson received the European Quality Award [EQA] in 1994). Nokia had received the Finnish National Quality Award in 1991, but this award did not convey the same prestige as the awards that its competitors had received. Nokia also noted that the customer's perception of quality was a significant driver for profitability — a lesson that was learned from the PIMS research conducted in the 1980s.[1] Because its customers were confused about the company, the management team reasoned that they would also be confused about the value proposition offered through its reputation for quality, as the customers didn't really understand their company's identity or its values.[2]

The NMP management team focused on a number of areas to grow its business. Product leadership was required: a broad R&D effort spent on creating intellectual property and a complete "Nokia branded" product line that could be recognized globally; operational excellence to allow the company to expand with profitable growth as the market passed the ini-

---

1. Robert D. Buzzell and Bradley T. Gale, *The PIMS Principles* (New York: The Free Press, 1987).

2. Today the European Foundation for Quality Management (EFQM), the organization that manages the EQA, operates a benchmarking group that coordinates sharing and learning among companies regarding areas of the award criteria that have been recognized as good practices. The EFQM also operates Communities of Practice (COPS), which are self-managed networks of practitioners who create an international forum for peer group networking, discussion, and learning on topics of specific interest (for information about these EFQM process, see http://www.efqm.org).

tial inflection point in its S-curve of growth and moved into the mass market; and, finally, customer intimacy to allow the company to deliver into the hands of consumers a product that was both intuitive and ergonomically aligned with the way people wanted the phone to work. It had to be designed to be held in a person's hand. In order to pull these ideas together into a coherent strategy, Nokia needed also to have a more concentrated focus on quality to integrate all of its efforts into a common value system or way of working that would characterize its own uniqueness to its people and truly separate itself from competitors.

CASE STUDY—CREATING COMPETITIVE ADVANTAGE FOR NOKIA MOBILE PHONES

As a participant in the HP study, the NMP management team was aware that they could create new perspectives by analyzing the quality strategies and methods taken by leaders in an industry. However, the HP study didn't help them as well as they needed because it did not provide specific insight into the greatly expanding cellular phone industry. Thus, the management team sought to extend the HP study into the cellular phone industry and become more specific in terms of creating an action plan to differentiate itself from its competitors through its management focus on quality. What could be learned about how Nokia's competitors were actually using quality management methods to differentiate the way their businesses operated? What choices and management moves were available to the NMP management team for them to differentiate themselves and achieve a greater degree of profitable growth?

CONDUCTING THE STRATEGIC BENCHMARKING STUDY

Because Motorola and Ericsson had received major quality awards, they were obligated to present information to the public about their systems that would be helpful in stimulating the improvement of other organizations. Both companies offered site visits to their plants producing products that were highlighted in their awards. Nokia visited both the

REDISCOVERING LOST LEARNING

THE ROLE OF FUJI XEROX IN THE XEROX DISCOVERY PROCESS

The Xerox benchmarking of mail-order giant L.L. Bean is history. However, one lesson has been lost in this history—what was the catalyst for doing this study, and how did it get exposed? The Xerox management team learned about their performance gap to their new competitors in Japan from their Japanese subsidiary—Fuji Xerox, a joint venture firm that had been established between Xerox and Fuji Photo Film. Yotoro "Tony" Kobyashi was the CEO of Fuji Xerox at the time, and it was his people who evaluated their Japanese competitors to allow a three-way comparison to be accomplished. By comparing scarce open-source knowledge of the Japanese competitors to the detailed knowledge of a fierce, but captive competitor (Fuji Xerox), Xerox Corporation was able to *triangulate*, which means to estimate performance of a third party using two known variables, and determine their standing against the competition. This is what Bob Camp would call *Step Zero* in their benchmarking study—a strategic discovery process that we call strategic benchmarking. Without this step and discovery, Xerox would not have the insight about what or where it must focus its benchmarking lessons to learn about what must change in its operations in order to make improvement endure.

THE ROLE OF HEWLETT-PACKARD IN THE NOKIA DISCOVERY PROCESS

Consider the way that this principle of triangulation was applied in the NMP benchmarking case study with Hewlett-Packard playing a key role in their discovery process.

Nokia made its discoveries about quality due to the enlightenment that came about the need to compete using quality based on the prior HP benchmarking study. While Nokia did not get a specific discovery about the process, it did realize that both of its key competitors had been included in the HP study and that they all met a common criteria for quality. This insight leads to a natural assumption that there may be no differentiable quality within the industry. So if the PIMS study indicates that customer-perceived quality is a key way to develop a competitive differentiator in an industry, then what opening existed for Nokia to pursue? Only by studying the approach to quality taken by these two leading companies would Nokia discover their options for creating a competitive advantage based on its quality performance. This is the key insight that

190

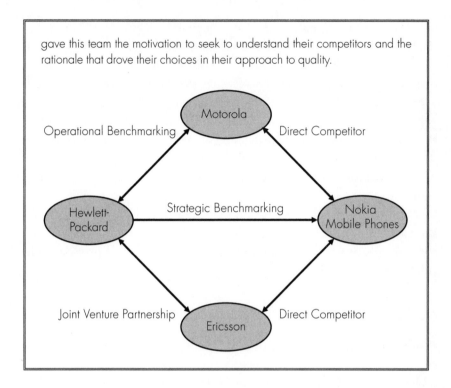

gave this team the motivation to seek to understand their competitors and the rationale that drove their choices in their approach to quality.

Boynton Beach pocket pager plant of Motorola, whose Bandit Project was a key feature of the initial Motorola Baldrige application and the Madrid, Spain, location of the Ericsson plant that was featured in their application for the European Quality Award. Both of these two facilities took very different approaches to quality management.

QUALITY AT MOTOROLA

Motorola was quite proud that its Bandit pocket pager stemmed the tide of market share loss to Japan for its pocket pager business and that they were actually able to win back some of this market share.[3] However, this

3. *Bandit* was the code name assigned to this project during R&D; however, the product's name was *Bravo* when it was launched into the market.

success story also signaled a new approach to quality within Motorola—the first product that was designed under a new system that they called Six Sigma. The Motorola engineers designed all the critical parameters to a Six Sigma tolerance level, and senior management was quite encouraged by the results of this product's reliability testing, which they claim exhibited a mean time to failure (MTTF) greater than 150 years! Indeed, according to this measure, the product would last many generations in its use! By comparison, Nokia had no stretch reliability goals for its products, and demonstration testing was just aimed at meeting the compliance standards of the major telecommunications suppliers (e.g., AT&T in the United States, NTT in Japan, and the major independents in Europe at this time), and each Nokia R&D project followed a roughly similar process, but the project manager could diverge from a fixed process if they could convince the R&D program manager to approve the deviation.

QUALITY AT ERICSSON

While Motorola emphasized product quality, Ericsson emphasized process quality and assured standardization among its production processes through the centralized management of process operating procedures and standards of performance in its corporate ISO9000 management system. Best practices were evaluated at Ericsson by a central committee composed of the plant quality managers who met to decide which of the internal practices was best and to convert all plants to the same process. Strength in the Ericsson production system was achieved through a high degree of standardization. All phones made anywhere in the world would be made with the same parts and using the same process. By comparison Nokia factories were developed with the latest technology that was available at the time of acquisition, and there was no commonality in the use of production software across its plants. Indeed, the Nokia value of "respect for the individual" was often interpreted to mean "don't interfere with our decisions or our right to make local choices about how we will produce our products!"

192

Developing a Creative Understanding of Strategic Benchmarking Information

Clearly, there were some significant distinctions between the ways these three companies approached their management of quality! Which approach was superior? Well, this was not really the most important question. Truly, the most important question was about the weaknesses that could be observed in the competitor's systems and how this weakness could be exploited to the advantage of Nokia as it redesigned its quality system.

The Basis for Beating Motorola

How was the Motorola quality system vulnerable? The insight to its weakness was provided during the site visit, when the local R&D manager made an offhand comment that all this attention to Six Sigma design that was dictated by corporate really slowed down the design process because it required so much more work to assure that all the critical parameters could be validated at this level of performance against the specified requirement for performance. Thus, Motorola had an internal conflict between the need to get products to the market fast and the need to assure that the quality of products released was Six Sigma relative to the performance they specified to customers. However, when asked what customer information this decision was based on, the local management team commented that they were designing a customer satisfaction survey at the moment and the "requirement for Six Sigma" was imposed by management as a surrogate for their customers. In other words, management made a decision based on Theory O, that the customer required this high degree of performance. But if you look at this goal from a different perspective, would you get the same decision? How many customers would want to pay for a pocket pager where the probability of failure is over 50 percent after 150 years and less than that prior to this time? Most customers only want to use these types of devices for a limited number of years and then replace them with more modern technology. In other words, this technology will become obsolete before the product becomes unreliable!

THE BASIS FOR BEATING ERICSSON

How was the Ericsson quality system vulnerable? The insight to its weakness was also obtained during the site visit. The local quality manager commented that changing their production process in any way required his submittal of a proposed change to the central committee that met quarterly. This committee then had to study the change and make a recommendation, and all related processes in the business had to change to adopt the common best practice. This degree of standardization assured consistent production, but it also slowed down the decision-making process and created a culture where it was acceptable to postpone decisions based on internal considerations alone. Changes induced on the production processes from external considerations (e.g., new technology or process capability) had to follow the same bureaucratic process. If this approach is compared to the Toyota Production System, then we can clearly observe the difference. At Toyota, many small experiments are conducted locally, and managers at the local level take responsibility for demonstration of the correctness of proposed work changes to assure that the change does represent the best way to perform standard work. When this change occurs at the local level, then the system of processes is updated, and change ripples through the entire system. The requirement for quality assurance of the proposed change is met without the bureaucratic delays of a management oversight committee from the entire corporation!

Interestingly, both companies possessed the knowledge of the weaknesses inherent to their quality systems, but due to each company's inability to listen to their people and act on their suggestions, the faults persisted, and this allowed Nokia an opportunity to take advantage of these structural limitations in their respective quality approaches.

APPLYING INSIGHTS TO INNOVATE BUSINESS POSITIONING

What should Nokia do to improve its quality management process? Nokia had to become faster in time to market than Motorola and more flexible in adapting operational process improvements than Ericsson.[4] Nokia's choices were based on some insights developed in a planning process with the new NMP Quality Vice President, Timo Hannukainen. In this process, the quality specialists in the company met to decide how to create a quality strategy that would truly differentiate Nokia.

INSIGHTS INTO BEATING MOTOROLA

One observation was made at the beginning of the NMP quality team's decision process: The goal for Six Sigma was originally set by Motorola in response to a Hewlett-Packard improvement objective to achieve a tenfold improvement in quality of its products during the decade of the 1980s. The question was asked, How did HP do? The answer was that in all divisions but one, HP actually achieved a 10X reduction in defect levels from their 1980 base. However, what HP didn't advertise was that the entire electronics industry had achieved a 7X reduction in defect levels over the same period, just due to improvements in processing equipment and the base technologies at the level of component production. Thus, the competitive advantage that resulted from HP's hard work was only the 3X better portion of their improvement that separated them as the gap to the rest of the industry! However, this marginal difference was more than enough to be perceived by its customers. On the other hand, the Motorola approach did not measure quality from a customer viewpoint (de-

---

4. Notice that this business requirement spans both value disciplines of product leadership (to beat Motorola) and operational excellence (to beat Ericsson). This is contrary to the recommendations of Michael Treacy and Fred Wiersema in their seminal book on this subject: *The Discipline of Market Leaders* (New York: Basic Books, 1995), where they state that management must choose one discipline in which to excel. Nokia required two because its two major competitors had chosen different paths to competitiveness.

fects reported is different from the compliance to a design specification, which is established by engineers to assure a level of performance is achieved in the product). Indeed, when the number of parts in a cellular phone or pocket pager is considered using the information about quality in the electronics industry, only a handful of parts actually do not meet a market-based standard of quality performance for a useful life as defined by customers. For these "dirty dozen" parts, there is a need for special engineering design to assure their reliability; however, for the vast number of standard components, their natural commercial reliability is sufficient for the product requirement. Thus, the perceived vulnerability of Motorola actually induces a cost in terms of time to market—more engineering time is required for superfluous levels of reliability, and this extends the time to market over the minimal set necessary to assure that the product is *designed for reliability*, when the standard of performance is *useful product life* as set by actual customer practice.

Insights into Beating Ericsson

The Ericsson benchmarking study indicated the potential disadvantages that could simultaneously arrive with the benefits of standardization. In a high-volume production business (today Nokia produces well over one million phones daily in its manufacturing processes), it is necessary to have standardized products and also to have standard work practices. At such high volumes, a company cannot afford the time to halt the flow of production in order to fix problems that had not been anticipated during the design process. Such megaproduction requirements enforce a business imperative: Design the product right and produce the product right, or you can't remain in this high-end business! The standard Ericsson production system had too much rigidity to be effectively extended to a high-volume production business. In order for the Nokia manufacturing system to work reliably over time, it was essential to develop a well-defined, bullet-proof production process that also could be rapidly cloned and replicated at distributed global production sites in order to meet the total world demand for these products. This meant that NMP had to combine

196

its central design capability with distributed implementation and flexible decision making at the local level to assure that this complex system could operate. In other words, Nokia had to design a complex, adaptive system that could organically reproduce mobile phones globally! This meant creating a proper balance between centralized and distributed levels of management and turning the vertical command and control system that Ericsson used into a lateral process that flowed with the stream of customer orders as each region of the world came online with their orders for these products with an asynchronous demand.

REALIZING THE RESULTS OF THE STUDY

Gaining insight about a potential competitive advantage is the objective of a strategic benchmarking study; however, executing a program to take advantage of that insight requires true leadership. How did Nokia use the information that this benchmarking research uncovered? Nokia pursued a number of simultaneous improvement projects to accelerate business success over these two competitors as it transitioned its technology from a base of analog telephones to digital telephones in the 1995 to 1999 time frame:

- *Nokia R&D Process Reengineering:* During this period, the NMP R&D engineering management team, led by R&D Senior Vice President Yrjo Nuevo and Pekka Valjus, Vice President for Development Programs, reengineered their process three times to streamline the design process and assure that principles of software reuse, modularization, standardized accessories, and other sound project management practices were tailored to the needs of the NMP concurrent engineering process. This process revolution created a disciplined product delivery process that was able to introduce three versions of digital technology products before Motorola was able to bring their first product to the market.
- *NMP Product Design Focus:* As Nokia moved to create a brand image, this was to be reflected in its "humanized technology" as the prod-

uct was to be made for holding in a person's hand and to interface intuitively with the user's mind through a friendly software design. One of the key people behind this effort to "out-Apple" the product form was Vice President Frank Nuovo, who served as the NMP design architect and whose California design team provided a fresh input to the style consciousness of the Finnish engineers.

- *NMP Manufacturing Technology:* Nokia also established manufacturing technology as a critical competence and staffed a manufacturing technology prototype development center in Salo, Finland, under Juha Lakkala to pursue the integration of its process technology with its launches of new product technology.

- *Nokia Reliability Management:* Hannukainen's NMP Quality Office set up a reliability group directed by Michael Grayeff with the objective of improving the reliability of its products to take advantage of the weakness in the blanket approach to reliability engineering used by Motorola. Instead of designing all customer features for Six Sigma performance, NMP focused on the most likely early failure items — those parts or functions that could fail during the expected lifetime that a customer would use the phone. This approach created a big difference allowing NMP engineers to focus on the dirty dozen parts for intense reliability engineering rather than spreading their efforts across the totality of all 400 or so parts that are included in the bill of materials of a typical cellular phone.

- *AT&T One-Rate Program:* At this time, AT&T approached NMP with a unique business opportunity. AT&T wanted to capture the new digital phone market in the United States as it was first emerging. To accomplish this, they wanted to create a strategic partnership with the leading producer of cellular handsets that could be sold in a bundled package with their service. They had an idea that was unconventional at this time — to sell airtime over the mobile network for 10 cents a minute without any further charges for roaming or long distance (within the territorial borders of the United States). This service would be substantially less expensive than alternatives, and with the national network coverage of AT&T, they expected to gain a mass market very quickly. AT&T approached Nokia with a business proposition — they could become the sole-source supplier for this new concept, provided they could demonstrate their ability to provide an unlimited number of digital phones to meet the expected demand that AT&T predicted. This opportunity and the prior work NMP had invested in its design and production processes opened the possibility to take on such a commercial challenge — provided the execution on the launch of the new Nokia digital phone could be conducted flawlessly — this called for a massive Six Sigma project.

- *The Nakola Manufacturing Six Sigma Project:* While the other projects set up the new design as reliable, there was still a need to assure that the implementation of the design and its production system was flawlessly executed so that there was no real limitation on the production volume or ramp-up capability of the factory. This was the basis for developing a Six Sigma megaproject at the Salo, Finland, manufacturing site (Nakola site) under Simo Salminen, Heikki Laurila, and Pekka Kytösaho. Salminen, Laurila, and Kytösaho led a Six Sigma team in conducting seven interrelated projects to streamline flow in the production line (so-called lean-sigma projects), eliminate defects from the production process, assure quality of parts from suppliers, mistake-proof the final assembly process, and guarantee that the testing of the products demonstrated their quality and caught problems as early as they could be discovered. When you are required to produce a million phones a day, then Six Sigma defect levels become a basic performance requirement of the process!

What results did this set of activities produce? Over the five years (1994 to 1999), NMP experienced exceptional growth: compound annual growth rates over 50 percent in terms of revenue, profit and units shipped that outpaced the growing market. Nokia rode the wave of increasing market size and gained increasing market share of this growing market. The cellular phone business grew from a total installed base of X units in 1994 to over Y units by the end of 1999. Nokia global market share grew from 8 percent in 1994 to 25 percent by the end of this period. Of course, it is clear that benchmarking was not the sole source of this gain—however, it was a catalyst that stimulated this growth by providing insights into sound decisions on the use of resources in alignment to remove vulnerabilities and capitalize on the weaknesses in the market. The combination of these strategic choices and the application of Six Sigma at the point of strategic implementation resulted in this success. (For a detailed insight into the performance of NMP during this period see the text box.)

What a change just five years made! As a footnote to this study, the European-Africa region of NMP (lead by Anssi Vanjoki and quality director Phil O'Neill) did indeed win the European Quality Award in the year 2000, achieving the highest score ever recorded in the history of either this award or underrelated criteria of the Malcolm Baldrige National Quality Award.[5] Notice, however, that the award came *after* the management decision to improve the business. Here, quality really was an enabler—a means to the business end—and the award was clearly not a strong management pursuit or end in itself.

LESSONS LEARNED: INTEGRATING BENCHMARKING INTO THE STRATEGIC PLANNING PROCESS

The investigation process of strategic benchmarking must engage the organization's best thinking assets in an inquiry process to develop the questionnaire used for the study, understand the implications of the observations, and create recommendations for action pathways to take advantage of these observations. The best timing for a management team to conduct these activities is in synchronization with its strategic planning

---

5. In its feedback report to Nokia, the examiners for the European Quality Award described the level of their scoring as between 750 and 800 points. In the 13 years that the MBNQA and MBNAQ had existed, no other company had scored at this level on the consensus review by the board of examiners. In recognition of his individual leadership in marshalling the human potential of NMP during this time, NMP CEO Pekka Ala-Pietilä was awarded the Kaoru Ishikawa Medal by the American Society for Quality.

THE GROWTH OF NOKIA MOBILE PHONES

Nokia released its first portable phone, the Mobira Senator, to the market in 1982, followed by Talkman in 1986. In 1987, the Cityman phone introduced the mobile handset format. The first GSM phone, a Nokia 1011, was sold in 1992. By then Nokia Mobile Phones had 3,147 employees, contributed less than 20 percent of the total revenue to the company's annual turnover of 3.056 billion euros, and had 17 percent of the global market share for cellular phone handsets. The next six years were marked by growth and turbulence, but by 1998, NMP had 18,627 employees, contributed 60 percent of the total annual revenue of 13.326 billion euros, and enjoyed almost 25 percent of the global market share—making it the industry leader!

This period is divided into three eras. In 1992 to 1996, NMP experienced extensive growth in mobile phone sales. In 1992, Nokia had adopted "Connecting People" to identify its brand and established a 25-year brand development strategy to become the global leader in mobile telephone market share. In 1994 to 1995, Nokia sold 20 million phones worldwide. The years from 1995 to 1997 were a period of growing pains and turbulence caused by both product quality and logistical issues, which made Nokia twice issue shareholder profit warnings. Nokia corrected these problems by reengineering its core business processes, while implementing the Six Sigma toolkit. Finally, in 1997 to 1998, NMP recovered to become the global market share leader.

Did NMP create an enduring heritage? This is a difficult question. This business changes within a period of months; therefore, unlike conventional businesses, this question must be answered within the span of relatively a few years. However, consider the results of the following four years (1998 to 2002). Just two years later, NMP European regional operations won the 2000 European Quality Award—receiving the highest-ever score from an assessment team. And by 2002, Nokia sales had grown to just over 30 billion euros, with 77 percent coming from the mobile phone operations that now enjoyed 38 percent market share. Based on this strong evidence, it may be concluded that the quality foundation NMP established has continued to mature and that it was one of the drivers behind this sustained commercial success.

What was the true reason for this exceptional success? It was the people who self-regulated their work and adapted to the many challenges that made this success happen!

process, as this would align the allocation of resources for these action pathways with a fresh view of the priority and availability of resources for an aggressive pursuit of the organization's top objectives. If these studies are not sequenced with the planning process, then they will result in a need to reprioritize resources and could potentially create managerial rework, as the business strategy and its underlying assumptions must be revisited to assure that they are being served properly. Greater synergy occurs in the process of management when strategic benchmarking is a prerequisite to creating a strategic plan. Additionally, when the projects derived from these studies are mainstreamed into an organization's priorities and commitments for its near-term plans then strategic benchmarking studies maximize their competitive contributions to the organization's success.

LESSONS LEARNED: STRATEGIC BENCHMARKING FOCUSES ORGANIZATIONAL RESOURCES

The result of those benchmarking studies that have an impact on strategy should be the creation of a project, or set of projects, to rapidly pursue the competitive advantage that is spotlighted by the study. As was the case in this Nokia study, change projects may involve a variety of project types, including capital equipment acquisition, development of new products or modification of the features of current products, entry into new markets or the pursuit of poorly addressed markets, and design or improvement of operational business or work processes. Managing such a complex system of change also requires new management styles and presents new challenges.[6] The way management chooses how to allocate its resources is one of its most important business practices as the scarce resources of time, money, and equipment does not readily lend itself to rework or an ability to recover waste as in physical processes. Once management dedicates its resources to a track of action, it is often unable to recover these same resources, and then it will need to reinvest additional resources on these

---

6. This subject was first pursued in *Business Systems Engineering* (New York: Wiley, 1994).

same objectives. Repeating this process represents a waste of both shareholder value as well the human energy of your people—and this will demotivate both investors and employees! Doing the right thing right the first time is always the least expensive way of creating success!

THE COMING ATTRACTION

In the next chapter, we dissect an operational benchmarking study to understand how the specific steps in this methodology are applied to investigate a business practice in order to improve performance results.

CHAPTER 8

Performing an Operational Benchmarking Study

Step by step walk the thousand-mile road.

— MIYAMOTO MUSASHI

LEAN PRODUCTION AS A BEST PRACTICE

In a study of over 275 participating organizations by the Aberdeen Group (Boston, MA), it was observed that 87 percent of the companies had some internal capability or expertise on the lean methods, while less than 40 percent had implemented all of the key elements of the Toyota Production System (TPS) throughout their organization.[1] This represents a similar finding for the level of dissemination than has been reported for Six Sigma, where an estimated 40 percent of the Fortune 500 companies have implemented an effective Six Sigma program.[2] This observation is a little difficult to accept, as Six Sigma methods also include these lean tools as part of their improvement toolkit and, thus, one would expect to observe a slightly higher level of lean deployment. However, two things are clear—first, lean production is broadly accepted as a

1. The Aberdeen Group, *Lean Strategies Benchmark Report* (June 2004). This free report is available to be downloaded as a PDF file from the Aberdeen Group at www.aberdeen.com.
2. This was reported by Michael Marx on www.sixsigmacompanies.com, 31 August 2006.

sound practice for operational excellence, and second, lean production is particularly interesting because it does not require the extensive training or the advanced statistical methods of Six Sigma. As a result, more companies find lean methods attractive — and the frequency of application for these lean methods has been increasing since the late 1990s. Thus, the operational benchmarking of the lean production system of Toyota is a particularly interesting case study.

Much has been written about TPS by both its originators and academic observers as well as by imitators seeking to emulate Toyota's success.[3] Some of these implementations have been highly successful — for instance, it is difficult to distinguish differences between a Honda factory and one operated by Toyota. However, not everyone finds that it is easy to put together all of the elements of TPS into a coherent company strategy for business improvement. The approach taken in this study will be to identify the TPS elements and then to put them into a process that may be assimilated in a Six Sigma DMAIC framework.

3. Masaaki Imai, *Kaizen: The Key to Japan's Competitive Success* (New York: McGraw-Hill, 1986); Masaaki Imai, *Gemba Kaizen* (New York: McGraw-Hill, 1997); Anthony C. Laraia, Patricia E. Moody, and Robert W. Hall, *The Kaizen Blitz: Accelerating Breakthroughs in Productivity and Performance* (New York: Wiley, 1999); Takashi Osada, *The 5 S's: Five Keys to a Total Quality Environment* (Tokyo: Asian Productivity Organization, 1991); Jeffrey K. Liker, *The Toyota Way: Fourteen Management Principles from the World's Greatest Manufacturer* (New York: McGraw-Hill, 2003); James P. Womach, Daniel T. Jones, and Daniel Roos, *The Machine That Changed the World* (New York: MacMillan, 1990); James P. Womach and Daniel T. Jones, *Lean Thinking* (New York: Simon & Schuster, 1996, 2003); David J. Lu, *Kanban-Just-in-Time at Toyota,* ed. Japan Management Association (Portland, OR: Productivity Press, 1989); Shigeo Shingo, *A Study of Toyota Production System,* trans. Andrew P. Dillon (Portland, OR: Productivity Press, 1990); Iwo Kobayashi, *20 Keys to Workplace Improvement* (Portland, OR: Productivity Press, 1995); Michael L. George, *Lean Six Sigma: Combining Six Sigma Quality with Lean Production Speed* (New York: McGraw-Hill, 2002); Michael L. George, David Rowlands, and Bill Kastle, *What is Lean Six Sigma?* (New York: McGraw-Hill, 2004); Shigeo Shingo, *Zero Quality Control: Source Inspection and the Poka-Yoke System* (Portland, OR: Productivity Press, 1986); Shigeo Shingo and Andrew P. Dillon, *Revolution in Manufacturing: The SMED System* (Portland, OR: Productivity Press, 1985); Shigeo Shingo, *The Non-Stock Production System: The Shingo System of Continuous Improvement* (Portland, OR: Productivity Press, 1988); Shigeo Shingo and Andrew P. Dillon, *Study of the Toyota Production System from the Point of View of an Industrial Engineer* (Portland, OR: Productivity Press, 1995); and Taichi Ohno, *The Toyota Production System: Beyond Large-Scale Production* (Portland, OR: Productivity Press, 1995).

Benchmarking lean business improvement practices will require an understanding of the story of Toyota and will focus on defining the key philosophies and methods of TPS as: (1) a means to understand what is important, and (2) how to creatively imitate the TPS by applying an imaginative understanding of the system. As Shigeo Shingo, the chief industrial engineer behind the TPS, said: "You have to learn not only the 'know how' but also the 'know why' in order to understand the system." This is similar to the quotation we cited earlier where Dr. Deming focused on the need for understanding the theory behind what is done in order to make improvements. How does one learn the theory?

This need to learn the theory behind the best practice presents one of the chief problems in benchmarking in such a large production system — the tendency to see only part of its whole. This is like the joke about the blind men who feel an elephant and try to explain what it is like from their local experience in touching the trunk, ear, leg, and tail!

Perhaps a real-world experience that happened while at HP while benchmarking the quality systems of the Japanese would help to explain this need better. The study team was visiting the Fujitsu factory outside of Tokyo and had been frustrated because over many trips they had seen many tools that helped to create quality, but they had not found an integrating principle. The team decided to take a fresh look at this factory and noticed one anomaly as they entered the factory. By the main entrance there were the obligatory charts tracking the performance of the factory, but above them was a Shinto Shrine. The Shire provided a unique cultural insight as there were offerings there to the ancestors and under the Shrine were the performance indicators of the factory — was this another type of offering? In Japan, natural resources are scarce, and the Japanese pay attention to how resources are used — so reducing waste is a very natural activity. It was almost as if the performance indicators were describing to the gods that we are careful in this factory about how we consume resources, and here is the evidence that we are not wasteful! Whether this interpretation is correct is not as important as the fact that the management team in the factory lived this way — reduction of waste was a religious quest for them—and each item of waste was avidly un-covered and conscientiously destroyed!

What is the key learning about Toyota that helps to unlock the intri-cacies of its many well-documented best practices? The first step to take is to recognize that the TPS is actually more of a learning system for mak-ing knowledge about processes explicit.

TOYOTA PRODUCTION SYSTEM—ACTUALLY TOYOTA LEARNING SYSTEM!

The learning system that is built into the TPS is based on the premise that one must know the profound detail about process knowledge. Perhaps the Japanese approach to lean starts with an attitude, just as we observed in the Fujitsu factory—that waste is evil and must be eliminated by the coordinated activity of everyone in the factory. Just what is this activity, and how does it get coordinated is the subject of this study? This study will talk about the TPS, as what I consider the Toyota Learning System (TLS)—this learning began at the turn of the twentieth century and was accelerated during a post-World War II benchmarking visit to Ford by the late Taichi Ohno (1912–1990), who was to become the future vice president for global manufacturing at Toyota. The five topics that I will use to help us understand the experience called the *Toyota production sys-tem* are the following:

- Improvement of TPS was stimulated by benchmarking Ford and a grocery store.
- Internal experience is captured in a learning system for continuous improvement.
- Continuous improvement maintains the performance of the TPS knowledge.
- Standards provide a base for holding gains and making further improvements.
- Personal accountability and work discipline hold the TPS process together.

BENCHMARKING AS A STIMULUS FOR CREATION OF THE TOYOTA PRODUCTION SYSTEM

The TPS actually began at the beginning of the twentieth century with the development of *jidoka* (man-machine integration) in their textile plants. Before Ohno worked for Toyota Motor Company, he worked as an entry-level engineer at their textile company Toyoda Boshoku (Toyota Spinning Company) where, in 1924, Sakichi Toyoda, founder of the Toyota Group, created jidoka (which is also called *autonomation* and together with Just-in-Time [JIT] is part of the TPS foundation). The innovation in this application that Toyota created was that the loom machine would run automatically, but it would stop whenever the thread broke or the machine ran out of material. The key is that this prevents the automatic loom from producing defects. This concept of built-in quality made this invention unique and established a key cornerstone of the TPS.[4]

In his book describing the development of the Toyota Production System, Ohno told of their post-World War II efforts at benchmarking:

> Following World War II, American products flowed into Japan—chewing gum and Coca-Cola, even the Jeep. The first U.S. style supermarket appeared in the mid-1950's. And as more and more Japanese people visited the United States, they saw the intimate relationship between the supermarket and the style of daily life in America. Consequently, this type of store became the rage in Japan due to Japanese curiosity and fondness for imitation.[5]

Indeed, when Ohno and a team of Toyota professionals visited America to observe the Ford Production System at its legendary River Rouge

---

4. Taiichi Ohno and Setsuo Mito describe much of this system in two books that are now out of print: *Workplace Management* (Gemba Keiei) (Portland, OR: Productivity Press, 1988) and *Just-in-Time for Today and Tomorrow* (Portland, OR: Productivity Press, 1988).

5. Taiichi Ohno (Setsuo Mito [editor]), *Toyota Production System: Beyond Large-Scale Production* (Portland, OR: Productivity Press, 1990), 25–26.

209

plant, the greatest lessons that they learned came from the first-hand observation of a supermarket! Undeniably, Ohno had adapted his personal observations of the supermarket by using their shelf restocking methods as an analogy for development of the Just-in-Time (JIT) inventory management system that is a hallmark of the Toyota system. "From the supermarket we got the idea of viewing the earlier process in a production line as a kind of store."[6] This supermarket analogy provided Ohno with an example of an enabling process from which he developed the kanban system for inventory flow management.

By all potential measures, the original Toyota benchmarking visit to the Ford River Rouge car factory was a dismal failure. Ohno had hoped to discover from Ford some improvement ideas about how to manage full-scale production while operating on limited resources; however, what they observed a factory characterized by waste. The River Rouge factory received raw material and produced automobiles on one continuous flow line. However, by-products of the output were scattered everywhere in a disarray of scrap, waste, and inventory. The conclusion that Ohno and his team made from their assessment was that they could not afford to have such a wasteful production system. It was from this benchmarking visit to Ford, triangulated with their observations of the supermarket, that Toyota shifted their focus to waste elimination.[7]

In a *Harvard Business Review* article, Steven J. Spear noted that at Toyota, the entire workplace is a laboratory for learning. The processes of work are observed with the same diligence as one conducts a scientific experiment in the laboratory. All proposed changes are structured as experiments with hypotheses that are tested using the scientific method to determine if the change causes a difference in performance results. Management seeks change by encouraging workers to conduct many small

6. Ibid.

7. *Triangulation* is a process by which you can determine one piece of knowledge by monitoring the location of three other observations or competitive positions. In benchmarking, triangulation studies a phenomenon by comparing three (or more) data sources or competitors to determine a previously unknown direction.

experiments as often as possible with the outcome of continuously improving their work processes. The job of managers in this learning system is to coach workers through this learning experience in order to discover how to improve the system. The job of managers is not to fix the system by their own activity, but to involve the workers as students who must be guided through the learning activity.[8]

OPERATING CHARACTERISTICS OF THE TOYOTA PRODUCTION SYSTEM

At Toyota, the work flows from the customer order to the production process to create the output that the customer ordered. In this process, design of the flow is perhaps the most important critical success factor. Indeed, the flow itself could be considered the key genetic material of this production system, and its DNA has been defined by Spear as a series of rules that are embedded in the specification of the work processes:

- "All work shall be highly specified as to content, sequence, timing and outcome.
- Every customer-supplier connection must be direct and there must be an unambiguous yes-or-no way to send requests and receive responses.
- The pathway for every product or service must be simple and direct.
- Any improvement must be made in accordance with the scientific method, under the guidance of a teacher, at the lowest level in an organization."[9]

These rules are applied to design of work processes and their continuous improvement. It is this structure that defines the Toyota learning

---

8. Steven J. Spear, "Learning to Lead at Toyota," *Harvard Business Review* May (2004).

9. Steven J. Spear and H. Kent Bowen, "Decoding the DNA of the Toyota Production System," *Harvard Business Review* September-October (1999).

experience—the student is never wrong; it is the teacher who hasn't explained well enough for others to learn. Dr. Deming called this "common-cause variation"—variation induced by the management system, which will restrict the capability of workers to perform. Thus, it is the obligation of management to eliminate those activities that restrict the capability of the workers to perform in an ideal way. How does the teacher guide the students to root out waste? One of the principles of the Toyota system is that "when the student is ready, the teacher will come."[10]

ELEMENTS OF THE TOYOTA PRODUCTION SYSTEM

How does the teacher know that the student is ready in the Toyota Production System? It is a simple answer—the visual factory shows the teacher that a student is ready—mostly because they have an urgent problem that they cannot resolve themselves! They had to stop production because they could not resolve the problem, and therefore it is time for the teacher to come to help the student. Stopping the production line is a signal of an out-of-control condition and also a request for help in applying the scientific method to fix a problem that the workers (students) cannot fix themselves. How does the teacher resolve these problems? This is the key focus of the Toyota system—eliminating waste in the process. Five actions are taken in this activity:

1. "Define value precisely from the perspective of the end customer in terms of a specific product with specific capabilities (features and performance) that is offered at a specific price and time.
2. Identify the value stream for each product or product family and eliminate waste.
3. Make the remaining value-creating steps flow.

---

10. Gregory H. Watson, "Cycles of Learning: Observations of Jack Welch," *Six Sigma Forum Magazine* 1 no. 1 (2001): 13.

4. Design and provide what the customer wants only when the customer wants it.
5. Pursue perfection."[11]

The TPS focuses on eliminating waste and adding value. In Japanese, the word for waste is *muda*. This single-minded concentration of the TPS on eliminating waste and adding value is achieved through application of a number of tools and methods that are dedicated to this effort. Different types of waste apply different tools and methods to achieve their ideal level of performance (perfection or the ideal is defined from the viewpoint of the final customer). The activities involved in this pursuit include the following:

- Identify the process flow, and define tasks as value adding or non-value adding from the perspective of the final customer.
- Eliminate the *eight wastes* from the process through use of lean tools.
- Minimize all required non-value adding activity remaining in the process.
- Assure constant flow of the remaining process steps so that everything works or nothing works and people are focused on improvement.
- Match the rate of flow of the process and the assignment of work to the people based on the flow of customer orders as the demand-pull signal.
- Seek perfection by continuously improving the process by eliminating waste.

With this strong focus on waste and its elimination it is clear that Toyota derives great improvement by matching tools to the types of waste that must be eliminated. Table 8.1 presents a breakdown of how the specific tools and methods employed in the TPS address each of the different types of muda that were identified by Taichi Ohno:

11. James P. Womack and Daniel T. Jones, "Beyond Toyota: How to Root Out Waste and Pursue Perfection," *Harvard Business Review* September-October (1996).

Table 8.1 Linkage of the eight wastes to the TPS tools and methods

Types of Waste	Elements of the TPS That Apply
1. *Transportation:* Excessive movement of people, information, parts, or products, resulting in wasted time, effort, and cost.	• Process and workflow analysis • 5-S housekeeping • Standard work and visual factory • One-piece flow, *kanban* pull system
2. *Inventory:* Excessive storage and delay of information or goods, resulting in poor customer service and unnecessary cost.	• Process and workflow analysis • 5-S housekeeping • One-piece flow, *kanban* pull system • Just-in-Time production • Load leveling
3. *Motion:* Poor workplace organization, resulting in poor ergonomics (excessive bending, stretching, reaching, etc.) and frequently misplaced work in process.	• Process and workflow analysis • 5-S housekeeping • Time and motion studies • *Jidoka* man-machine integration • *Heijunka* workload management
4. *Intellect:* Failing to engage, apply, and use the knowledge, skills, competence, or capability of workers to improve the quality of the work they perform, which results in decreased motivation and lack of commitment to the quality of the work they do.	• Process and workflow analysis • 5-S housekeeping • Time and motion studies • Suggestion systems • *Kaizen Blitz* • Standard work and visual factory • Autonomous maintenance • Quality responsibility
5. *Waiting:* Long periods of inactivity for people, information, or goods resulting in poor work flow and long cycle times.	• 5-S housekeeping • Time and motion studies • One-piece flow, *kanban* pull system • Just-in-Time production • Single minute exchange of die (SMED) • Total productive maintenance (TPM) • *Heijunka* workload management

(continued)

214

Table 8.1 (continued)

Types of Waste	Elements of the TPS That Apply
6. *Overprocessing:* Applying too much technology or using the wrong tools or procedures in a work process when a simpler and less costly approach may be more effective.	• 5-S housekeeping • *Jidoka* man-machine interface • Value analysis • Just-in-Time production • *Heijunka* workload management • Poka yoke mistake proofing • Skills charting
7. *Overproduction:* Producing too much or too soon, resulting in poor information flow and excess inventory.	• 5-S housekeeping • One-piece flow, *kanban* pull system • *Heijunka* workload management • Just-in-Time production
8. *Defects:* Frequent errors in paperwork, product quality, or delivery performance, leading to excessive cost and decreased customer satisfaction.	• 5-S housekeeping • Six Sigma DMAIC analysis • Standard work and visual factory • Poka yoke mistake proofing

The next step in the operational benchmarking of the TPS is to define what each of these tools and methods does and how they are used to continuously improve Toyota. This is summarized in Table 8.2.

This collection of best practices is a potpourri of improvement methods. How does it fit together as a repeatable system? What should one do to make improvement at a work-process level? How are these tools integrated into an improvement methodology? Should a manager choose one tool and deploy it—followed by another one? Which tools should be chosen in what priority order? What works best?

Gaining profound knowledge of how this system operates requires creative imitation to develop of a sound theory for process improvement based on the integration of these methods into a consistent practice for work-process management. This requires a new effort in operational benchmarking to integrate and streamline the observed best practices prior to recommending them for implementation. How does this work? Let's apply this principle to these methods and practices of lean production.

Table 8.2 The tools and methods of the TPS

Tools and Methods of the TPS	Description
Process and Workflow Analysis	Mapping the activities of the work process to determine travel time, flow, cycle time, inventory location, and also to identify the tasks as value adding or non-value adding.
5-S Housekeeping	The process of organizing the environment of work so it is clean, safe, ordered in a rational structure, and easy for operators to perform their tasks.
Waste Reduction	The dedicated removal of all types of waste from the work process, plus minimization of all required non-value adding work.
Single Minute Exchange of Dies (SMED)	The streamlining of set-up or change-over time in the production process—the time it takes to transition from one product or part to another at the full production line level or just at the location of an individual piece of production equipment.
One-Piece Flow	Eliminating the batch-and-queue process from production by making all work flow in single production units and only using minimal buffer inventory to maintain the smooth flow of production.
Heijunka *Workload Management*	Balancing of production line activities to the takt time, equalizing workloads, and synchronized, level production.
Just-in-Time Production	Reduction of lead times, reducing levels of defects toward zero, minimizing inventory, and working at minimum cost.

(continued)

Table 8.2 (continued)

Tools and Methods of the TPS	Description
Kanban *Pull System*	A visual record that helps to maintain the flow of parts inventory or work.
Jidoka *Man-Machine Interface*	People make judgments—equipment does the work. Failsafe equipment operations to keep it from making defects. People stop production to fix any defective conditions.
Standard Work	The one best way to perform a job. Also, standard work is the basis from which any process improvement is judged. Standard work includes the takt time, standard work in process (buffer inventory), standard operating procedures (SOP) or tasks to be done by the operator, and the control plan that allows operators to self-regulate the quality of their own work.
Visually Controlled Factory	Visual controls help to communicate the key requirements for producing standard work—these controls are reinforced by operator cross-training and self-inspection for quality of your own work outputs.
Poka Yoke Mistake-Proofing	The process for striving to eliminate the opportunity for mistakes at the source by using controls, warnings, or shutdowns to prevent errors from occurring.
Kaizen *Continuous Improvement*	A system for continuous, incremental work process improvement that focuses on the responsibility of the workers to improve the quality of their own output by reducing waste, improving consistency, and checking the conformity of their work.

LEARNING FROM EXPERIENCE AND CONTINUOUS IMPROVEMENT

We will follow a two-step approach in seeking to define a system of tools and methods for integration into another organization's continuous improvement program. First, we must provide a structure for how these tools may be applied in a continuous improvement project, and then we should fit them into the Six Sigma generic problem-solving process so that the lean tools are integrated with the statistical tools for process improvement.

Of course, it is not necessary that the TPS toolkit be used with the Six Sigma DMAIC framework in any particular problem-solving situation. The system that is presented in the following can be used for process improvement without linking it to Six Sigma; however, a generic problem-solving method must be capable of addressing all problems — even the ones that cannot be solved at the workplace. Thus, the most powerful problem-solving approach would be to integrate the toolkit for both workers with the methods used by their technical support team, which must attach those problems that the workers are not able to solve themselves.

The first step toward developing this integrated problem-solving approach was performed in a workshop of Master Black Belts that was conducted in late 2005. The team studied the affinity of the lean production tools and methods and their sequencing in a number of situations for problem solving in order to determine a natural flow for these improvement methods. The result of this effort was the development of what we called a 10-S approach to lean management. This approach builds on the elements of the TPS and is a natural extension of the 5-S housekeeping method that is fundamental to all of the waste elimination methods identified above. The 10-S approach can be summarized in Table 8.3.

What is the specific activity that occurs in each of these 10 steps?

1. *Study:*
   - Conduct a lean maturity self-assessment of your processes.
   - Develop an as-is state value stream map of key focus areas.
   - Analyze the lean performance measures of your process.

Table 8.3 The 10-S approach to integrating the tools of the TPS

Elements of the 10-S Approach	Summary Description
Study	Analyze work to find waste and value losses.
Sort	Divide work into categories according to value.
Sanitize	Clean the workplace to make waste visible.
Systematize	Organize the flow of the work activity.
Streamline	Eliminate unnecessary activities.
Simulate	Check work performance prior to change.
Synchronize	Set the timing for optimal work flow.
Safeguard	Eliminate the possibility of mistakes.
Standardize	Assure all work follows the standard.
Self-Discipline	Consistently perform and improve.

- Identify issues and performance concerns regarding waste.
- Identify problem areas in cycle time flow.
- Identify areas of process variation (ANOVA).
- Test significance of performance differences (hypothesis test).
- Brainstorm potential root causes of problem areas (5 Whys).
- Prioritize areas of improvement opportunity.

2. *Sort:*
   - Perform a spaghetti map of your organization's work flow to determine the distance traveled for the value stream flow.
   - Sort work activities into categories of value according to the customer benefit: value added, essential, set-up, non-value added, administrative, and unnecessary work.
   - Identify the time spent in each category along the work flow of the process.
   - Calculate the ideal or theoretical cycle time only by using all optimized value added and required activities.
   - Calculate differences between actual and theoretical times.

219

3. *Sanitize:*
   - Remove all unnecessary items from the work environment (i.e., tools, equipment, etc.) and place in a red-tag zone for disposition.
   - Return all unnecessary, usable parts and material to their correct location in inventory for in a first-in/first-out basis.
   - Clean the operating equipment and work space so all dirt is removed and the environment appears spotless visually.
   - Paint equipment to return it to its original operating condition.
   - Develop a sanitization schedule to maintain cleanliness and link this schedule to routine equipment maintenance.

4. *Systematize:*
   - Publish visual images of good and bad actions for workers.
   - Paint the work area to clarify the flow of work, identify the standard locations for storage of required equipment and material, and define areas that are hazardous to workers.
   - Identify set-up kits of tools and material used at changeover.
   - Organize material and parts at the workstation for ease of access, and assure that material and parts only arrive as they are needed to fulfill the daily operational demand.
   - Arrange tools in shadow boxes for easy visual identification.
   - Post performance measures to summarize work outcomes.

5. *Streamline:*
   - Evaluate all work procedures to eliminate red-tape policies.
   - Eliminate all unnecessary work activity from the operations.
   - Reduce the transportation distance in all material flows.
   - Minimize time expended on essential or required work.
   - Organize all human activity for minimal motion and effort.
   - Automate repetitive activity to improve performance.
   - Automate the flow of material using *kanban* system logic.
   - Reduce the amount of paperwork and reports prepared.
   - Automate measurement recording and monitoring by alarm.

6. *Simulate:*
   - Prepare a simulation model of the work process for use as a test bed for process improvement suggestions.

- Validate the simulation model against actual process results.
- Identify potential process changes for hypothesis testing.
- Perform many small experiments to indicate impact potential of proposed changes on the operating process.
- Confirm simulation results with process demonstration tests.
- Conduct worst-case analysis at the extremes of the process operating envelope to assure robustness of the process at its most severe operating conditions.

7. *Synchronize:*
   - Define the takt time for the operation based on order rate.
   - Establish targeted cycle times for all of the work processes.
   - Map the relationship of process cycle time and takt time.
   - Identify bottlenecks where cycle time exceeds takt time.
   - Evaluate work tasks that can be reordered to smooth flow at the bottleneck process: then redistribute and balance tasks.
   - Cross-train operators to assure that tasks can be distributed.
   - Test operators to assure process capability for new skills.
   - Conduct a pilot run of production process changes before the process is released for full-scale operations.

8. *Safeguard:*
   - Evaluate work activities to determine where potential failure opportunities exist and their impact on customer activity.
   - Eliminate opportunities for inadvertent mistakes at the origin of the opportunity before it escapes to become an error.
   - Reduce the severity of inadvertent errors so that the impact is not felt by the customer.
   - Improve the detection systems so that error conditions may be anticipated and preventive actions taken.
   - Design mistake-proofing devices into the production system by applying "Design for Manufacturability and Assembly."

9. *Standardize:*
   - Establish work standards for each task to be performed.
   - Document work standards as operating procedures, and use visual methods to define their limits of quality performance.

- Develop standardized measurement systems that predict the outcome of work that deliver business results.
- Assure that each job has a well-defined procedure, a testing method to assure compliance with the procedure, and means to self-regulate and adjust work when performance diverges.
- Establish performance monitoring and reporting systems that make accomplishments visible and encourage rapid action.

10. *Self-Discipline:*
    - Continue efforts for work improvement day-in and day-out.
    - Develop self-assessment processes for operators to accept the personal responsibility to perform self-service activities at their workstation — this supports management monitoring.
    - Conduct regular communication meetings to review progress and provide feedback on continuous improvement efforts.
    - Develop a sharing mechanism so that lessons learned from improvement projects and actions are distributed widely.
    - Develop a recognition process to assure that all improvement activities are reinforced by positive management attention.

How should this 10-step process be implemented in a factory environment?

Implementing Lean in a Factory Environment

Creation of a lean production system requires that improvements be made at two levels of performance: the factorywide production-system level and the workstation-task level. At each of these levels, there are slightly different performance measurement systems that are employed as well as different artifacts that identify the environment as belonging to a lean production system. In addition, there are also different sets of assessment questions that would be used to evaluate progress on the lean journey. The following sections will describe how these two levels of lean operation are distinguished.

First, we will look at the performance of the lean factory as an entire operation. We should note that lean production should follow lean design in order to maximize the full commercial opportunity for a product. Lean must be a total system, as products that are late to the market can never really achieve their full potential profitability, and emphasis on lean never gains enough momentum because they don't endure in the market long enough for the time-based, incremental improvements of lean systems to drive enough of an effect.[12]

How should an organization measure its own performance in order to determine if it is in need of a further dietary dose of lean projects? Consider Table 8.4, which presents a set of measures that can provide insight into lean performance from the viewpoint of the entire production operation.

While the measurement of the factory will demonstrate how lean it is performing, direct observation of its operations should also expose the lean artifacts that indicate the degree of leanness at which that the factory is being operated. Some of these artifacts are described in Table 8.5.

In a similar manner, lean measurements and artifacts may be observed at the workstation level when a lean production system has been fully deployed to the frontline level of the operational environment. The lean performance indicators of the workstation and artifacts that are associated with lean production at the workstation level are illustrated in Tables 8.6 and 8.7.

After establishing this degree of understanding how lean production relates to the factory environment, we can turn our attention to how the 10-S process is integrated into the five steps of the Six Sigma DMAIC problem-solving process. This is an essential aspect of the lean theory as lean methods, by themselves, do not offer a conceptual framework or an integrating principle that defines how the individual methods operate synergistically to produce sustained performance gains. It seems that there are two aspects to such a long-term systems integration — one involved in the execution of the lean tools as part of an improvement project (this

---

12. Robert S. Kaplan and David P. Norton, *The Balanced Scorecard: Translating Strategy into Action* (Boston: Harvard Business School Press, 1996), 101–104.

Table 8.4 Lean performance measures

Lean Organization-Wide Operational Measures

Operational performance measures monitored at the factory level in monthly increments using a 12-month rolling trend.

Measure	Definition
Customer Takt Time	Time available for production divided by number of customer-shippable units required during a specified time period (typically one month).
Order Turnaround Time (OTAT)	Time from placement of the order by a customer to delivery fulfillment of the order to the customer (installed and certified for operation).
Factory Cycle Time	Time from the initiation of the production process (ordering of parts) to placing the product in finished goods inventory.
Operational Availability (A_o)	Uptime divided by uptime plus downtime.
Production Throughput	The delivery rate of products that are matched to customer sales.
Rolled Throughput Yield (RTY)	The product obtained by multiplying the first pass yield of each independent step in the sequence of the flow of production operations.
Product/Model Changeover Time	The cycle time from production of the last unit of the prior product or model made in a manufacturing facility to the production of the first unit of the next product or model.
Process Cycle Time Efficiency ($A\Delta T$)	The ratio of the actual cycle time (factory cycle time) to the theoretical cycle time (the cycle time for only the value adding steps of the production flow).
Product Travel	The distance that raw materials and product assemblies flow from the initiation of production to the final movement to ship a product from the factory.

(continued)

Table 8.4 (continued)

Measure	Definition
Floor Space Required	The amount of floor space reserved for operations related to the production of a specific product.
Number of Job Categories	The number of unique job descriptions or work categories whose skills or competence are required to produce a product.
Operator Cross-Training	The number of jobs that an operator is trained to perform in a production operation.
Finished Goods Inventory (FGI)	The number of production units that have been completed and are ready for shipment to fulfill customer orders.
Total Inventory (Value)	The total financial value of raw material, work-in-process, and finished goods inventory.
Work-in-Process	The amount of inventory that supports the current production of units and that may be measured in terms of pieces in queue or days on hand of inventory that are supporting the productivity of throughput.
In-Process Defects Detected	The total number of defects detected in the production process, which is decomposed by the root cause, failure code, or type of observation (e.g., mechanical, process, electrical, etc.) and is typically displayed using a Pareto diagram.
In-Process Scrap	The cost of the material that has been scrapped or rejected during the process of production.
Cost Per Transaction	The total cost of production for a product-model combination as divided by the total number of units produced over a fixed period of time.

(continued)

Table 8.4 (continued)

Measure	Definition
Breakeven Time (BET)	The time to achieve payback of an investment from the time of project initiation to the time it returns the investment, plus the cost of capital (as calculated using the discounted cash flow method).
Production Effectiveness	The product obtained by multiplying availability (A_o) by efficiency ($A\Delta T$) and yield (RTY).

Table 8.5 Lean evidence—Factorywide level

Lean Artifact	Description
Visible Factory	Location of *andon* lights, tool shadow boards, painted floors, quality standards, *kanban* cards, performance summary records, and photo boards.
Material Flow Lines	A single piece flow moving in a straight line with little to no inventory between work stations and no evident material bottlenecks in the flow.
Online Supply Storage	Required consumable supplies are stored online and readily accessible to operators for replenishment.
Online Part Storage	Production parts are provided to operators as they are needed to produce the assembly. Material handlers support production by replenishing parts prior to depletion.
Discrepant Material Segregation	Incoming material that does not conform to quality requirements is segregated from material that is approved for production and is kept separate so that it cannot possibly be converted into production use.

(continued)

Table 8.5 (continued)

Lean Artifact	Description
Workstation Ergonomics	The work environment is designed for ease of use by the operators to assure that it is both safe and physically stress-free.
Equipment Layout	Equipment is laid out so that it is flows in a straight line or a *U* shape and minimizes the interoperator distance for material flow.
Work Standards	Visible work standards including quality check procedures are used to train workers in the right way to conduct work operations and evaluate goodness of the work output.
Performance Records	Performance documentation and reports are visible and maintained current.

Table 8.6 Lean performance—Workstation level

Lean Workstation Operational Measures

Operational workstation level measures are monitored daily with weekly increments that are reported using a quarterly trend analysis.

Measure	Definition
Cycle Time	Time from initial acceptance of input from the prior process to passing of the completed work to the next process.
Operational Availability (A_o)	Workstation uptime divided by uptime plus downtime.
First Pass Yield	The percentage of production produced at the workstation that passes the in-process quality test for performance without being scrapped, rerun, reworked, retested or returned, or diverted for off-line repair.

(continued)

Table 8.6 (continued)

Measure	Definition
Process Cycle Time Efficiency (A∆T)	The ratio of the actual cycle time of the workstation to the theoretical cycle time (the cycle time for only the value adding actions of the operator).
Value Added Time	The time component of the workstation cycle time, which is value adding based on customer value perceptions.
Non-Value Added Time	The total of all time that is not value added.
Required Time	The component of non-value adding time that is required and cannot be eliminated from the process (it must be kept for legal, regulatory, or for pragmatic reasons and, therefore, must be minimized in any improvement strategy).
Waiting Time	The component of non-value adding time that the flow of material is halted and no value adding activity is being performed.
Material Movement Time	The component of non-value adding time that the material is in transit or moving on the line, and no value adding activity is being performed.
Product/Model Changeover Time	The component of non-value adding time that the workstation is down due to the need to reconfigure the equipment or material flow, in order to accommodate the production requirements of a new product or model.
Product Travel	The distance that raw materials and product assemblies flow from the beginning of a process step to the start of the next production step (this may be measured in inches or centimeters).

(continued)

Table 8.6 (continued)

Measure	Definition
Floor Space Required	The amount of floor space (square feet or square meters) that is reserved for the operation of a workstation and its related material flow activities.
Operator Cross-Training	The number of job categories that operators are trained to perform so that there is no reliance on a single person to do a single job.
Work-in-Process	The amount of raw material and subassemblies that supports the current at the workstation and that may be measured in terms of pieces in queue or days on hand of inventory that are supporting the conversion of input into output.
In-Process Defects Detected	The number of defects by failure code that are produced at the workstation.
In-Process Scrap	The amount of scrap by part number produced at the workstation.
Cost Per Transaction	The incremental cost that is added to a product during the total cycle time at the workstation (activity-based cost), net allocated costs.
Workstation Effectiveness	The product obtained by multiplying availability (A_o) by efficiency ($A\Delta T$) and yield (RTY) for the specific workstation.

Table 8.7 Lean evidence—Workstation level

Lean Artifact	Description
Visible Work Standards	Where appropriate, *andon* lights, tool shadow boards, painted floors, quality standards, *kanban* cards, performance summary records, or photo boards are used to increase operator awareness of production and quality issues.
Performance Measurement System	Measurement of the performance of a workstation in terms of key indicators (productivity, quality, safety, etc.), which are visible to the workers and maintained on a regular basis.
Ergonomic Operator Station	The conditions of the workstation have been adjusted to the physical stature of the operator and steps have been taken to eliminate repetitive stress by introducing fatigue-reducing and injury-prevention methods.
Workstation Material Flow	Material moves across the workstation continuously in a one-piece flow.
Work-in-Process and Raw Material Buffers	Workstation inventory has been reduced to a minimum, and material buffers are managed to assure smooth flow of production.
Tool Layout	Tools are easy to access and stored in the proper place, so they are ready for use as needed.
Maintenance Records	Maintenance records are kept up to date by the operator, and all routine tasks are performed by the operator on a regular schedule.
Operator Safety	All unsafe or hazardous conditions have been mistake-proofed at the workstation.

is addressed by their integration into DMAIC), and the second is how lean projects are identified and prioritized—the subject of Chapter 9 in this book.

Merging the Toyota Production System Elements into Six Sigma DMAIC

Most lean production systems use observation and common sense to focus improvement efforts. A major distinction between lean production management and Lean Six Sigma is the use that Lean Six Sigma makes of statistical tools to identify statistically significant process performance differences and focus on areas that must be improved (e.g., using tools such as multi-vari analysis, hypothesis testing, and ANOVA).

To develop such a Lean Six Sigma system, it is often convenient for organizations to merge the lean production improvement methods into the DMAIC statistical problem solving framework. How does the 10-S process map into the DMAIC framework so they may be used in a collaborative way to generate performance improvement? The mapping of 10-S into DMAIC is straightforward and is illustrated in Table 8.8.

Just as DMAIC requires an interaction between workers and managers at the project level to keep focus on achieving business results, the same interaction is required if DMAIC is integrated with lean tools, but the purpose here is to encourage workers and also to maintain the busi-

Table 8.8 10-S integrated with DMAIC

Six Sigma DMAIC Step	10-S Lean Management Steps
Define	Study
Measure	Sort—Sanitize
Analyze	Systematize
Improve	Streamline—Simulate—Synchronize
Control	Safeguard—Standardize—Self-Discipline

ness focus. Indeed, the Define task in the 10-S process (Study) requires deep participation of management to assure that the improvement tasks, and the plan for attacking different process areas are aligned with their interpretation of what must be done. The Measure and Analyze phases of the Lean Six Sigma projects can be conducted by line workers as they tend to focus on individual workstations and then build up a collaborative environment by increasing the scope of participation of workers. The tasks for Improve and Control can be undertaken as a *Kaizen Blitz* to force rapid improvement and assure that standard work is performed as normal operating procedure.

The scientific method requires not only the building of a theory, but also demonstration that the theory is generally applicable. Has this improvement system worked over the long term for other companies—or is it unique to Toyota?

EXTENDING LEAN LEARNING

The true sign of maturity in applying any business improvement methodology is that the organization no longer views it as something separate from its normal way of working. In other words, the process of improvement has become a natural act or part of the organization's genetic makeup, which defines what it is and how it works. A number of companies have achieved this transition and have developed their own version of lean learning from Toyota and other Japanese companies who practice the elements of lean thinking. Here are a few examples of companies who have walked the thousand-mile lean road one step at a time:

- Following the award of the Deming Prize to its Japanese subsidiary in 1982, Hewlett-Packard began an intensive study effort to apply the methods that advanced Yokagawa Hewlett-Packard (YHP) from its least profitable division to its most profitable one in just five years. Many study visits to leading Japanese companies were arranged (Toyota, Hitachi, Fujitsu, Nippon-Denso, Honda, Komatsu, and Fuji Xerox were just a few of the companies visited during this period), and the HP lessons learned about application of Total Qual-ity Control and Just-in-Time management were transferred to YHP's American sister divisions throughout the world. Implemen-tations of these lessons learned were documented by consultant Richard J. Schonberger as an honor roll describing dozens of ex-amples of JIT breakthroughs in various HP divisions.[13] Hewlett-Packard led the way for transfer of knowledge about JIT and time-based competitiveness from Japan to the United States by over two decades prior to generation of the current fascination with this topic. Hewlett-Packard influenced many other manufacturers to take a lean approach to their management and take the lean journey.

- Like HP, Xerox traces its quality history back to a stimulus pro-vided from Japan—its Fuji Xerox organization, which won the Deming Prize in 1980. Xerox based its first integrated quality program (called "Leadership through Quality") on the methods it learned from Fuji Xerox and also triangulated their performance by comparing the details of their internal performance against that of Fuji Xerox and then compared this baseline against the public statements about Canon in order to infer how competitive Xerox was against Canon. This formed the basis of the Xerox benchmark-ing program. Later, Xerox reinvigorated its quality program in 1993 when it updated its management model to define "Business Excellence" and again in 2002 when it introduced Lean Six Sigma. The entire quality journey at Xerox has been influenced by quality improvements. Indeed, Lawrence Zimmerman, CFO of Xerox com-mented in an August 12, 2005 statement in *Forbes* that "Xerox has become a Lean Six Sigma company. We're focused on efficiencies in our operations and in the way we deliver value to our customers. Lean Six Sigma projects have already contributed hundreds of mil-lions of dollars in cost savings, cost avoidance, and revenue to the

---

13. Richard J. Schonberger, *Japanese Manufacturing Techniques: Nine Lessons in Simplicity* (New York: Free Press, 1982) and *World Class Manufacturing: The Lessons of Simplicity Applied* (New York: Free Press, 1986).

company. More than 1,500 projects have been completed or are underway with the assistance of more than 600 Xerox Black Belts and Master Black Belts."[14]

- Boeing began its fascination with Japanese production techniques in the 1980s when Dave Packard, cofounder of Hewlett-Packard, was on its board of directors. Packard encouraged Boeing to pursue quality improvement as a business strategy and to evaluate the methods of the Japanese for application into their production processes. In the early 1990s, Boeing sent study teams to Japan to evaluate how to take this advice, and by 1993 it had started to apply these lessons learned and began its step-by-step journey. Workshops were held for employees in 1992 to 1994, and the first lean production cell was built in 1993 for the escape hatch of the 737 commercial aircraft. In 1994, Boeing started a formal 5-S program and initiated *Kaizen* events in 1995. By 1996, lean was a formal part of the organization with establishment of a Lean Manufacturing Office and engagement of the Shingijutsu Consulting Company from Japan. By 1999, Boeing was moving its aircraft through a production line at one-half an inch each hour, and they instituted another moving line for the 737 in 2001. As Boeing says "lean is a mindset" and comes from a journey with increments of a thousand small steps.[15]

- General Electric followed a 20-year history of business improvement under its CEO, Jack Welch. The journey embraced variety reduction, simplification of its work processes, workout to focus on rapid decision making, and Six Sigma to improve process consis-

---

14. The early history of the Xerox quality story was described by Xerox executives Richard C. Palermo and Gregory H. Watson in *The World of Quality: A Timeless Passport* (Milwaukee: ASQ Quality Press, 1994). The story of the Xerox application of Lean Six Sigma is described by Arthur Fornari and George Maszle in "Lean Six Sigma Leads Xerox," *Six Sigma Forum Magazine* August (2004): 11–16. A discussion about lean Six Sigma at Xerox is also presented in a white paper available from their web site: "Xerox Lean Six Sigma" (http://www.xerox.com/downloads/usa/en/n/nr_XeroxLeanSixSigma_2004May.pdf).

15. Richard G. Roff, "Fans of Six Sigma," *Boeing Frontiers On-Line Newsletter* 3 no. 10 (2005): http://www.boeing.com/news/frontiers/archive/2005/march/i_ca2.html, and Paul V. Arnold "Boeing Knows Lean," *MRO Today Magazine* February-March (2002).

tency. Following this journey, GE added lean methods and design for Six Sigma, with its emphasis on innovation to its basic Six Sigma program as a means to reinvigorate its performance and meet a new challenge to grow organically at three times the rate of the American economy's gross national product.[16] Over the years, GE has proven itself adept at change—it even has a process it calls "change acceleration" to force itself to move quickly. The lean methods, with their step-by-step disciplined implementation, complement all this fast action by providing a stabilization base in standard performance that serves as the baseline for future change.

How can you begin your company's transition to a lean operating system? Well, first study the theory of lean to discover how to apply the results of operational benchmarking study to the culture and business model of your organization. Then, do a two-pronged self-assessment of your performance—capture the results of your performance using a set of lean performance measures that are most appropriate for your company, and establish this as a performance baseline from which you may evaluate your improvement. Then do a self-assessment of your business practices to evaluate how well you have addressed the practices of improvement that are hallmarks of a lean production system. This reflection period (*hansei*) allows your organization to consider how it may improve and create new ideas about how to move forward. Conducting a lean self-assessment is the subject of the next section in this chapter.

EVALUATING MATURITY OF YOUR LEAN SYSTEM

Reflection is a key ingredient in *Kaizen* and is one of the three ways that Confucius said man could gain wisdom: "First, by reflection, which is noblest; second, by imitation, which is easiest; and third by experience, which is the bitterest." Conducting a formal self-assessment permits this

---

16. Gregory H. Watson, "Cycles of Learning: Observations of Jack Welch," *Six Sigma Forum Magazine* November (2001): 13–17: "Growth As a Process: Interview with Jeffrey R. Immelt," *Harvard Business Review* June (2006).

Table 8.9 Factorywide self-assessment questions

1. What is the relationship between customer orders and the production build plan?
2. How is production material replenished on the line?
3. How does work flow through the production line?
4. How flexible is your workforce performance capability to do different jobs?
5. What is the relationship of your total cycle time to the incoming order rate?
6. What percentage of your total cycle time is value added?
7. What percentage of factory space is dedicated to storage of material or inventory?
8. Is the production bottleneck used for production control to manage throughput?
9. How is the quality of incoming material assured—does it meet this requirement?
10. How have workstations been modified to assure operator safety and efficiency?
11. How is worker input solicited in order to improve process performance?
12. What visual cues show that the production line is operating in a lean manner?

reflection, which separates those organizations that create history from those who are doomed to repeat it! This self-assessment or reflection is a means to conduct the review element in a policy deployment management system (see Table 8.9 and see Chapter 9 for more details on how benchmarking should be linked to this method).

While the factorywide self-assessment is the job of the senior management team, local area supervisors can lead their workers in doing a workstation audit to self-assess their own lean performance capability. The real purpose behind this self-assessment is to build involvement and commitment to improvement among the frontline workers. A positive outcome of this self-assessment would be a list of *Kaizen* improvement projects that the workers are committed to perform. (See Table 8.10.)

Of course, this self-assessment and reflection period is just a beginning, a departure point for creation of lean improvement projects and diligently executing them to achieve all of the potential net improvements. In the final analysis, the value of the TPS comes from its disci-

Table 8.10 Workstation level self-assessment questions

1. Is the standard operating procedure for work visible to the operator?
2. Are there clear, visible standards for acceptable and unacceptable quality?
3. Are tools and production equipment configured for ease of access and safety?
4. Is the workstation adjustable to the operator's physical requirements?
5. Is all required production equipment available at the point of use?
6. Are the incoming and outgoing inventory buffers balanced to smooth throughput?
7. Is the production time (*takt* time minus cycle time) enough for operators to work?
8. Are operators trained in multiple tasks so they may rotate to other workstations?
9. Do operators have ability to self-regulate quality and productivity in their work?
10. Have all potential failure modes at the workstation been mistake-proofed?

plined approach to doing the daily work of the organization—from putting rigor into the processes by which the organization produces its output. The effort behind the TPS is focused on defining the one best way to assure that customers get what they order.

CONCLUDING COMMENTS

Writing about the TPS reminds me of a story told by my friend Noriaki Kano. Kano observed that today Japan is experiencing fourth-generation sushi. First-generation sushi was prepared in the traditional way by a Japanese chef on the Ginza using fresh fish. Second-generation sushi was exported from Japan to America, where we could observe a Japanese chef making sushi with fresh fish. In the third-generation sushi, the chef is now an American preparing the sushi in a more-or-less traditional way. The fourth generation of sushi finds the American chef serving sushi on the Ginza using fresh beef. At the end of this product migration, one can ask (with sincere apologies to the creators of the old hamburger advertisement), Where's the sushi?

What is important in the adaptation of operational benchmarking lessons is not just the "know how" but also the reasons behind the method—the "know why" that builds a theory of profound knowledge about how the process should really operate. With a theoretical basis, we can extend the application of the "know how" from one business environment to another by seeking those leverage points of learning and adapting the theory to a different company's culture, business model, or commercial environment.

PART 4
Conducting Benchmarking Studies

CHAPTER 9

Mainstreaming Benchmarking into Strategic Planning

The neglect of the future is only a symptom; the executive sights tomorrow because he cannot get ahead of today. That too is a symptom. The real disease is the absence of any foundation of knowledge and system for tackling economic tasks in their business. There are three different dimensions to the economic task: (1) the present business must be made effective; (2) its potential must be identified and realized; and (3) it must be made into a different business for a different future.

—PETER F. DRUCKER

INTRODUCTION TO POLICY MANAGEMENT

As Drucker observes, effective business must control the environment for today while preparing itself for a different future—or to paraphrase the late Austrian economist Joseph Schumpeter and his concept of innovation—prepare to abandon the past in order to have the freedom to choose your future. Schumpeter observed that profits are linked to innovation, and as the innovation becomes undifferentiated, then profit margins will disintegrate proportionally. As this transition occurs, then the customer and market gradually gain power over product pricing, and the product transitions into a low-margin commodity. As this transition is inevitable for competitive products, it is essential that the business maintain tight control over its costing during the initial production ramp-up

241

toward maturity in order to maximize the lifetime profit potential of the product because profit is not uniformly distributed over the life of the product. The requirements of such business control include a sound system of performance measurement, knowledge of performance requirements and the competitive targets that must be achieved, and an ability to self-regulate performance in order to achieve the desired end state.[1] The requirements of creating the future cannot be stated with the same degree of certainty as observations of the past because it rests upon assumptions and is calculated in terms of probability. Policy management applies a systems approach to manage organization-wide improvement of key business processes.

Policy defines the purpose or idea of the business; identifies the specific excellence, competence, or capability that it must attain to be successful; establishes the definition of success; and selects the priorities that must be managed in the pursuit of opportunities that create a sustained and continuing state of success. Management is the mechanism for control and improvement of work outcomes. Drucker noted, "for full effectiveness all the work [of an organization] needs to be integrated into a unified *program for performance*."[2] The policy management program for performance improvement is designed by the top management team to provide a very specific, effective course of action to achieve its desired results. In order to achieve these results, then all the dimensions of the business must be consistent with each other and work together in harmony as an engineered system. This is exactly what a board intends to happen when it establishes the policy and delegates implementation to manage-

---

1. Business control should not be interpreted as controlling performance to reflect past experience. If this is the case, then business will only attempt to repeat the reality of its past experience. Business control is different from statistical control, which focuses on reducing variation and maintaining standard performance. Business control requires managed change — change is a mandate — current processes must be monitored in order to determine when change is required to keep up with the emerging realities of technical and commercial developments. Otherwise, business controls and statistical controls are compatible. Drucker also described the requirements for business accountability in Chapter six of his early book *The Practice of Management* (New York: Harper & Row, 1954).

2. Peter F. Drucker, *Managing for Results* (New York: Harper & Row, 1964), 195.

ment. However, it is easy to describe this state, but it is execution and management of time and effort that determine ultimate success.

PROGRAM FOR PERFORMANCE MANAGEMENT

The process of policy management initially will engage senior management with the organization's board of directors to focus on a policy regarding the future, and then it integrates strategic planning, change management, and project management with performance management methods that focus on delivering results. This is the policy-setting process. Once a policy has been set, the next challenge is to align the strategic direction with the work that must be performed to change the daily management system and to cascade the objectives throughout the organization so that resources and efforts are expended in the most efficient and effective manner to accomplish the policy. This is the deployment of policy in which change projects (such as Six Sigma projects or implementation of benchmarking study recommendations are defined and implemented in the daily management system of the business). These change projects are designed to improve the way the routine business operates by creating a discontinuity of change, rather than contributing to the incremental improvement, which is the responsibility of the entire workforce.

Policy management (also called *policy deployment* or by its Japanese name *hoshin kanri*) is a strategic management process that begins with the top-down organization vision of its desired future state, employs the measurement capability of the organization to shape and refine the approach to achieving this vision, and engages the entire organization in a dialogue that focuses the attention and energies of the organization on achieving results that are congruent with the desired direction. How does this work, and what is the role of benchmarking in this performance management process?

Performance management is the means to achieve the three objectives that Drucker proposes for the business: making the present business more effective, identifying the potential performance of the business and realizing that potential, and creating the organization of the future that is capable of meeting emergent needs. In the language of strategic benchmarking and Six Sigma, this means that the organization must do those things necessary to assure profitable growth by identifying its hidden process capability and eliminating the barriers that hold it back from effective application of its resources. Because business policy definition is the responsibility of the top-most management of an organization, we should examine how this policy is shaped and what role benchmarking can plan in the process of strategy-setting.

Throughout the policy management process, senior management (executive management team plus the board of directors) concentrates on defining the policy and strategic intent, while operational management focuses on translating policy into improvement projects and full-scale implementation in the daily management process. Jointly, the executive team and the board of directors should conduct reviews of the organization's activities to assure that implementation reflects the intent of their policy. Some specific activities that provide unity in this program for performance management include the following:

- Identifying critical business assumptions and areas of vulnerability
- Identifying specific opportunities for long-term improvement
- Establishing business objectives to address the most imperative policies
- Setting performance improvement goals for the organization
- Developing change strategies to address business objectives
- Preparing an annual policy implementation plan for the organization
- Defining project charters for implementing each change strategy
- Implementing the change projects

As the senior management creates its annual policy implementation plan to reflect the high-priority areas for investigation, they address five elements to establish a plan for individual improvement projects:

1. *A statement of the desired end or objective:* Statement of an improvement policy or objective that is to be accomplished.

244

2. *Metrics with which to measure progress:* The measurement that describes progress toward a desired result (expressed as a target value).
3. *A goal that describes the measure of the desired state:* The target value or level of the metric or the result that you want to attain.
4. *A deadline date:* A scheduled date by which the target value must be achieved.
5. *Activities to achieve the objective:* A strategy (approach) to accomplish the target—the content of what must be done to achieve the goal.

What should be the role of benchmarking in this process? Benchmarking is one of two methods that act as catalysts working symbiotically to stimulate strategic change. The other catalyst is measurement, and having a sound measurement system is a prerequisite to effective benchmarking. Indeed, effective measurement is the foundation of the entire management process, while benchmarking provides a means for challenging performance targets to stimulate improvement. Measurement allows management to determine if it needs to change, assess its progress in making changes, and evaluate the effectiveness of changes that have been made.

Measurement is the key to sound performance management that results in competitive advantage. How does this work? Let's review how a policy management system is designed in order to understand the requirements for an effective measurement system.

The Japanese Approach to Policy Management

Enduring competitive advantage has a better chance to be achieved if benchmarking is mainstreamed into the strategic planning process and used on a regular basis to detect changes in critical business assumptions, technology applications, or other emerging differentiators. The relationship between these methods and the approach for merging these concepts in the context of the organizational business model is the foundation for policy management systems. Thus, strategic benchmarking finds an organizational home in the management process alongside long-range planning and business development.

Shigeru Mizuno defined *hoshin kanri* as the process for "deploying and sharing the direction, goals and approaches of corporate management from top management to employees, and for each unit of the organization to conduct work according to the plan."[3] *Hoshin kanri* is a comprehensive, closed loop management planning, objectives deployment, and operational review process that coordinates activities to achieve desired strategic objectives. The word *hoshin* refers to the long-range strategic direction that anticipates competitive developments, while the word *kanri* refers to a control system for managing the process.[4] Some of the key terms in this Japanese management method and their definitions follow:

- *Policy:* A general rule or operating principle that describes a management-approved process to approach a business condition or situation based on how it chooses to control its work and manage risk. Once the right policy has been determined, then the organization can handle similar situations with a pragmatic response by adapting its policies to the concrete situation that it faces. Truly unique business situations that run counter to the critical business assumptions require the full attention of the senior management team to evaluate how these situations challenge the boundary conditions of the business model and threaten its policies of operations with change that is imposed from externalities. Policies consist of targets and means.
- *Target:* The measurable results that are to be achieved within a specific time frame for performance. Targets have checkpoints.
- *Checkpoints:* A measurement point that is used to evaluate an intermediate state in the policy deployment process to demonstrate that

---

3. A concise and comprehensive treatment of policy deployment is presented in Gregory H. Watson, "Policy Deployment: Consensus Method of Strategy Realization," in Tito Conti, Yoshio Kondo, and Gregory H. Watson, eds., *Quality into the 21st Century: Perspectives on Quality and Competitiveness for Sustained Performance* (Milwaukee: ASQ Quality Press, 2003), 191–218.

4. Gregory H. Watson, "Introduction to Hoshin Kanri," in Yoji Akao, ed., *Hoshin Kanri: Policy Deployment for Successful TQM* (Portland, OR: Productivity Press, 1991), xxix–xxx.

progress is being made. The data collected at a checkpoint can be reported to management in interim project status reports. The check-point of one process is the control point of the next process—the checkpoints and control points work together to formulate a "wa-terfall" that cascades across the implementation plan flow and is part of the business measurement system.

- *Check Items:* Check items and process or project variables that are evaluated in order to enable organizations to understand the causes that contribute to the outcome of a particular policy.
- *Means:* The sequence of actions that an organization will take to im-plement a policy or choice of the management team that is an out-come of the strategic direction setting process. Means have control points. In the language of process benchmarking, a means is called an *enabler*—the set of activities that created the observed change in the business practice of a benchmark organization.

From this description of the elements of *hoshin kanri,* it should be clear that measurement is the critical ingredient to focusing this management system and that comparative analysis is the means to achieve dissatisfac-tion with a poorly performing present state. Because measurement is the precursor to benchmarking, then we should consider how to develop a sound measurement system.

MEASUREMENT SYSTEM DESIGN

Three elements are required to create an effective business measurement system: a model of the way the entire enterprise operates as a coherent process, a system of performance indicators that is linked to the actions required to produce the results desired of the enterprise, and assignment of accountability for work-process performance.

An enterprise map illustrates the sequence and relationship of the busi-ness activities as well as the way that organization is managed using key performance indicators. The first step in developing an enterprise mea-surement system is to model the core business processes and determine the location of its critical business control points—those places where the process performance may be checked, analyzed, and regulated using feedback from its real-time operations. The following sequence of steps describes the detailed approach for constructing an enterprise model:

- Identify the key business processes, and model them as a chain of sequential processes to illustrate what the organization does and how it achieves its outcomes.

- Identify the key perspectives of the key customer stakeholders in the organization, and determine what is important about the organization's output from each of their viewpoints—those things that enable them to get their own work accomplished. These factors that are important to the quality of your customers are critical to their satisfaction (CTS) and are key contributors to their success.

- Translate the high-level process diagram into a detailed model that is organized into "centers of excellence" (a core business process that conducts key repetitive tasks in the business on behalf of customers, such as production operations, distribution, etc.) and "communities of practice" (a functional organization that supports the core business processes but operates in a way that performs only a professional practice that is essential for the mainstream process to operate smoothly, such as purchasing, human resources, information systems, etc.) in order to show how collaboration occurs across your organization in delivering performance results.

- Identify the decisions that enable a hierarchical flow of the process maps—where detailed process maps of work activities are combined into a set of higher order thought maps that define the relationship of the CTS factors to your organization's own critical-to-quality measures of success.

- Determine what decision rights have been delegated for each major decision, who participates in these decisions, the perspective they have regarding the context of the decision, what information or measurements they use to evaluate their perspective, and what accountability and responsibility has been allocated for the specific decision.

248

- Assess the validity of these measurements by conducting a process audit.
- Carry forward all learning into creation of a measurement specification that defines all the critical ingredients of each customer measure.
- Conduct a measurement analysis to determine the linkages and prediction capability of these performance indicators.
- Build a linked and aligned measurement system from the customer perspective back to operational process indicators of quality, cost, and time using the $Y = f(X)$ logic of the Six Sigma DMAIC process.
- Determine the degree of control available for the real-time measurement system. Of the performance indicators that track production throughput in the process map, which indicators are measured at a point in the process where the throughput can be regulated for controlling the production flow of the system?
- Apply the measurement system in the strategic planning process, regular management reports, and work performance analysis.

This sequence of actions not only creates an enterprise model but it also identifies the key performance measures and measurement control points that may be used to manage business performance. The next task is to map the measurement system.

A measurement map specifies the linkage of the strategic measures of business performance at the enterprise level with the operational measures of work-process control at the functional level of the business. Using the language of Six Sigma, the basis for specifying the measurement system is a $Y = f(X)$ measurement map that links the business Ys (e.g., shareholder value and brand value) to the process level Xs (quality, cost, and time) by determining their functional relationship. This analysis makes a deliberate stratification of the top-level business measures into component work-process measures in a way that meets two conditions: the measures are mutually exclusive and completely exhaustive within each measurement tree. Several trees can exist at the same time to represent "confounding" or interactions among variables (e.g., this occurs between the three major branches of quality, cost, and time).

The sequence of steps that a team will follow to develop a measurement map of the enterprise business system includes the following steps:

- Establish management measurements for top-level (business Ys).
- Assess current state of measurement system and its linkage to business Ys.
- Accumulate work process Xs into intermediate Ys to deliver business Ys.
- Operationally define all key measurements and each opportunity for defects.
- Determine the sources of variation for the work process Xs.
- Identify management-controllable factors for each X measure.
- Select both the sampling methods and frequency of reporting for Xs.
- Create the graphical methods for presentation and interpretation of Xs.
- Assign accountability for performance of Xs, Ys, and business Ys.
- Choose owners for business Ys to assure implementation compliance.
- Document the measurement specification for each business Y.
- Assign managerial oversight for the entire business scorecard.
- Align business decision processes to the measurement system.
- Reduce work complexity that adds variety without customer value.
- Apply the measurement system to streamline value added work.
- Implement the measurement system in business information systems.

The intermediate Ys referenced in the preceding are similar to a scorecard. For example, one set of these intermediate Ys includes the following four indicators: system delivery flexibility (delivery of the maximum production volume to meet requirements of market delivery mechanisms and customer demand), deliver-to-promise (accuracy of delivery on promises made to customers), profit maximization (production of the maximum profit capability from the contributions of capital investments and operational work processes), and first-time quality (rolled throughput yield of business demonstrating the ability to deliver quality results without losing productivity due to poor quality). However, unlike the scorecard, each of these indicators is linked together using a $Y = f(X)$ analysis, which may be expressed as a mathematical relationship using probability to illustrate strength in the relationship between the factors. In the language of Six Sigma, a business Y (such as *profitable growth*) that must be achieved is the strategic goal, while a process X (such as *creditworthy customers*) delivers this performance through a transfer function $Y = f(X)$ and is therefore a business fundamentals measure in the daily management system. This transfer function can be measured and monitored and used to predict its contribution to the business objective of profitable growth.

The development of this transfer function is a key enabler of great benchmarking as it provides a linkage between the strategic and operational performance indicators for the entire organization. Strategic benchmarking seeks knowledge and insights into decisions that affect the leverage points of the organization. When a measurement system has been developed using this Six Sigma process, then it specifies the key leverage points of the organization through the investigation and analysis that produce the enterprise model and measurement map.

Once a measurement map has been created, then the two intermediate products of this analysis (the enterprise model and measurement map) are ready to specify the customer dashboard system and deploy it for business management. Of course, it must be recognized that the manner in which these two elements are built will establish an organizational bias for acceptance or rejection of the measurement system. The real trick in measurement system design is to build the system collaboratively! This creates an atmosphere of acceptance by the organization because they have helped to design it and understand the rationale behind its component parts. There are four activities that help to assure companywide acceptance:

- Using a workshop format for creation of the enterprise model and measurement map builds acceptance and establishes credibility among the middle managers.
- Applying consensus management to define the measurement specifications with the active participation of all related process owners will assure they apply the result.

- Cascading the measurement system by business process area and across functional groups will assure integration of the measurement system into the fabric of the work activities (using both dimensions of the process thread and the functional thread).
- Embedding the measurement system into the information management system will assure compliance with structured measurement by eliminating the opportunity for calculation error and creative interpretation of the measurement definitions.

The third and final element required to establish a measurement system is accountability for performance of the processes in the enterprise model as defined by the indicators in the measurement map. This system of accountability is established through ownership of the core business processes as assigned by the executive management team. In addition to the typical profit and loss responsibilities of a line manager, the job of a process owner includes the following activities:

- Deliver total system performance expectations.
- Manage work as a process.
- Document procedures for standard work.
- Establish standards of performance.
- Measure work performance.
- Initiate improvement activities.
- Establish teams to enhance work outcomes.
- Establish projects that improve results.
- Train team coaches in facilitation and Six Sigma.
- Monitor process performance.
- Implement corrective actions and countermeasures.
- Initiate performance enhancing projects.
- Encourage creative innovations for results advantage.
- Review progress of improvement projects.

Once the measurement system is operational, then it can be used to define a performance baseline for the organization, and this baseline can be used as a basis for comparison in the conduct of benchmarking studies.

The comparative analyses and critical from benchmarking are used to define the strategic direction of the organization.

DEFINING DIRECTION

What are the essential ingredients in choosing strategic direction? This process of management integrates strategic planning, change management, and project management with the performance management methods that focus on delivering results. Some specific subprocesses include the following:

- Identifying critical business assumptions and areas of vulnerability
- Identifying specific opportunities for improvement
- Establishing business objectives to address the most imperative issues
- Setting performance improvement goals for the organization
- Developing change management strategies for addressing business objectives
- Defining goals-project charters for implementing each change strategy
- Creating operational definitions of performance measures for key business processes
- Defining business fundamental measures for all subprocesses to the working level

Once a strategy has been set, the next challenge is to align the strategic direction with the work that is being performed in the daily management system. In this activity, all work is viewed across a planning horizon. What is a planning horizon? It is the distance that an organization "sees" into the future in order to study and understand the potential impacts of events on its policies and prepare it for evolving situations that may impact its performance. In general, organizations have four distinct planning horizons:

- *Business Foresight:* Managing for the long term to assure that the organization is not surprised by changes in the assumptions that it has made in the design of its business model and product-line strategy (focusing on a 3- to 10-year business outlook).

- *Strategic Direction:* Managing for the intermediate-term changes in technology and competitive dimensions to assure that vulnerabilities in the business model are not exploited and to bridge the chasm that may exist between product-line introductions (focusing on the next three to five years of business operation, depending on the degree of change that is anticipated in the business environment).
- *Business Plans:* Managing the short-term fluctuations of the market — a planning horizon that delivers against short-term fluctuations in demand or supply (focus on quarterly and annual operating plans).
- *Business Controls:* Managing the current state of a business — a planning horizon that delivers today's performance and assures rapid responses for corrective actions required to sustain advertised service levels (focus on the short-term operating plans that are measured in daily, weekly, monthly, or quarterly increments).

Strategic benchmarking tends to focus on the first two planning horizons, while operational benchmarking studies focus on the more near-term activities supporting specific business plans and controls. In order to maximize the capability in strategic direction setting, all benchmarking studies should be coordinated across these planning horizons using the enterprise model and the measurement map to coordinate the selection of study topics. Strategic studies must examine critical assumptions and vulnerabilities of the organization, while operational studies must deliver best practice for adaptation into the organization's operating system for business and process control. How is opportunity recognized?

IDENTIFYING OPPORTUNITIES FOR DISRUPTION

Opportunity is the obverse side of the managerial coin from risk. Risk may cause an organization to become more conservative and resist taking chances, in other words, to focus on sustaining technology by extending proven product lines in known markets. However, the opportunity for exceptional growth and profit is also a great motivator for taking risks—and the bigger the perceived opportunity, the more risk people may be willing to accept in order to realize these potential commercial gains. These risks involve exploring new technologies, product applications or functional capabilities, and features in order to disrupt an established commercial market. Opportunity management is thus a critical success factor for organizations desiring high growth. Managing opportunities focuses on the front-end of the *hoshin kanri* process—the selection of the focus areas for business improvement that define the opportunities that the organization has chosen to accept.

However, management may tend to get so locked into their measurement system that they fail to identify the ingredients of change as they occur. Thus, the measurement system of an organization will support operational management, and operational benchmarking will provide an understanding of how to extend sustaining technologies, but a wholly different approach is required to identify opportunities for disruption.

Drucker commented, "Relevant outside events are rarely available in quantifiable form until it is too late to do anything about them."[5] The most important events outside of an organization are not the trends of the historical performance that support understanding the pathway for sustainable business developments. Rather, the most important events are the changes in the trends—the inflection points—that mark a new opportunity due to the disruption of the market.

In order to transition to successful operations under disruptive conditions, an organization must first perceive and understand the opportunity, as distinguished from the way it has been operating in the past to sustain its growth. Thus, the role of strategic benchmarking is to seek out the trigger events that identify inflection points and allow early discovery of those technology, market, regulatory, or competitive factors that are defining the emergent opportunities as they happen. Thus, management

5. Peter F. Drucker, *The Effective Executive* (New York: Harper & Row, 1967), 16.

255

of strategic benchmarking must be included in the management planning system as a stimulus for identifying and capitalizing upon potentially disruptive events in order to do something about them.

APPLYING BENCHMARKING FOR POLICY MANAGEMENT

While strategic benchmarking identifies what to change, the most significant purpose of operational benchmarking is to identify how to change. The discovery of best practice (or better practice than what your organization uses) is the critical outcome of operational benchmarking studies. These studies should result in the incorporation of improvement opportunities in the standard work practices and operating procedures of the organization. Because in most organizations their routine work is defined in operating procedures that are documented in their quality management system, it is only natural that operational studies result in changes to the standard operating practices and management of organizational resources to support these practices. Thus, operational benchmarking supports the deployment aspect of policy management and strategic benchmarking supports the formulation of policy.

CONCLUSION

Policy management should be coupled with a statistically based business measurement system and an approach for identifying discontinuities in historical trends to define and execute the policy of an organization's management team. This requires integration of the measurement system with the benchmarking process and strategic planning process. By doing this, an organization assures line of sight from the strategic goals of the organization to the operational tasks that workers perform at the frontline as they do the work that produces the organization's goods or services. The nature of this process can be described using the term *robustness* — a statistical state in which a process is able to accept variation in its inputs, without influencing the variation of its outputs. Such a process is capable of performing consistently — delivering consistent results according to its design intent.

Because policy deployment engages the workforce in achieve the common goal of sustained success, it is a strategic tool for assuring sustained competitive advantage over both current and potential business rivals.[6]

The emphasis of the next chapter will be on the execution of benchmarking studies by organizing an effective management process for conducting them.

6. In addition to the previous references in this chapter, the following books are recommended for anyone seeking more in-depth understanding of *hoshin kanri* or policy deployment: Peter Babich, *The Hoshin Handbook*, 2nd ed. (Poway, CA: Total Quality Engineering, 1996); Joseph F. Colletti, *A Field Guide to Focused Planning: Hoshin Kanri—American Style* (East Granby, CT: The Woodledge Group, 1995); Brendan Collins and Ernest Huge, *Management by Policy: How Companies Focus Their Total Quality Efforts to Achieve Competitive Advantage* (Milwaukee, WI: ASQ Quality Press, 1993); and Michael Cowley and Ellen Domb, *Beyond Strategic Vision: Effective Corporate Action with Hoshin Planning* (Boston: Butterworth-Heinemann, 1997).

CHAPTER 10

Creating a Sustainable Benchmarking Capability

To know you don't know is best. Not to know you don't know is a flaw.

— LAO TZU

SUSTAINABILITY — KEY TO ENDURANCE

If benchmarking is to become part of your institutional management process, then it must become a sustainable capability and find a home in your organization. What does it mean to have a *home* for benchmarking? Both external and internal perspectives must be used to define the home for benchmarking. The external perspective leads to establishing benchmarking networks to facilitate participation in collaborative studies. The internal perspective focuses on developing both centers of benchmarking excellence to do the studies and communities of practice to apply the findings of benchmarking.

COLLABORATION TO ENHANCE COMPETITIVENESS

How can learning be encouraged across firms — to establish a sustained interaction that results in organizational learning? The most enduring capability will be established in external relationships as functional networks or collaborative clusters that operate as either a center for excellence or a community of practice. What are these relationships, and how are they formed?

Benchmarking works best when a *society of firms* establishes a collaborative network to address topics of mutual interest in benchmarking studies. Typically, the organizations involved in such a collaborative are not competitors and are of similar size, although the similarities can end at this point. The types of studies conducted by the collaborative also tend to be generic due to the distribution of business models, but the value of these studies is great because the diversity of perspectives used in the approach to the study will help to uncover general principles that may be adapted into each organization's learning environment. Organizations that maintain a stable membership in their intercompany network can have a significant advantage as they build trust and knowledge in each other's operation and obtain deeper insights into how the different approaches to business improvement work out over the long term (e.g., General Electric maintained a network of 16 noncompetitive companies for over 10 years from the middle of the 1980s to the end of the 1990s). This long-term learning enables a sustained capability for understanding how business must change through the course of economic cycles and product life cycles. Gaining such a long-term perspective can facilitate better short-term decisions. Such external networks can be either formal or informal.

What reason do organizations have for forming a benchmarking alliance or partnership? There are several compelling reasons for creating an informal alignment:

- Expanding learning perspectives about the process that is under investigation
- Combining complimentary resources to achieve related objectives
- Sharing costs of training and research investigations
- Gaining access to a wider source of information than obtainable internally

On the other hand, formalized networks are created with members of the organization's value network (key suppliers or customers) who have relationships such as joint ventures, strategic alliances, preferred suppliers, long-term suppliers, major accounts, and so on. These companies have a natural affinity for sharing as it is in their best interest to develop a strong mutually supportive capability to further their own economic performance. So one objective (the so-called what's in it for me consideration) of a benchmarking network is the concept of reciprocity — mutually beneficial goals to further each participants' own ability to perform. Other objectives for establishing such a network include the following:

- *Efficiency:* Achieve higher productivity
- *Stability:* Better face the challenge of an uncertain future
- *Legitimacy:* Enhance brand reputation by formal association

Examples of the formal benchmarking networks include the International Benchmarking Clearinghouse at the American Productivity & Quality Center in Houston, Texas, and the Global Benchmarking Network.

INTERNAL CAPABILITY AND COMPETENCE DEVELOPMENT

In addition to developing an external capability, organizations must also build internal strength in their benchmarking competence by establishing both centers of excellence and communities of practice. What does this mean?

A center of excellence defines a functional organization that delivers a specific competence for the entire company — such as specialists in market research or purchasing. A center for benchmarking excellence would provide specialized support for conducting benchmarking studies. Some of its activities would include the development of specialists who manage the benchmarking study, provision for teams who are participating in a benchmarking study, relationship maintenance with the external networks, administration of benchmark measurements for input into the balanced scorecard or customer dashboard, management of logistics for benchmarking studies (both for visitors and for benchmarking teams going on site visits), and maintenance of the corporate archives of benchmarking studies and records. These activities are best administered from

261

a central perspective in order to reduce the investment in overhead resources applied for benchmarking. Appendix C identifies web-based benchmarking resources that can aid in the development of this benchmarking capability. Since centers of benchmarking excellence define the functional organization, the community of benchmarking practice must define the lateral process for application of the methodology.

A community of benchmarking practice would involve all the managers who sponsor the benchmarking studies, as well as the team members who participate in the studies. The *community* could be defined as an informal network that applies the practice to its core business processes and integrates benchmarking methods into the organization's culture. The degree of identity that is formed by such a community of practice will depend on the effort that is made in the center of excellence to create a visible and vibrant community. One of the activities that could foster the development of a community of practice is the distribution of a periodic newsletter to describe events of interest, report summaries of the studies performed, spotlight the use of tools or methods, and so on. Another factor that could help to build a sense of community is holding a quarterly or annual internal conference that brings the participants together, reports on studies, features external speakers from the network companies and internal senior managers, and provides a vehicle to recognize the efforts of the community members on behalf of the company.

How can the maturity of an organization's benchmarking effort be judged? Perhaps the best way is to investigate the vitality of its center of excellence and its community of practice! Do these two organizational constructs form a learning system that integrates the new knowledge into the organization's process for strategic thinking and planning? Does this new knowledge cause the organization to adapt to changing environment or the stimulus of external ideas? Benchmarking maturity is best judged by the ability of new studies to influence the strategic direction and operational activities of the organization. If an organization acts like an adaptive learning system, stimulated by new knowledge that is generated from new studies, then the benchmarking system has become mature.

ADAPTIVE LEARNING SYSTEM

In many companies, the business systems appears to be like the horse designed by a committee (this is a definition of a camel). The business system itself has not been designed to operate in a specific way; it is haphazardly constructed and is a disjoint conglomeration of management practices that are fragmented and create internal conflict as the improvement efforts sponsored by different functions do not create a coherent approach to define the future. In such an organization, the loyalty that is provided to the strong functional managers drives them to promote their biased solutions for business improvement as the best for the organization as a whole (i.e., activity-based costing for finance, business process reengineering for information technology, and team-based employee empowerment for human resources). This conflict provides an unhealthy foundation for process improvement. When such a conflagration exists, then the practice of benchmarking becomes yet one more tool in the box and loses its capability to make a coherent contribution in helping to define the organization's strategic interest or those best practices that the organization needs to stimulate its internal improvement efforts.

These fragmented approaches to business improvement should give way to a more focused and comprehensive approach that consolidates the best of all practices into a coherent system that focuses on both "fitness *of* purpose" or the objectives to be achieved (this is also called *doing the right thing*) as well as "fitness *for* purpose" (sometimes called *doing things right*) or the actions to be accomplished to achieve the objective. In my experience, the best way to integrate all the improvement tools and methods of an organization is in a comprehensive Six Sigma program that is linked with management practices for process benchmarking, business planning, managerial accounting, and information technology. When this is done, then the organization has effectively established an adaptive learning system by linking its process improvement methods with its business analysis and strategic planning processes to form a means to continuously refresh its strategy and thereby challenge the appropriateness of its action plans. This process relies on the organization's capability to continuously benchmark and scan its environment for new ideas that stimulate it to think differently and adapt itself to the changes in trends that affect its business, while at the same time maintaining constancy of purpose in its long-term business pursuits.

Today, fragmentation is all too frequent in management systems. Six Sigma approaches, which link customer and stakeholder goals to process indicators, have largely contributed to overcoming the problem, but still the importance of measurement alignment between benchmarking, planning, process management, and self-assessment is underestimated. As a starting point, business leaders should reflect upon some questions to see if they have prepared their organization for the adaptive learning system that is enabled by integrating benchmarking with the planning and management processes of their organization:

- Is our company networked well enough with leading organizations to allow us to learn about best practices and develop improvements to enable us to accomplish our strategic goals?
- Are we doing enough to develop network capabilities that will allow us to maintain a continuous learning effort that can feed our organization's learning engine?
- In what ways are we leveraging learning to achieve enhanced benefits in all of the applicable areas?
- How well does our networking contribute to our portfolio of new ideas about how to manage our business?
- Are we investing enough time and effort in creating a cross-organizational learning collaborative?

Learning is an adaptive and collaborative process whereby lessons come from both our success and failures—as well as through the success and failure of others—so we steer our future direction more soundly and do not repeat historical catastrophes. Where patterns exist in learning, it is important to understand how these patterns are created and what they imply. To an analytical thinker, such patterns can identify potential root causes of process failure. When a business or work process is continuously changing, it is necessary to generate adaptive learning in order to discern the meaning of the entire system in which the process exits as it undergoes transformation and thereby learn the potential effects of change on the system as a whole. This is the problem that businesses encounter—a continuously changing environment that its working processes must learn and then adapt to their desired strategy so business may maintain progress toward achievement of its chosen performance target. Adaptive learning helps to discern meaning in continuously changing systems that are undergoing transformation. This is a persistent challenge for most businesses—a continuously changing environment that requires its working processes to learn and adapt to rapidly shifting market and technological conditions so that the business may maintain its progress toward achieving its performance objectives.

Change is being accelerated by the global technological shift toward interconnectivity. As the world moves from relationships based on "atoms," where value comes from the physical products, to one based on "bytes," where value is a function of services or software provided to support products whose functions have become more generic, customization becomes deliverable concurrently by mass production processes. Today, this phenomenon occurs in the cellular phone industry where both aftermarket custom cases and user programmable ringing tones and games allow the phone to become truly unique and personalized. But how will value be delivered in the future as we learn more? Will the knowledge of customer needs become so complete that appropriate insights are always gained into customer requirements and value becomes taken for granted? Will flawless execution of work become possible so that customers consistently receive the value that they desire, not just require? These two conditions define a utopian state that is potentially closer now than it has ever been before.

When learning occurs across firms, there is a greater opportunity to gain insights that lead to development of breakthrough concepts simply because the diversity of viewpoints will spawn an enriched interpretation of the practices that stimulate change.

ADMINISTRATION OF BENCHMARKING

Just creating external relationships and internal capabilities is not enough to ensure success in an organization's approach to benchmarking. The organization must also have a culture that is open to learning from others. Effective benchmarking requires external, adaptive learning, and this is not a natural ingredient in many organizational cultures. Indeed, the cultural heritage of many organizations seems to be focused on the not-invented-here syndrome—which specifically devalues learning from external sources. So what can be done to build a culture that is open to benchmarking? Some of the elements of business culture that may be influenced by benchmarking include the following:

- Teamwork
- Achievement
- Customer satisfaction
- Decision making
- Competence development

Figure 10.1 indicates several capabilities that can enable improved outcomes from the process of benchmarking by enhancing the organization's capabilities.

What can an organization do to administer its center of benchmarking excellence while also facilitating its community of practice? First, we must focus on how to build a center for benchmarking excellence. There are five ingredients in successful administration of a center for benchmarking excellence:

- Business measures and benchmarking procedures to define a framework for studies
- Benchmarking specialists who can facilitate study teams and perform the analyses
- Training to increase the effectiveness of teams who are doing the benchmarking studies

Capability Area	Capabilities That Enable Effective Benchmarking
Performance Skills	• Project management • Team facilitation • Meeting management • Statistical analysis (Black-Belt or Green-Belt level)
Management Systems	• Six Sigma/Lean enterprise • Customer dashboard • Formal project selection process
Technical Systems	• Enterprise resource planning software • Relational database
Cultural Values	• Process orientation • Attitude of continuous improvement • Fact-based management • Goal-directed behavior • Accountability for performance • Standard work practices

FIGURE 10.1 Capabilities that enable effective benchmarking

- Information technology to enable relational analysis of your data warehouse
- Continuous benchmarking as part of your business environmental scanning

Each of these elements must be understood in its own right.

BENCHMARKING METRICS AND PROCEDURES

Benchmarking measures must be aligned with the business measurement system of the organization. Thus, strategic studies should focus on those factors that influence the total corporate performance or create discontinuities that lead to breakthrough change. These types of studies should respond to the value measurement dimensions of the organization.

Organizations produce value in three different dimensions: value for markets and customers, value for shareholders and investors, and value for society. In this final area, there are no real measurement systems that define the overall "balanced scorecard" for performance. Many small indicators are used to determine if an organization is fulfilling its responsibility to employees, communities, government, and the public, in general (including the future generations of mankind). Will there be an indicator for the social value added contribution of a firm as there are for market value added (MVA or the brand value added contribution) and economic value added (EVA or the shareholder value added contribution)?

Leaders will not be credible quality champions if they do not convert their unique focus on the bottom line into a focus on a multiple bottom line that extends the scope from financial results to people and society related results. Perhaps the almost exclusive focus of many American companies on shareholder value will become a big obstacle on the road to sustainable excellence. Conversely, many European countries focus more on stakeholder value than on shareholder value — and that, too, is an obstacle to excellence. Society as a stakeholder is going to become particularly important whenever the interest of mankind in a global world is at stake, not just protection of the environment and social responsibility, but also in the areas of biogenetics and international relations. Mastering these changes will become more and more a quality-related issue. Quality will assume the role of protecting humanity from the risk of disruptive changes to the environment.

Customer satisfaction is the final goal of quality activities and the ultimate enabler of enduring competitiveness. While we have discussed stakeholder satisfaction, there is a distinction between these two types of satisfaction that must be made. *Stakeholder value* focuses on intrinsic characteristics of an organization — display creativity within the framework of restrictive conditions that are imposed by society. It is compliance or obedience-based. However, *customer satisfaction* is based on extrinsic characteristics and is the aim of work. It is achievement based. While the importance of stakeholder satisfaction will rapidly increase in the near future, it must be emphasized that when we achieve stakeholder satisfaction, this performance is nonsense if we have not first achieved customer satisfaction.

After a strategic measurement system has been defined, it must be cascaded into a linked and aligned system of measures to permit line-of-sight connectivity from the strategic direction of the company to the operational processes that deliver the actions to drive in that direction. Thus, the measurement system must link key results measures for overall organizational performance to the key process measures, describing a level of operational performance that generates these intended results. Benchmarking studies are appropriate if targeting all of the measurements along this performance chain.

BENCHMARKING SPECIALISTS TO FACILITATE STUDIES

The concept of a benchmarking specialist was first developed at Xerox, where people from the company's quality network established a companywide capability to conduct benchmarking studies. Today, such a capability exists in many organizations through their distributed network of Six Sigma Black Belts. These individuals have the skills, knowledge, and business experience to act as specialists and facilitate benchmarking studies. It is essential that they be used to do these studies in addition to their DMAIC and design for Six Sigma improvement projects.

BENCHMARKING TEAM TRAINING

A benchmarking team should be convened to perform the external study after the process has been documented internally and all of the secondary research is completed. All of this preliminary work should be facilitated by the benchmarking specialist in conjunction with work groups in processes that are affected by the proposed study. This work is best accomplished as part of a Six Sigma DMAIC project in order to assure that there is a rigorous internal definition of process performance. The appropriate timing to convene the team is following the completion of the DMA phases of the Six Sigma project after a *Kaizen Blitz* has been conducted to capture the quick wins from the initial analyses. In addition, the benchmarking specialists should assure that the project leverages its learning by examining all related improvement projects that have been conducted in the past and conducting a postmortem assessment on them so that the learning is preserved from this work for their study.

When the team is formed, the benchmarking specialist along with the sponsoring manager should kick-off the formal study with a workshop to provide team training. What should be the training subjects included in this team workshop? Here is a sample agenda:

- What is benchmarking?
- Business reasons for benchmarking
- Linking benchmarking to other activities: Six Sigma, business excellence, ISO9000
- Benchmarking code of conduct
- Description of the business challenge presented to the team
- Process of benchmarking and team activities at each phase of the project
- Interpretation of analysis methods
- Assessment of "leverage in" information and secondary research results
- Development of criteria for benchmarking partners
- Delineation of team actions and benchmarking specialist activities
- Project reporting requirements

This one- or two-day workshop moves the team from the point of interested observer in the study process to active participants in a coherent team.

TECHNOLOGY AND BENCHMARKING

Organizations will evolve over time as stimulated by the catalyst of technological change that makes possible new directions and challenges the horizon of today's business goals. It will be the challenge of management to stimulate meaningful innovation that makes a difference to their targeted customers—to find what future markets will value—and then define what will be their own organization's unique value proposition or promise to the market. The operational challenge of management will remain essentially the same. Once a promise has been made to the market in the form of a new product or specified service, then management must assure that it has processes that will consistently keep their promise to their customers. However, the underlying challenge of business leaders will be to engage the power of their people to develop a collaborative effort that facilitates the shared vision.

Benchmarking is becoming integrated into management systems where the best of all approaches are merged into unique quality systems that engage the entire business, rather than a single function, and an entire related operating philosophy and organizational culture is developed by the management team as the core dimension of its way of working. The formalization of toolkits and bodies of knowledge are only the beginning steps toward this integration. Development of customized business models based on quality system models, such as business excellence and ISO9000, is another step in this direction. The resultant business systems integration will be centered on the human cultural dimension of an organization and based on a process model for its critical business processes using measurement control points to link balanced scorecard metrics to indicators of actionable operating conditions that drive the routine performance, which produces the desired output of the business value chain.

Such business system integration will not be driven by selection of an Enterprise Resource Program (ERP), but it will represent a choice for doing business that is identified and desired by management (process definitions, measurement systems, and people systems) and then be embedded into the ERP. While the current generation of ERP systems can provide consistency of operation across a business, their generic solutions to operational problems may not provide competitive advantage if all the competitors are using the same process. Competitive advantage will come when the organization chooses a direction—different from the competition, yet aligned with realities of the desired customer experience—and then focuses its energies and talent in making this choice work well.

271

While the current emphasis in business is on application of "fashionable" technology, technologies will become increasingly integrated as a convergence occurs to create a personal electronic appliance[1] that is able to deliver application-specific required knowledge electronically to the point of need. In the near future, technology will enable quality—placing solutions into the hands of workers at the time that they are needed—and anticipate problems through smart monitoring of all process performance parameters that contribute significantly to the customer-perceivable output. In order to achieve this integration, organizations will become knowledge-based learning centers in their efforts to maintain a competitive edge.

For business improvement to be driven to the next level of performance, it must be comprehensively applied and assimilated into the entire business system equally at the grassroots level of organizations and the strategic apex of its senior leadership and their process of management. Continuous learning must be a value of the organization of the future—leaders must create an environment where everyone is a learner, everyone is a teacher, and everyone takes responsibility to mentor those who need development. Such a proactive, human-focused business environment can only be developed when both the "hard, analytical disciplines" and the "soft, psychological disciplines" merge into a unified approach for managing results through people. How will the future migrate from the current state to establish the context for this integration?

CONTINUOUS BENCHMARKING

One thing we know, however, is that the future will not be sluggish. It will be fast paced and complex as markets produce alternative technol-

---

1. By personal electronic appliance, I mean a device that represents the ultimate in convergence of the technologies of laptop computers, personal data assistants, mobile phones, electronic books, along with the spectrum of electronic entertainment and recording devices. I described this vision and its potential in an article written in *Quality Progress Magazine* called "Digital Nails and Electronic Hammers: Tools of the Next Generation" July (1996).

ogies and applications diverge from the traditional knowledge base. This means that rapid choices must be made in the face of many types of risk—not just financial risk, but also operational risk, market risk, and technological risk. Managing in this complex web of interrelated opportunities for both success and failure will become a strain on business leaders. The complexity of the environment will force leaders to address new or emerging business issues such as quality in governance and ever-improving the management of organizational change. It seems as though organizations have become proficient at defining the changes that they want to make, but fail during the implementation. Excellence in the future will be observed only through the actions taken by organizations as all these dimensions of quality are addressed simultaneously.

While the current age is technological, technologies will become increasingly integrated and able to deliver electronically to the point of need, the knowledge required for specific operating work. In the near future, technology will enable quality—placing solutions into the hands of workers at the time that they are needed—and anticipate problems through smart monitoring of all process performance parameters that contribute significantly to the customer-perceivable output. In order to achieve this integration, organizations will need to become knowledge-based learning centers.

In order for quality to be taken to the grassroots level of organizations, it must be assimilated into the entire business system and, most especially, into its senior leadership and their process of management. Continuous learning must be a value of the organization of the future. Leaders must create an environment where everyone is a learner, everyone is a teacher, and everyone takes responsibility to mentor those who need development. Such a proactive, human-focused business environment can only be developed when both the "hard, analytical dimension of quality" and the "soft, psychological dimension of quality" come together in a unified approach for managing results through people. How will the future provide the context for this integration?

BENCHMARKING PROCESS AUDIT

The following is a self-assessment of capacity to network effectively:

- Have we developed a strategy for external company networking relationships?
- Who is responsible for this strategy, and how effectively is it being executed?
- Do we know all of the relationships we have, their nature, and performance results?
- Have we exploited all possible networking opportunities and kept the best?
- Do we have a policy to encourage key employees to participate in these networks?
- How are we capturing and applying the learning and knowledge from these networks?

Some organizations find that doing a quick assessment of their business control system to encourage the use of benchmarking is an effective reminder of the need for using this business practice. This assessment should be planned like any other audit. The team to conduct it must be identified and a standard questionnaire should be used to query the organization and collect information about the progress in benchmarking implementation. A quick review of results should be conducted immediately after the audit is completed, followed by a detailed report describing areas of strength and opportunities for process improvement and specific recommendations. As a guideline, some of the questions that should be considered in evaluating your benchmarking capability could include the following:

1. What is the vision for deployment of benchmarking in your business unit? How broad an application of benchmarking is planned? For instance, is it limited in scope to operational benchmarking of production processes, or will it used to improve all key business and support processes?

2. How is benchmarking helping to define your business unit goals? Do business leaders clearly understand the linkage between benchmarking and their business unit goals?

3. What actions have your business leaders taken to demonstrate their support for benchmarking? Is there evidence in the form of memoranda on benchmarking? Are meetings held that focus the benchmarking study selection process? Has a core group of Six Sigma Black Belts been developed as benchmarking specialists?

4. Have your business leaders taken any specific steps to benchmark the performance objectives of process owners in order to establish their accountability for delivering breakthrough improvements?

5. How are benchmarking projects selected? What is the process used? What are the criteria for selection of projects? How can you be assured that you have identified those projects that have the greatest impact on business improvement?

6. What process measurement system has been defined for your organization? How do you benchmark your top-tier measures? Have you linked these top-tier measures to the operational measures of work processes? Do your operational measures also have external benchmarks? Is there a defined relationship between the benchmarking of your operational measures and your indicators of strategic business performance?

Only when we seriously examine our key business factors on a regular basis can we be sure that they will be refreshed and improved as required to keep our competitive edge.

CONCLUDING COMMENT

When business improvement methods such as strategic benchmarking and Six Sigma are integrated into everything that your company does, then they have become a critical part of your organization's DNA—the genetic strain that defines the difference that your organization makes in its marketplace. As organizations depend more and more upon their ability to learn and know, the business need for integrated business improvement methods will become stronger, and the imperative to reload all management methods with the science of Six Sigma will drive the redefinition how business is done—by working smarter, not just working harder. I will offer one story in closing.

During 1999 to 2001, I worked with Taizo Nishimuro, then chairman of Toshiba Corporation in the deployment of Six Sigma in a program that he called *Management Innovation 2001*. The program was actually a major-change management initiative designed to transition Toshiba into a more capable organization who could deal more effectively with the changing business environment of the coming century. It was a far-reaching program. One day in his office, I noticed that Nishimuro had a single Japanese *kanji* character framed on his wall. I asked him what it was. He told me that it meant *flexibility*—that as the CEO he had to be able to see the world many different ways and be able to process this information in order to understand how it could influence the organization's future direction. Later, he presented me with a single *kanji* character—he told me it meant *work smart*—I interpreted this to mean that as the CEO it was his job to be flexible and my job to work smart. Another business sage, Dr. W. Edwards Deming, would have agreed with this interpretation. Deming said that hard work is not enough; we can't improve processes by just working harder—organizations must learn to improve by working smarter at all levels. Strategic benchmarking is a business tool that stimulates working smarter.

The Benchmarking Code of Conduct

PREAMBLE

Benchmarking—the process of identifying and learning from best practices anywhere in the world—is a powerful tool in the quest for continuous improvement.

To guide benchmarking encounters and to advance the professionalism and effectiveness of benchmarking, the International Benchmarking Clearinghouse, a service of the American Productivity & Quality Center, and the Strategic Planning Institute Council on Benchmarking have adopted this common Code of Conduct.[1] We encourage all organizations to abide by this Code of Conduct. Adherence to these principles will contribute to efficient, effective, and ethical benchmarking. This edition of

---

1. This code of conduct was adapted from an earlier version that was originally created by the Council for Benchmarking of the Strategic Planning Institute. It was originally developed by SPI Executive Director Jim Staker and Sam Bookhart of DuPont Fibers. This version of the code of conduct was further edited by Sam Bookhart and Gregory H. Watson for use by the International Benchmarking Clearinghouse in 1992.

the Code of Conduct has been expanded to provide greater guidance on the protocol of benchmarking for beginners.

BENCHMARKING CODE OF CONDUCT

Individuals agree for themselves and their company to abide by the following principles for benchmarking with other organizations.

1. *Principle of Legality*
   - If there is any potential question on the legality of an activity, don't do it.
   - Avoid discussions or actions that could lead to or imply an interest in restraint of trade, market, or customer allocation schemes, price fixing, dealing arrangements, bid rigging, or bribery. Don't discuss costs with competitors if costs are an element of pricing.
   - Restrain from the acquisition of trade secrets from any means that could be interpreted as improper, including the breach or inducement of a breach of any duty to maintain secrecy. Do not disclose or use any trade secret that may be been obtained through improper means or that was disclosed by another in violation of a duty to maintain its secrecy or limit of use.
   - Do not, as a consultant or a client, extend one benchmarking study's findings to another company without first obtaining permission from the parties of the first study.
2. *Principle of Exchange*
   - Be willing to provide the same type and level of information that you request from your benchmarking partner to your benchmarking partner.
   - Communicate fully and early in the relationship to clarify expectations, avoid misunderstandings, and establish mutual interest in the benchmarking exchange.
   - Be honest and complete.
3. *Principle of Confidentiality*
   - Treat benchmarking interchange as confidential to the individu-

als and companies involved. Information must not be communicated outside the partnering organizations without the prior consent of the benchmarking partner who shared the information.

- A company's participation in a study is confidential and should not be communicated externally without its prior permission.

4. *Principle of Use*
- Use information obtained through benchmarking only for purposes of formulating improvement of operations or processes within the companies participating in the benchmarking study.
- The use of communication of a benchmarking partner's name with the data obtained or practices observed requires the prior permission of that partner.
- Do not use benchmarking as a means to market or to sell.

5. *Principle of First-Party Contact*
- Initiate benchmarking contacts, whenever possible, through a benchmarking contact designated by the partner company.
- Respect the corporate culture of partner companies, and work within mutually agreed upon procedures.
- Obtain mutual agreement with the designated benchmarking contact on any hand off of communication or responsibility to other parties.

6. *Principle of Third-Party Contact*
- Obtain an individual's permission before providing his or her name in response to a contact request.
- Avoid communicating a contact's name in an open forum without the contact's permission.

7. *Principle of Preparation*
- Demonstrate commitment to the efficiency and effectiveness of benchmarking by completing preparatory work prior to making an initial benchmarking contact and following a benchmarking process
- Make the most of your benchmarking partner's time by being fully prepared for each exchange.
- Help your benchmarking partners prepare by providing them

with an interview guide or questionnaire and agenda prior to benchmarking visits.

8. *Principle of Completion*
   - Follow through with each commitment made to your benchmarking partners in a timely manner.
   - Complete each benchmarking study to the satisfaction of all benchmarking partners as mutually agreed.

9. *Principle of Understanding and Action*
   - Understand how your benchmarking partners would like to be treated.
   - Treat your benchmarking partners in the way that each benchmarking partner would like to be treated.
   - Understand how each benchmarking partner would like to have the information he or she provides handled and used, and handle and use it in that manner.

Standard Operating Procedure

Benchmarking Process

PURPOSE

This standard operating procedure describes the philosophy, approach, methods, and management process for conducting benchmarking studies at both the strategic and operational level of the company's activities.

SCOPE

This is a mandatory procedure that applies to all internal and external studies that compare performance between different parties in order to discover best practices that may be implemented to improve performance results.

REFERENCES

1. Gregory Watson, *Strategic Benchmarking* (New York: Wiley, 1993).
2. Gregory Watson, *The Benchmarking Workbook* (Portland, OR: Productivity Press, 1992).

DOCUMENT OWNER

The document owner is the director of corporate quality.

DEFINITIONS

- *Benchmarking:* A process of comparing the performance and process characteristics between two or more organizations in order to learn how to improve.
- *Strategic Benchmarking:* A benchmarking study whose objective is to discover ideas for improvement that will trigger breakthrough changes and may be leveraged across the business to enhance an organization's competitive advantage.
- *Operational Benchmarking:* A benchmarking study that is focused on the way that a specific work process is performed, with an objective of improving the performance of that specific process (e.g., improving a sales process, printed circuit board production process, or distribution process).
- *Critical Success Factor (CSF):* A key results performance indicator that differentiates the relative success of two organizations at performing the same process. The CSF must also relate to the internal balanced scorecard performance reporting system, and a CSF should relate to the output of the process for performance that is critical to satisfaction of the process customer.
- *Process Enablers:* Specific operational activities that contribute directly or indirectly to the observed process performance. Measures of process enablers should be linked to the output or results measures (those describing performance of critical success factors in the process) and be demonstrated as statistically significant causes for the observed best-practice performance of the process.
- *Best Practice:* The specific activity, capability, or technology application that has been demonstrated as an enabler of the observed performance excellence. For a specific enabler to be classified as a *best practice,* the management practice must have been rated in the top

282

fifth percentile of all observed practices. Good practices can also be a source of learning but should not be placed into the same category as a best practice when describing study results.

- *Operating Committee:* An executive management committee charged with executing oversight for performance management and operation of the core business processes.
- *Benchmarking Process Owner:* The benchmarking process owner is assigned with responsibility for the long-term development and improvement of the organization's capability to perform benchmarking studies and apply their results. Responsibilities include management and conduct of benchmarking-related training, management of benchmarking records and documents, and the management of all standard operating procedures related to benchmarking. The benchmarking process owner will also serve as an executive coach to guide benchmarking project sponsors through the steps of the study process and will assign a benchmarking specialist to facilitate the entire study process.
- *Benchmarking Project Sponsor:* The benchmarking project owner is responsible for the cradle-to-grave conduct of a single benchmarking study and will assign a study advisory team to provide process-level guidance to develop study details, interpret the study results, and assist in formulation of recommendations. The benchmarking project sponsor will also be charged with the timely implementation of the project recommendations.
- *Benchmarking Study Team:* The benchmarking study team will operate under the leadership of the benchmarking specialist to design and execute the benchmarking study. The team will be composed of representatives from all affected work-process areas, as well as technical support staff to assist in their specialty areas (e.g., materials engineers, information technology, manufacturing technology, etc.).
- *Study Advisory Team:* A study advisory team consists of business specialists and process owners who are charged with maintaining the study realism and assuring its applicability as the project progresses through its phase-gate milestones. The study advisory team will perform four major reviews to assist the benchmarking study team in

its efforts: Study Plan Approval (review of study plans, partnership criteria, and proposed partner organizations); Information Transparency Approval (review of the detailed operational definitions of performance measures, including the draft questionnaires and interview guidelines prior to contacting external study partners); Preliminary Results Review (an assessment of the preliminary study results to help generate ideas for adaptation to the organization); and Approval of Study Report (review of the final study results including the final report and plan of action for implementing the recommendations). Note that the milestone for approval of study recommendations is reserved for a joint meeting of the operating committee with the study advisory team, prior to the approval of the study report.

- *Benchmarking Specialist:* A Six Sigma Black Belt who is charged with responsibility for conducting the preliminary Six Sigma DMA process study and then facilitating the benchmarking study team through the entire project. Benchmarking specialists are responsible for following the benchmarking standard operating procedure and assuring the technical and statistical validity of the study. Benchmarking specialists will be supported by other technical specialists (e.g., from information technology or engineering), as required for the specific project.

PHILOSOPHY AND APPROACH

The benchmarking process will begin by identifying the focus areas where performance advantage is desired in the business. Once the management team has identified a focus area, then measures of enabling performance will be defined and related to the business critical success factors that are reported for guiding overall performance results for the organization. A Six Sigma project will be initiated to characterize process performance in this focus area and determine baseline capability. Once our baseline performance is known, then a management review by the operating committee will be conducted to authorize a formal study based on a study plan and measurement specification. Once a study has been approved, then the operating committee will specify the objectives for the study and provide supporting information as required in the benchmarking study template. The final report and recommendations from the study must be submitted to the operating committee within one month of the study initiation.

MANAGEMENT PROCESS

Once a benchmarking study has been authorized by the operating committee, then the benchmarking project sponsor (a manager designated as the business lead for the study) will meet with the director of corporate quality (the benchmarking process owner) to establish a specific plan of action for conducting the study and will assign team members who are most suitable to pursue the study in a timely manner.

BENCHMARKING METHOD

The overall process for conducting the benchmarking study will apply the following steps.

- *Identify the Topic:* The topic will be assigned by the operating committee based on an initial assessment of opportunities for organizational development or improvement.
- *Plan the Study:* The study plan will be developed jointly by the benchmarking project sponsor and the benchmarking process owner. A formal study plan will be issued to the benchmarking project team that they assign to conduct the study. The director of quality will assign a benchmarking specialist to facilitate the study.
- *Define Performance Criteria:* The performance criteria for the benchmarking study will be established during a preliminary process characterization study that uses the Six Sigma DMA process to baseline the performance and establish the theoretical base case performance of the business focus area.
- *Establish a Baseline:* The baseline performance of the study subject will be defined in the preliminary Six Sigma DMA study. The baseline will

include the historical trend of data, process capability calculations, customer specification of tolerance in process variation, and operational definitions of key terms used to describe the measurements.

- *Solicit Study Participants:* The benchmarking project sponsor will establish a study advisory team to define the criteria for soliciting study partners and approve the set of organizations that will be contacted for participation. This study advisory team will execute managerial oversight for the benchmarking project team.

- *Prepare Questionnaire for Survey:* The benchmarking specialist will facilitate the benchmarking study team in developing a questionnaire for initial screening of the potential study partners. This questionnaire should be reviewed by a specialist to assure the questions are objective and are phrased so their meaning is not ambiguous.

- *Conduct Preliminary Interviews:* The benchmarking specialist will conduct all of the preliminary interviews (via e-mail or telephone) and will prepare a summary report for the team. The team will identify those organizations that they wish to pursue for data analysis.

- *Collect Performance Data:* The benchmarking specialist will coordinate all external data collection with partner organizations and will evaluate this information to assure it is feasible to make meaningful cross-comparisons among the partner organizations.

- *Analyze Performance Results:* The benchmarking specialist will analyze submitted performance results and establish performance envelopes for each organization, as well as performing appropriate statistical comparisons to assure that the results have been sustained over time.

- *Identify Benchmark Practice:* The team will apply the company's decision criteria to the analysis of the performance results in order to determine which study partners are benchmark practices. Permission for a site visit will be requested from these partners.

- *Conduct Site Visits:* The benchmarking specialist will lead a subgroup of the total benchmarking study team in conducting a site visit at the identified best practice for the purpose of developing an understanding of the practice in operational detail.

- *Document Benchmark Practice:* At the completion of each site visit conducted, the team will document the benchmark practice as soon as possible to assure that they capture all the necessary lessons to be learned.

- *Adapt Benchmark Practice:* The benchmarking study team will meet with the study advisory team to adapt the study learning into a recommendation for internal change. This joint team recommendation will be presented to both the benchmarking project sponsor and the operating committee for final approval and implementation.
- *Prepare Final Recommendations and Report:* The benchmarking study team will prepare two final reports—comprehensive report for internal distribution and a final report for sharing with external partners.
- *Share Report with External Partners:* The report that is shared with benchmarking partners should include the following items: the performance survey results with participant identity blinded; statistical analysis of best-practice performance; documentation of best practice (performance indexed value stream map); and operational definitions of the critical process enablers.

PROCESS FLOW DIAGRAM

The following process diagram assigns this sequence of benchmarking steps into a series of five project phases:

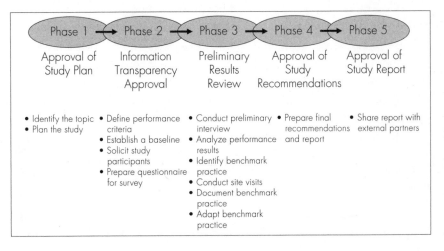

Record and Storage Retention Policy

Benchmarking records (study plan, trip reports, report to partners, and final report) are to be stored at the corporate quality office for a period of seven years. After this period, a review shall be conducted jointly by the director of strategic planning and the director of corporate quality to determine if any of the items are of sufficient historical interest to be filed in the corporate archives. If they are not transferred to the archives, then these documents need no longer be retained.

Control Plan

The following business controls will apply to all external benchmarking studies:

1. All studies must be initiated with the approval of the operating committee or by a corporate executive who will act as the benchmarking project sponsor.
2. Each external study will be assigned a director-level executive as corporate sponsor and charged with the oversight of the study to assure transparency in all activities.
3. All external studies will comply with the Benchmarking Code of Conduct.
4. Each benchmarking team will be facilitated by a member of the corporate quality staff who has been expressly trained in good benchmarking practices.
5. All surveys will be reviewed prior to external release to assure both good format in the questions and sensitivity to corporate governance issues.
6. Performance measures used for study results must be related to the corporate system of operational measures.
7. Identified benchmark-level performance must be at least top quartile in a statistically validated performance analysis.
8. Any confidential information gathered will be marked as "Company Confidential" at the time it is accepted, and a formal, written

receipt will be issued specifying both the use of this information and the record and storage requirements that must be followed.

PRACTICAL ADVICE

- Benchmarking studies should be designed before starting the data collection process. If you can align study topics to those areas that are strategic imperatives to improve your business, then you will get the maximum leverage from the learning you gain.
- When considering what to benchmark talk to your customers, talk to noncustomers that you would like to become customers, and also talk with the customers of your competitor in order to learn what improvements are necessary within your industry.
- Understand how the benchmarking topic that you have identified for study is linked to the characteristics of your organization's outputs that are critical to the satisfaction of your customers.
- The champion or sponsor of your study should be in a position to implement results of your study and should be involved in the study process from the initiation of the plan to the interpretation of the data and establishment of the implementation plan for improving your processes to incorporate the process learning.
- Team members should be identified early in the study to assure that they are available to help and that they are free to travel. Team membership may change as the project progresses in order to assure the right mixture of skills and competence on the team.
- Fix what you find broken now to capture what is called "low-hanging fruit," but remember that you should concentrate on developing the long-term solution that will be based on the process observations from leading companies.
- Remember to characterize your own process before seeking to learn about how others approach their process design. You will discover many quick wins just from simple actions, like tracking how you perform the process currently and establishing baseline performance for the process.

- Take time to carefully develop your performance measures and assure that they are truly critical success factors that are important to the process output. Measures of the process enablers should be linked to the output or results measures in order to be able to demonstrate causation in the process characteristics.
- Collect all of the information about critical success factors, but apply the logic of the Six Sigma DMAIC process to reduce the number of factors down to the vital few.
- Do not ask your benchmarking partners for inappropriate or sensitive business data.
- Do not waste time in gathering information that is available from public sources.
- Spend time designing the data collection plan, sample size, sampling frequency, and demonstration of measurement effectiveness.
- Conduct a pilot data collection effort to demonstrate efficacy of interview questions, data collection plan, and analysis methodology. Assure you know how to interpret it!
- Debrief your site visit or interview immediately following the session, as there is a great loss of detail in observations as the time lengthens from the experience.
- Think outside the boundaries of your normal process and use creative imagination to adapt the learning you have observed at other organizations to your own work.
- Benchmarking is not a process about copying the processes of others. It requires that recognized leading practices be adapted to the business model, industry, and culture of the firm.

APPENDIXES

- Study Plan Format
- Measurement Specification Template
- Benchmarking Study Template

Web Resources for Benchmarking

BENCHMARKING AND QUALITY ORGANIZATIONS

American Society for Quality
www.asq.org

GOAL/QPC
www.goalqpc.com

International Benchmarking Clearinghouse at American Productivity & Quality Center
www.aqpc.org

Profit Impact of Market Strategy
www.pimsonline.org

Global Benchmarking Network
www.globalbenchmarking.com

Robert C. Camp
rcampbpi@att.net

The Benchmarking Network
www.benchmarkingnetwork.com

Best Practices LLC Global Benchmarking Council
www3.best-in-class.com/gbc

The Benchmarking Exchange
www.benchnet.com

STATISTICAL ANALYSIS SOFTWARE

Minitab Software Package
www.minitab.com

JMP Software Offered by SAS Institute
www.imp.com

PRIMER ON WEB-BASED SEARCH LOGIC

http://www.internettutorials.net/boolean.html

Glossary of Terms Used in Lean Production

Andon: [Japanese] From the word meaning "light"—a visual control device to indicate production process status—it may be either a flashing light that signals problems (e.g., yellow for off-rate production and red for line stoppage), or it may be an overhead video display that provides visual and numerical indicators of flow in production. An *andon* is used to describe the current status of production and to alert everyone to changes in status or emerging problems (line slowdown, etc.).

Autonomation: A form of automation in which machinery automatically inspects each item it produces for defects and then stops production if a defect is detected and notifies the operator of this condition (see *Jidohka*).

Autonomous Maintenance: [*jishu hozen* in Japanese] The self-management of routine equipment maintenance tasks by the operators. This approach may also include participation of operators in the repair and service of their equipment.

Baka yoke: [Japanese] A manufacturing method for preventing mistakes by designing the production process, equipment, and tools so operations cannot be performed incorrectly. In this system, the device not only prevents incorrect operation, but it also provides a warning to the operator of incorrect performance (see *Poka yoke*).

Balanced Production: A manufacturing condition where the capacity of the production resources is matched exactly to the market demand for the product. Work is distributed in the production line to avoid underutilization or overburden of individual activities and to assure a shorter flow time as both bottlenecks and downtime are avoided.

Batch and Queue: Producing more than one unit of production at a time and then moving the units to the next operating step before it has a need to produce using these units. This style of production creates waiting time as parts are moved in batches and wait in queues for the next operation to be conducted.

Bottleneck: The step in the production process that restricts the smooth flow of output to the customer—a production resource whose capacity is equal to or less than the demand that is placed upon it is a bottleneck.

Breakthrough: A dramatic change in process performance that removes an old barrier or surpasses milestone performance by achieving a significant increase in efficiency, cost reduction, quality level, or some other measurable performance indicator.

Cell: An arrangement of people, machines, material, and equipment so that processing of the production unit are colocated in their sequence of operation with minimal delay time between process steps.

Chaku-chaku: [Japanese] "load-load"—a method of conducting single-piece flow (*Nagara*) in which the operator moves from machine to machine taking the part from a previous machine and loading into the next machine to decrease the intermachine waiting time.

Changeover: The act of converting a production line or equipment to produce a new part, product, or model and which may require a new setup of the facilities such as changing of tooling, material replacement, or rearrangement of people and equipment.

Changeover Time: The time required to convert a workstation to achieve a part, product, or model changeover—it includes teardown time to remove a previous set of production conditions and setup time to assemble the new production conditions (see *Setup Time*).

Constraint: Anything that reduces the capacity of a system from achieving its throughput capability. The bottleneck that most severely restricts the continuous flow of production.

Continuous Flow: The production process where units are produced sequentially moving one unit at a time through the processing steps. Continuous flow is also called *one-piece flow* or *single-piece flow* production (see *Nagara*).

Cycle Time: The time required to complete a cycle or sequence of production operations from start to finish. When cycle time for each operation is equal to or less than takt time, then products can be produced in a single-piece continuous flow.

Dantotsu: [Japanese] Being the best of the best—sometimes translated as "world class" or "best practice."

Downtime: Any loss in production time due to equipment operating capability resulting from breakdown, maintenance or repair, power failure, operator availability, etc. (see *Operational Availability* and *Uptime*).

Error-Proofing: A process to prevent errors from moving down the production line and being delivered to customers as defects. When errors are not passed down the line, then both quality and productivity improve (see *Baka yoke* and *Poka yoke*).

First Pass Yield (FPY): The percentage of production that completes the final quality test for performance without being scrapped, rerun, reworked, retested or returned, or diverted for off-line repair (also called the *Right the First Time Yield (RFTY)* or *outgoing quality level*).

Gemba: [Japanese] The shop floor or workplace where production operations occur.

Hanedashi: [Japanese] Automatic part ejection.

Hansei: [Japanese] Reflection—reflecting on ideas or experiences in order to learn from successes and failures and improve either oneself or work processes in the future.

Heijunka: [Japanese] A method for load leveling of production rate or line balancing to smooth the flow of production by avoiding batching of different product categories, mixing production processes, or fluctuating volume produced for the same product.

Hinshitsu Kanri: [Japanese] Quality control management system.

Hoshin Kanri: [Japanese] Strategic planning and business control system that assigns the resources and people to complete projects that achieve breakthrough on the focus areas for improvement and achieve measurable goals for performance gains.

Jidohka: [Japanese] Transferring human intelligence to automated machinery so machines are able to detect production of a single defective part and immediately stop production and request help. In Toyota, this also includes the responsibility of each operator to inspect the quality of their own work and when a problem is detected to stop working until the cause of the defect has been corrected.

Just-in-Time (JIT): An optimal material flow system whereby material is brought to the point of processing or consumption at a rate such that it arrives just when it is needed.

Kaikaku: [Japanese] Radical improvement of any business activity to eliminate waste by reorganizing process operations to achieve *Dantotsu* or breakthrough results (see *Hoshin Kanri*).

Kaizen: [Japanese] Continuous, incremental improvement—always doing little things to consistently set and achieve higher work standards of performance.

Kanban: [Japanese] A signal that authorizes production or movement of a product using a card, sign board, container, or other signal to control the flow of production material.

Lead Time: The total time a customer must wait from submitting an order to receiving the ordered item (see *Order Turnaround Time*).

Lean: A systematic approach to identifying and eliminating waste (non-value added activities) through continuous improvement by making the production flow according to the rate of pull by the customer demand. Lean maximizes production of products to be sold to customers while minimizing operating and inventory costs.

Line Balancing: A process for distributing work in a production line so that tasks and staff are evenly balanced to coordinate individual workstation cycle times to meet the takt time (see *Takt Time*).

Little's Law: Named after MIT Professor John D. C. Little, who is considered the father of queuing theory in operations research—the average number of customers in a system (work in process) over some time interval is equal to their average arrival rate (throughput), multiplied by their average time in the system (cycle time).

Muda: [Japanese] Waste—all non-value adding activity is waste.

Nagara: [Japanese] One-piece production flow.

Nichijo Kanri: [Japanese] The daily management control system implementing 5-S, visual controls, and standardized work. This system is monitored using fundamental measures of quality and cycle time to assure balanced flow of production to reliably meet customer demand.

Non-Value Added Activity: Any activity for which a customer would not willingly pay and has no need. These activities add no real value to a product or service and are a form of waste (e.g., waiting time, transportation and handling time, or repair time) See *Value.*

One-Piece Flow: The opposite of batch production. Instead of building several products and holding them at the workstation before passing them on to the next operation, the operator passes each product to the next station without interruption of the production flow, and the products are presented one piece at a time to their subsequent process (see *Continuous Flow* and *Nagara*).

One-Touch Changeover: The reduction in work change over or setup time so that the task is completed in a single step (see *Single Minute Exchange of Dies*).

Order Turnaround Time: The total time from placement of a customer order to delivery of the ordered item in a usable state.

Operational Availability (A_o): The percentage of time during which production equipment is available to operate—also called *uptime*. It is calculated as machine operating time, as divided by available time (net planned nonworking time for training, breaks, vacations, or holidays) See *Uptime* and *Downtime*.

Pitch: Pace and flow of production—the amount of takt time it takes to produce a single, shippable unit of production (see *Takt Time*).

Poka yoke: [Japanese] Mistake-proofing techniques for avoidance, error elimination, and defect prevention at the point of process design. The method uses devices and detection methods to identify inadvertent mistakes and prevent them from occurring. Mistakes are activities that are wrong at the point of occurrence (within operation activity); errors are mistakes that have been passed on to the next workstation and reduce its productivity; and defects are errors that have failed detection in the process and are delivered to the customer (also called *safeguarding*—see *Error-Proofing* and *Baka yoke*).

Production Status Board: An electronic status board that displays production information, such as hourly targets and units produced. Information about problems and abnormal conditions relating to continuous flow are recorded for visual observation by the entire workforce.

Productivity: A measure of process outputs given the rate of production inputs.

Pull System: A system of production scheduling whereby the demand for production is set by the withdrawal of a finished item from inventory by a customer order, thereby setting a signal to replenish this item in inventory by producing an additional unit (this produces the trigger signal for a one-piece production flow).

Queue Time: The amount of time that a product spends in line waiting for the next step in the operation to be performed.

Quick Changeover (QCO): The ability to change either the product or model rapidly on a production line — switching tooling and fixtures rapidly so that multiple configurations or products may be produced using the same resources (see *Single Minute Exchange of Dies* and *One-Touch Changeover*).

Required Activity: A category of non-value added work that cannot be eliminated from a production process because the work output is required by a third party for legal, safety, environmental, or any other nonnegotiable business reason that affects good governance of the organization.

Rolled Throughput Yield (RTY): The product of the first pass yield of the individual steps in a continuous flow process. RTY is the probability of producing the final production unit right the first time without rework, repair, or retesting.

Seiri: [Japanese] The first of the five *S*s used to create a workplace that is suitable for the visual control of a lean production system — sort, structure, screen, or sift — to put in order the work environment by separating necessary tools, parts, and instructions from those that are not necessary and removing the unnecessary ones from the production environment. The activity simplifies the organization of the workplace.

Seiton: [Japanese] To set in order or systematize — to arrange neatly and identify parts and tools for ease of use. By organizing essential materials, operators are able to find what is needed, when it is needed because everything is in its correct location (see *Shadow Board*).

Seiso: [Japanese] To sanitize, sweep, or shine — to conduct a cleanup campaign. A dirty environment is often the source of problems in reliability, safety, or quality.

Seiketsu: [Japanese] To standardize the work process — to conduct the first three steps of the 5-S process (*Seiri, Seiton,* and *Seiso*) as part of the daily routine in order to maintain the orderliness of the workplace. Standard work is documented using visual controls so that operators have clear communication of the daily routine and are able to follow the policy and procedures unambiguously.

Sensei: [Japanese] A teacher who has a profound mastery of a body of knowledge (lean production or Six Sigma).

Setup Time: The time for conversion or changeover of a production operation. It includes both external setup (work done off the line while production continues) and internal setup (work that requires stopping the line and loss of productivity to complete the changeover).

Shadow Board: A visual management method that indicates the proper placement of a tool by its painted outline in order to identify its storage location and assure fast sighting of any misplaced tools.

Shitsuke: [Japanese] To sustain or maintain self-discipline — to form a habit of using the four Ss of the 5-S system to collectively assure an orderly, clean, and efficient working environment.

Shojinka: [Japanese] Continuously creating personnel capability improvement requirements of skills, training, or knowledge in order to enhance the performance capability of a production cell.

Simulate: The development of a model (either physical or computer based) of a production environment in order to examine alternative ways to conduct the work and eliminate non-value adding activities.

Single Minute Exchange of Dies (SMED): A process developed by Toyota industrial engineering manager Shigeo Shingo to effect rapid changeover of production equipment in less than 10 minutes. The objective of SMED is to achieve such a rapid changeover of tools that it is virtually instantaneous and does not interrupt the continuous flow of the production operations.

Standard Work: A precise description of the "one best way" of working that specifies the cycle time, takt time, and minimum quantity of parts that should always be available for use during or between processes (buffer stock). All work is organized around the human activity to assure that human motion is performed in an efficient sequence without waste.

Statistical Process Control (SPC): A statistical methodology developed by Dr. Walter E. Shewhart that evaluates process performance data to determine if new observations come from the same population that produced the previous results. A control chart plots the data history and the average performance of a process parameter of interest. The upper and lower control limits are calculated to compare new process data, and also a series of probability-based pattern recognition tests are used to determine if performance of the process is operating in a state of statistical control (e.g., no unusual events that are outside the range of reasonable probability). When "out of control" events are detected, a "special cause" of variation is identified that must be investigated in order to determine what changed from the common-cause system of natural process variation. Investigation of a special cause of variation may lead to the root cause of a process performance problem.

Streamline: Synonym for *lean*—a process for eliminating waste and cycle time from the production environment in order to assure the continuous flow of production.

Takt **Time:** [German] The rate of customer demand that is calculated by dividing the time that is available for production by the quantity of products ordered by customers during that time. *Takt* is a German word that describes a beat as in a heartbeat or the beat of a metronome that defines the tempo of music.

Teiem: [Japanese] An employee suggestion system used to solicit, analyze, and implement ideas for continuous improvement from frontline workers.

Theory of Constraints (TOC): Developed by management consultant Elihu Goldratt, this theory holds that resource flow is constrained at bottlenecks, which should be managed to improve throughput (salable output), while decreasing both inventory (nonsalable output) and operating expense.

Throughput: The rate at which a production system generates cash through sales or the conversion rate of inventory into shipped product.

Total Productive Maintenance (TPM): Use of reliability prediction, planned maintenance, and autonomous operator responsibility for equipment upkeep in a systematic process to reduce or eliminate equipment degradation or breakdown.

Touch Time: That portion of the total cycle time where an operator is handling a product.

Uptime: The time that production equipment is available for operation—the total time it is available, minus downtime (see *Operational Availability* and *Downtime*).

Value: A judgment of utility by a customer—either an item is worth what they paid for it, or it is useful to get their job done at a cost that is tolerable. Judgments of the value of a product are subjective and typically are based on a comparison with alternative goods or services that could become a substitute.

Value Adding Activity: Activities that transform inputs into customer usable output where the customer may be either an external consumer or an internal associate who is part of the flow sequence that delivers value to the ultimate consumer.

Value Stream: All activities, both value adding and non-value adding, that transform a raw material into a finished product that is ready for shipment to a customer. A value stream may be described from order to delivery (or installation), or it may be described from customer requirements through design to product launch.

Value Stream Map (VSM): A graphical representation or process map of the value stream of a production line.

Visual Controls: Any devices that allow workers to quickly manage the routine processes of production. These devices increase operator ownership for their work, clarify actions that are required, inform them of critical production information, or indicate the standards of work performance. Visual control devices include andon lights, painted floors, photo boards (e.g., for quality inspection requirements, recognition of employee achievements, or specification of work standards), production status boards, shadow boxes, and *Kanban* cards.

Waiting Time: The time that equipment, people, or material is idle and not involved in an activity of production.

Wa: [Japanese] Harmony within the workplace—a state achieved when all elements are in balance and synchronized.

Waste: Any activity that consumes resources and produces no value for the product or service that the ultimate customer desires (see *Muda*).

Work in Process (WIP): Production assemblies waiting to be processed or material that is in queue and idle. That part of the material inventory that is found between raw material and finished goods in the production process.

Chronological Bibliography of Books about Benchmarking

1. Porter, Michael E. 1980. *Competitive Strategy.* New York: The Free Press.
2. Deming, W. Edwards. 1982. *Out of the Crisis.* Cambridge, MA: Massachusetts Institute of Technology, Center for Advanced Engineering Study.
3. Fuld, Leonard M. 1985. *Competitor Intelligence: How to Get It — How to Use It.* New York: Wiley.
4. Porter, Michael E. 1985. *Competitive Advantage.* New York: The Free Press.
5. Corporate Quality Office. 1987. *Competitive Benchmarking: What It Is and What It Can Do For You.* Stamford, CT: Xerox Corporation.
6. Furey, Timothy R., Robert M. Fifer, Lawrence S. Pryor, and Jeffrey P. Rumberg. 1988. *Beating the Competition: A Practical Guide to Benchmarking.* Vienna, VA: Kaiser Associates.
7. Camp, Robert C. 1989. *Benchmarking.* Milwaukee, WI: ASQ Quality Press.
8. Corporate Quality Office. 1989. *Benchmarking for Quality Improvement.* Stamford, CT: Xerox Corporation.

9. Verity Consulting Group. 1991. *Benchmarking.* Los Angeles: Verity Press.

10. GOAL Research Committee. 1991. *Benchmarking Research Report.* Methuen, MA: GOAL/QPC.

11. Balm, Gerald J. 1992. *Benchmarking: A Practitioner's Guide for Becoming and Staying Best of the Best.* Schaumberg, IL: Quality and Productivity Management Association.

12. Codling, Sylvia. 1992. *Best Practices Benchmarking: The Management Guide to Successful Implementation.* Beds, UK: Industrial Newsletters.

13. Hooper, John A. 1992. *Borrowing from the Best: How to Benchmark World-Class People Practices.* Beaverton, OR: HR Effectiveness.

14. Leibfried, Kathleen H. J., and C. J. McNair. 1992. *Benchmarking: A Tool for Continuous Improvement.* New York: McGraw-Hill.

15. Miller, Jeffrey G., Arnoud DeMeyer, Jinichiro Nakane, and Kasra Ferdows. 1992. *Benchmarking Global Manufacturing.* Homewood, IL: Business One Irwin.

16. Spendolini, Michael J. 1992. *The Benchmarking Book.* New York: The American Management Association.

17. Watson, Gregory H. 1992. *The Benchmarking Workbook.* Portland, OR: Productivity Press.

18. Bosomworth, Charles E. 1993. *The Executive Benchmarking Guidebook.* Boston: The Management Roundtable.

19. Bourque, Daniel P. 1993. *The Benchmarking Process: An Approach for Improving Quality, Cost, and Clinical Performance (A Guide).* Irving, TX: Voluntary Hospitals of America.

20. Czarnecki, Mark T. 1993. *Benchmarking Strategies in Accounting and Finance.* New York: American Institute of Certified Public Accountants.

21. Fitz-Enz, Jack. 1993. *Benchmarking Staff Performance: How Staff Departments Can Enhance Their Value to the Customer.* San Francisco: Jossey-Bass.

22. Hammer, Michael, and James Champy. 1993. *Reengineering the Corporation.* New York: Harper.

23. International Benchmarking Clearinghouse. 1993. *Benchmarking the Best.* Houston, TX: American Productivity & Quality Center.
24. Karlof, Bengt, and Svante Ostblom. 1993. *Benchmarking: A Guide to Productivity and Quality Championship.* Borga, Sweden: Svenska Dagbladet Förlags AB.
25. Watson, Gregory H., and Joseph M. Wexler, eds. 1993. *The Benchmarking Management Guide.* Portland, OR: Productivity Press.
26. Watson, Gregory H. 1993. *Strategic Benchmarking.* New York: Wiley.
27. Xerox Quality Solutions. 1993. *Benchmarking for Process Improvement.* Rochester, NY: Xerox Corporation.
28. Bogan, Christopher E., and Michael J. English. 1994. *Benchmarking for Best Practices: Winning through Innovative Adaptation.* New York: McGraw-Hill.
29. Boxwell, Robert J. 1994. *Benchmarking for Competitive Advantage.* New York: McGraw-Hill.
30. Czarnecki, Mark T. 1994. *Benchmarking Strategies for Healthcare.* New York: Aspen Publishers.
31. Gift, Robert G., and Doug Mosel. 1994. *Benchmarking in Healthcare.* Chicago: American Hospital Publishing.
32. Watson, Gregory H. 1994. *Business Systems Engineering.* New York: Wiley.
33. Camp, Robert C. 1995. *Business Process Benchmarking.* Milwaukee, WI: ASQ Quality Press.
34. Demelio, Robert. 1995. *The Basics of Benchmarking.* New York: Quality Resources.
35. Thor, Carl G. 1995. *Practical Benchmarking for Mutual Improvement.* Portland, OR: Productivity Press.
36. Andersen, Bjorn, and Per-Gaute Pettersen. 1996. *The Benchmarking Handbook.* London: Chapman & Hall.
37. Finnegan, Jerome P. 1996. *The Manager's Guide to Benchmarking: Essential Skills for the New Competitive-Cooperative Economy.* San Francisco: Jossey-Bass.
38. Harrington, H. James, and James S. Harrington. 1996. *High*

Performance Benchmarking: Twenty Steps to Success. New York: McGraw-Hill.

39. Harrington, H. James. 1996. *The Complete Benchmarking Implementation Guide.* New York: McGraw-Hill.
40. Keehley, Patricia, Stephen Medlin, Sue MacBride, and Laura Longmire. 1996. *Benchmarking for Best Practices in the Public Sector.* San Francisco: Jossey-Bass.
41. Camp, Robert C. 1998. *Global Cases in Benchmarking.* Milwaukee, WI: ASQ Quality Press.
42. Tweet, Arthur G., and Karol Gavin-Marciano. 1998. *The Guide to Benchmarking in Healthcare.* New York: Quality Resources.
43. Czarnecki, Mark T. 1998. *Managing by Measuring.* New York: The American Management Association (AMACOM).
44. Grayson, Jack, and Carla O'Dell. 1998. *If Only We Knew What We Know.* New York: The Free Press.
45. Zairi, Mohamed. 1998. *Effective Management of Benchmarking Projects.* London: Butterworth-Heinemann.
46. Ahmad, Munir, and Roger Benson. 1999. *Benchmarking in the Process Industries.* New York: Institute of Chemical Engineers.
47. Jackson, Norman, and Helen Lund. 2000. *Benchmarking for Higher Education.* Buckingham, UK: Open University Press.
48. Reider, Robert. 2000. *Benchmarking Strategies: A Tool for Profit Improvement.* New York: Wiley.
49. Coers, Mardi, Chris Gardner, Lisa Higgins, and Cynthia Raybourn. 2001. *Benchmarking: A Guide to Your Journey to Best Practice Processes.* Houston, TX: American Productivity & Quality Center.
50. McCabe, Steven. 2001. *Benchmarking Construction.* London: Blackwell Science.
51. Wober, Karl W. 2002. *Benchmarking in Tourism and Hospitality.* Cambridge: MA: CABI Publishing.
52. Graafland-Essers, Irma. 2003. *Benchmarking e-Government in Europe and the U.S.* Santa Monica: Rand Corporation.

53. Kozak, Metlin. 2004. *Destination Benchmarking: Concepts, Practices and Operations*. Cambridge, MA: CABI Publishing.
54. Mard, Michael J., Robert R. Dunne, Edi Osborne, and James S. Rigby. 2004. *Driving Your Company's Value: Strategic Benchmarking for Value*. Hoboken, NJ: Wiley.
55. Saul, Jason. 2004. *Benchmarking for Non-Profits: How to Measure, Manage and Improve Performance*. St. Paul, MN: Amherst H. Wilder Foundation.
56. Wireman, Terry. 2004. *Benchmarking Best Practices in Maintenance Management*. New York: Industrial Press.

About the Author

Gregory H. Watson is president of Business Excellence Solutions, Ltd., a global consulting company dedicated to improving the performance of its clients through the application of strategic benchmarking, business assessment, breakthrough planning, and systems engineering using the Six Sigma methodologies. In addition, he is an adjunct assistant professor in the Department of Industrial Engineering and Management at Oklahoma State University, where he teaches distance learning courses on engineering technology and management. Previously, Mr. Watson was vice president of quality for Xerox Office Document Products, vice president of benchmarking at the American Quality & Productivity Center, director of quality at Compaq Computer, and manager of the Quality Leadership Development Program in the corporate office of Hewlett-Packard. Before his commercial career, Mr. Watson was a lieutenant commander in the United States Navy. He was also a cofounder of the International Benchmarking Clearinghouse at the American Productivity & Quality Center and the Six Sigma Advisory Committee to the International Standards Organization Technical Committee on Statistical Matters.

Mr. Watson was inducted as an Academician into the International

Academy for Quality in 1996 and is currently its vice president of publications. He was elected to the College of Fellows of the World Productivity Science Council in 1997. Mr. Watson is a past president and fellow of the American Society for Quality (ASQ), companion of the Institute for Quality Assurance in the United Kingdom, and has been elected a fellow of the Australian Organization for Quality, the Quality Society of AustralAsia, and the Royal Statistical Society. In a 2000 *Quality Progress* survey, he was named one of the world's "21 voices of quality for the 21st century." In 2001, he was awarded the Lancaster Medal by the American Society for quality in recognition of his global efforts in extending the body of quality knowledge and the Association for Quality & Participation (AQP) presented him with the President's Award in recognition of his career contributions to the quality profession. Also in 2001, Mr. Watson delivered a 50th Anniversary Deming Lecture to the Japanese Union of Scientists and Engineers. In 2003, Mr. Watson presented the 25th John Loxham invited lecture to the Institute for Quality Assurance in Glasgow, Scotland. In 2005, his book *Design for Six Sigma* was awarded the Crosby Medal as the outstanding book of the year by the American Society for Quality, and he was named an honorary member of the Benchmarking Club of Russia.

Mr. Watson completed his Master Black Belt credential in 1998 under Dr. Mikel Harry of Six Sigma Academy; has twice served on the board of examiners for the Malcolm Baldrige National Quality Award; and has been a judge for the state quality awards of Texas, Florida, and New York. He holds masters degrees in systems management, legal studies, industrial engineering, and business administration. Mr. Watson has been elected to honor societies for academics (Phi Kappa Phi), scientific research (Sigma Xi), engineering (Tau Beta Phi), and industrial engineering (Alpha Pi Mu), and he has been certified as a Quality Engineer, Reliability Engineer and Six Sigma Black Belt by the American Society for Quality. Mr. Watson has authored or collaborated on 10 quality-related books that were translated into 11 languages. He may be contacted at greg@excellence.fi.

Index

Index